ID0975512

Becoming Gentlemen

BECOMING

Gentlemen

Women, Law School, and
Institutional Change

LANI GUINIER

MICHELLE FINE

JANE BALIN

Beacon Press

Boston

Beacon Press
25 Beacon Street
Boston, Massachusetts 02108–2892

Beacon Press books are published under the auspices
of the Unitarian Universalist Association of Congregations.

Text design by Christopher Kuntze
Composition by Wilsted & Taylor

Library of Congress Cataloging-in-Publication Data

Guinier, Lani.
    Becoming gentlemen : women, law school, and institutional change / Lani Guinier,
Michelle Fine, and Jane Balin.
        p.   cm.
    Includes bibliographical references and index.
    ISBN 0-8070-4404-0
        1. Women law students—United States.   2. Women law teachers—United
States.   3. Law—Study and teaching—United States.   I. Fine, Michelle.   II. Balin,
Jane.   III. Title.
KF287.G85   1997
340'.071'173—dc21   96-39142

CONTENTS

I

Why Isn't *She* President?

Lani Guinier

1

II

Becoming Gentlemen: Women's Experiences
at One Ivy League Law School

*Lani Guinier, Michelle Fine, and Jane Balin,
with Ann Bartow and Deborah Lee Stachel*

27

III

Models and Mentors

Lani Guinier

85

Afterword

98

Notes

103

Index

171

Becoming Gentlemen

∞ I ∞

Why Isn't *She* President?

Lani Guinier

*I*N THE FALL of 1995, President Bill Clinton explained his veto of a congressional bill containing stopgap spending measures. He had to act as he did, he told us, because this bill raised fundamental issues about the role of government. Government, he announced, is not "a one-size-fits-all bureaucracy," but a way to organize society to help everyone realize his or her full potential. "We don't want a winner-take-all society," he declared. "We want a society in which everyone has a chance to win together." That goal—*a chance to win together*—and that critique—the answer is *not one-size-fits-all*—are foundational to the arguments in this book.

The essays in this volume tell the story of women's experience with legal education as a way to begin a wider conversation in which we rethink conventional norms. Based on our research and on the personal accounts of women participants, my coauthors and I argue that formerly all-male institutions cannot incorporate and take advantage of difference without changing from within. We argue that by reconsidering the fairness and functionality of an educational culture that trains, teaches, or evaluates everyone using a one-size-fits-all approach, these institutions can transform themselves to benefit women, others who have historically been outsiders, and, most importantly, *all* consumers of their services.

At the center of this volume is a study analyzing women's experience at the University of Pennsylvania Law School, conducted by Professor Michelle Fine, Professor Jane Balin, and myself with the able assistance of Ann Bartow, class of 1990, and Deborah Stachel, class of 1993. We found that women come to the school with credentials virtually identical to those of their male counterparts, but that many women do not perform as well academically, do not participate as much in class, and do not graduate with comparable honors and awards. Using written first-person narratives, interviews, questionnaires, and quantitative research data, our study tells a poignant story about the insidious effects of gendered stratification.

Because law school's educational mission is so intertwined with the goal of selecting students for entry into a competitive profession, much of its pedagogy, including examination formats, is designed to rank students. The idea is that those who succeed in this highly competitive and individualistic culture will do well as lawyers. As a result, the law school valorizes sorting, rewards people who think fast but not always those who think deeply, and relies upon uniform rules and standards that may appear to treat all students the same but do not necessarily develop each student's true potential. We conclude that law schools such as the one we studied not only reflect or reproduce larger sets of social stratifications, they create and legitimize them.

This book focuses on the experience of a law professor who is a woman of color and on women law students of all colors. It chronicles the disappointments of women as they enter previously male-dominated institutions and, to a surprising extent, remain isolated, marginalized, and dissatisfied. In a crucial sense, however, this account is a critique, not a complaint. It is narrated by women, yes, but it contains lessons for all of us.

We learned, for example, that a standardized, hierarchical, competitive approach to training lawyers inhibits many women *and some men*. Such an approach sets in motion a peer culture that also intimidates and silences many women, in a process with which faculty interfere too rarely. We learned that too many women internalize their failure and begin to question their own abilities. At the same time, conventional approaches to legal education do not necessarily educate or evaluate everyone based on their capacity either to learn or to do the job of a lawyer well. Indeed, the very women who resist "playing the game" in law school do graduate. Most go on to become important, often distinguished, members of their profession.

We also learned about new ways of teaching from studying the way women, as "outsiders," perform in law school—many, for example, prefer group-based learning teams and participatory, student-initiated learning projects. Like certain of the most daz-zling Olympic gymnasts, some women "can always do it when it's for the team" but struggle when it's for themselves.[1]

Interestingly, the preference of some women students for coop-erative styles of learning parallels findings about members of other underrepresented or marginalized groups. For example, Professor Uri Treisman studied African-American undergraduates who were having difficulty in learning calculus.[2] His faculty colleagues as-sumed that these difficulties stemmed from "underprivileged" backgrounds, low motivation, weak academic records, and lack of family support, but Treisman found that all four of these assump-tions were incorrect. The black students were actually studying as much as the Asian-American students who were excelling. What the black students were not doing, however, was studying in groups, whereas the Asian-American students were reinforcing what each learned individually by constantly talking about math in social settings—as they studied, over lunch, even as they walked to class.

Treisman did observe friendly competition among the Asian-American students—individuals would strive to come up with the best solution to a problem or to come up with a solution first—but in the end they shared what information they had so they all could excel. By contrast, few of the black students, many of whom were academic loners in high school, came to the university adept at learning mathematics or science from their peers. Especially for those black students whose self-reliance had been a resource in the past, social isolation from peers and the institutional culture of the university was now an important deficit to be overcome, as was their self-consciousness in asking for help even when they most needed it.

Treisman discovered that learning math was often best accom-plished as an interactive, cooperative venture and went on to design a successful program using peer study group sessions. Through these faculty-sponsored workshops, the black students' academic needs were addressed in an informal setting, which helped remove social barriers as well. The basic premise was that through the reg-ular practice of testing their ideas on others, students can develop the skills of self-criticism that are essential not only for the develop-ment of mathematical sophistication, but for all intellectual growth.

Because he found that the best students were independent but not isolated learners, Treisman also encouraged workshop participants to assume leadership roles in other campus activities.

The issue, then, is not individual capacity to learn but that all individuals learn differently and some learn even better when their peers are their teachers. In the course of our study, we discovered that we cannot use a single set of criteria or a single pedagogical style to measure or teach a complex set of skills. We learned, in other words, the limitations of one-size-fits-all thinking.

We also discovered that an educational approach that emphasizes ranking rather than learning limits the range of skills that students are encouraged to bring to the profession. Not only does such an approach denigrate certain insights and perspectives, all too often it undermines the wonderfully complex and kaleidoscopic understanding that comes from integrating mainstream *and* marginal viewpoints. Problem solving, especially the solving of complex problems, may require individuals who not only value but need the input of diverse perspectives and skills, including the ability to listen not just speak, the ability to synthesize not just categorize, and a willingness to think hard about nuance and context even when that slows down the process of decision making. Indeed, among highly competent lawyers, successful performance often depends on a team of individuals, no single one of whom possesses all of the necessary expertise but all of whom, working together, are able to accomplish their task in a reliable way.

The most important lesson we learned, therefore, is that we must listen to the voices of those whose experience is both marginal and central to our understanding. The experience of many women is marginal in that women have traditionally been outsiders in the field of law,[3] but the experience of these same women is also central because they offer us an opportunity to rethink the nature of the job we all want done. If we are committed to becoming a society that values inclusive decision making and genuine opportunity, the kind of we-all-can-win-something-together society to which President Clinton referred, we must learn that bringing in new perspectives, especially from those who have been underrepresented, is not only fair, it is functional.

In listening to women's voices, we tried to follow the admonition of Harvard scholar Ronald Heifitz, who writes about leadership without easy answers, as the process of "adaptive work"—of getting people to tackle tough problems, of getting people to take the risk of challenging conventional assumptions. We asked, for example, what does the present approach to legal education accomplish? Are conventional teaching methods and assessment techniques predictive of the kinds of work, the kinds of relationships, the kinds of collaborative approaches to solving private and public problems that lawyers will need in the future? The twenty-first century may require fewer litigators and more negotiators, fewer solo practitioners and more in-house counsel, fewer brilliant advocates and more brilliant collaborators. If that is the case, we can learn how best to meet the challenge of the future if we heed the words of social critic bell hooks: "With creativity and an open mind, we can use information from the margin to transform the way we think about the whole."[4]

In using our research into the experience of women law students as the foundation for adaptive work, Michelle Fine, Jane Balin, and I considered three sets of questions. The first centers on what it means to be qualified as a law student or a legal practitioner in the first place: Are we using measures of qualifications that are functional, not just efficient or purportedly objective? Can we assess qualifications in advance and can we accurately predict the performance of lawyers using a single standard or a one-size-fits-all approach to assess performance of law students?

The second set of questions concerns fairness. Many are committed to an equality which they interpret as formally uniform treatment. Is that our goal—to treat everyone exactly the same? Or do we want to treat everyone fairly and productively? Are we confident that when we treat everyone the same we are treating everyone in a way that nurtures each one's potential?

The third line of inquiry begins with the question of what we can learn from diversity. Can diverse approaches to legal education help us adapt to the changing demands of legal work as well as our changing demographics? Can we begin a new conversation about the needs of twenty-first-century America for lawyers who cooperate and collaborate in ways that draw from a diverse set of experiences and perspectives? Can our diversity help us find "adaptive" or creative or innovative approaches to training legal problem solvers? What can we learn from those who have been left out?

Our study suggests three related answers to these questions. First, we conclude that functional merit, meaning the ability to do a job, cannot always be measured by paper-and-pencil tests, whether they are nationally standardized ones like the LSAT (the standard admissions test for law school) or timed, in-class examinations administered at the end of a law school semester. The LSAT in particular may appear to be an efficient predictor of first-year law school grades, but it is not necessarily useful in identifying those who can actually do the job of lawyer, and, more importantly, do it well.

Second, we conclude that sameness is not necessarily fairness. Often the same treatment is not just or fair treatment. In particular, promoting real learning may require treating people differently, using different techniques depending on the topic, the motivation and experience of students, or the dynamic of the classroom.

Third, and perhaps most important, our study suggests the need to reconsider the nature of the job and the nature of the learning environment, not just to be more inclusive, but to do the adaptive work that we will need to do in the next century. Those women who are less competitive in the aggregate than men may fail in a competitive, highly stratified and individualistic law school culture, yet succeed in a cooperative, team-oriented environment. Their participatory, interactive style prepares them to be effective negotiators, corporation counsel, and transactional lawyers. And evidence suggests that lawyers who collaborate will often be those who are most valued in the twenty-first century.[5] Teamwork, listening skills, and creativity in problem solving may be equally important, and sometimes even more important than argumentativeness, aggressiveness, or individualism as we prepare to enter a new era. As John P. Fernandez writes in *The Diversity Advantage: How American Business Can Out-Perform Japanese and European Companies in the Global Marketplace*, "[I]t is increasingly clear that a key to [corporate] success will be [the] ability to develop diverse, well-trained work forces that can function effectively as high-performance teams and produce quality products and services at a competitive price."

*   *   *

Our research began when Ann Bartow, then a third-year student at the University of Pennsylvania Law School, approached me to supervise an independent study. She wanted to shoot a videotape in which she reversed by gender all of the roles of professors and students. Ann had seen a video treatment parodying the experience of medical students, one in which all the professors were women and all the more vocal students were female. The medical school videotape, entitled *Turning Around*, contained several pointed role reversal vignettes. For example, "a female doctor leers at a male nurse, admires the fit of his uniform, pats him on the rear and calls him 'a good boy.'" The video parody presents the female body as typical; the professors draw from it all their examples about the effects of a disease. In one scene, a male medical student raises his hand tentatively to ask, "What happens when a male develops this disease?" The female professor wheels around and says dismissively, "You're smart. Extrapolate. Figure it out."

Knowing nothing about video at the time, I was nevertheless intrigued by Ann's project and agreed to supervise her independent study. I suggested that she first draft a script, which she did. The scenes were poignant depictions of subtle as well as blatant sexual harassment, but they all revolved around Ann herself. "I don't doubt your stories, but are they representative?" I asked. "Is it possible you have been a lightning rod for negative comments?" We agreed that before she invested any more energy into producing a video we should identify the extent to which Ann's experiences were typical. To that end, she drafted a seventy-question survey which she placed in the mail folders of all law students then enrolled at the school.

We were both pleased and troubled by the response—delighted that over half the student body responded but dismayed that the survey answers showed an institution deeply divided by gender. Many of the women respondents had entered law school full of self-confidence, one-third of them eager to practice public interest law when they graduated; by contrast, only 10% of their first-year male counterparts intended to practice in public interest.

But what was most surprising was the difference—an apparent change over time—between the responses of the first-year women students and the responses of third-year women. Only 8% of the third-year women who responded to the survey intended to practice public interest law. Furthermore, these third-year women, just like their first-year counterparts, did not participate much in class, but unlike their first-year classmates, they were not bothered by their lack of participation. The third-year men, like the first-year men, voiced some concerns and expressed criticisms of the way some professors intimidated them into learning, but they tended to see law school as a game or contest in which they simply had to fight back. One female student reported, "Guys think law school is hard, and we just think we're stupid"; some women, another said, sink "deeper and deeper in a mire, and just keep sinking lower and lower."

Ann suggested that we look at the academic performance of these women to see what, if any, impact the gendered dynamic had on women's grades as well as their attitudes. Ann, who graduated with honors, raised this possibility after looking at her own graduation program and discovering that few women in her class were also graduating with honors or had received the prestigious awards distributed by the predominantly male faculty. With the cooperation of Dean Colin Diver, professors Michelle Fine, Jane Balin, and I examined the academic performance of 981 law students at the University of Pennsylvania Law School over a period of three years.

We found that many women who come to law school with virtually identical entry-level test scores as men nevertheless do not perform as well *in law school*. These "neutral" entry-level credentials are not very predictive of actual law student performance. Our findings reinforce Supreme Court Justice William Douglas's earlier observation in a case involving university admissions. "Certainly the tests do seem to do better than chance," Justice Douglas wrote. "But," he added, "they do not have the value that their deceptively precise scoring system suggests. . . . [F]or example, most of those scoring in the bottom 20% on the test do better than that in law school—indeed, six of every 100 of them will be in the top 20% of their class."[6]

Our study confirms the findings of others that the LSAT alone is not a very good predictor of performance for all students, not just women or minorities. Some women underperform compared to their scores on the LSAT. Many males overperform compared to their LSAT scores. But *very few students actually performed in ways predicted by the LSAT*. LSAT "explains" at most 21% of performance at Penn Law School in the third year.[7] For students in their first and second years, the LSAT explains even less: 14% and 15% respectively. Moreover, above an LSAT threshold score of 34 or 35 on a scale that goes to 48, LSATs just don't matter as a predictor of performance in this law school.[8] In other words, the LSAT test does not in fact predict performance for *most* law students regardless of race or gender.[9]

Entry-level criteria of this kind also fail to take into account variables that predate taking the test, such as how often you were exposed to the test before you took it,[10] and variables that postdate the test, such as study habits, interest in the subject matter, or the "culture" of the school—which turn out to be more important in determining law school performance than either test-taking skills or women's stronger undergraduate academic performance.[11] The law school culture—meaning what gets measured, how people are rewarded, and what kinds of mistakes are not forgiven—represents a set of beliefs and values that emphasizes aggressiveness, legitimizes emotional detachment, and demands speed. The LSAT provides only limited predictive information regarding an applicant's potential to do well in this kind of environment; LSAT scores do, however, correlate with an applicant's family income, status, and gender.[12]

Our data reflect the reality that many women are able to excel academically in law school. But our data also suggest, as recently confirmed by a 1996 report analyzing quantitative data from a national sample of 29,000 law students, that "law school is not an environment that nurtures the academic development of women."[13] There is something about the law school *environment* that has a negative academic impact on female law students.[14]

What would happen, we asked, if we used the experience of women as a point of critique and data for institutional change? Would we need, for example, to rethink the use of the LSAT as either a standard for admission or a predictor of success as a lawyer? Should we begin to examine critically both the pedagogy and the evaluative techniques that law schools use to rank students? Indeed, those admitted to Penn Law School graduate and become excellent lawyers without regard to their entry-level credentials. And—although those of us invested in teaching law may hate to admit this—many who graduate also become accomplished professionals without regard to their law school grades.

The managing partner at a large New York law firm confirmed this to me when he described a study his firm conducted of all the lawyers they hired over a thirty-year period. They found that those who were superstars in law school were also likely to be outstanding lawyers and to become partners in the firm. There was a relationship between the very top students in law school and the top 1% of their lawyers, but below the top 1 or 2% of law school performers the results were random. There was little or no correlation between law school grades and actual performance in the profession for most of the lawyers this firm had hired.[15] In other words, he confirmed that what we in legal education often tout as "merit" is a baseline or minimum set of requirements upon which one builds the capacity to do the job. These requirements may be linked to certain skills, but they do not predict the ways in which these skills manifest themselves and especially do not permit us to make fine distinctions between people with essentially comparable credentials.

Efforts to predict in advance who will be successful often fail because they do not simulate well enough all of the conditions involved in the actual job. Moreover, success often reflects qualities of persistence, zeal, and initiative that are not measured by any paper-and-pencil test at any stage in one's career. A study of three classes at Harvard College reinforces both these intuitions. The study, which looked at three classes of alumni over three decades, found a high correlation between "success"—defined by income, community involvement, and professional satisfaction—and two criteria that might not ordinarily be associated with Harvard freshmen: low SAT scores and a blue-collar background. Marilyn McGrath Lewis, director of admissions for Harvard and Radcliffe, said, "We have particular interest in students from a modest background. Coupled with high achievement and a high ambition level and energy, a background that's modest can really be a help. We know that's the best investment we can make: a kid who's hungry."[16] In fact, those with the lowest SAT scores and the poorest parents, who nevertheless convinced Harvard that they should be given a chance to succeed, did just that. In fact they succeeded not only beyond their parents' status but beyond what was achieved in the real world by their "more qualified" peers. It is not surprising, therefore, that college admissions officers at elite universities report that intense involvement in extracurricular activities, in part because it correlates with "initiative," is one of the best predictors of achievement.[17]

Performance on a single test is not what correlates with success in life, as measured by financial rewards, professional satisfaction, and contribution to the community. Attempting to predict achievement using a one-size-fits-all standard fails to account for the multiple kinds of intelligence, motivation, self-confidence, and relationship to law school culture that likely affect performance. It is not simply a problem of predicting performance of law students, not simply a problem of identifying the right test in advance; it is also a problem that reveals the limitations of uniform tools of prediction. We often can't know in advance how a person will perform in a new setting, or what it will take to do well in a job whose functions are in flux.

It is *the opportunity to learn*—a job, a craft, a skill—*and the motivation* or drive to take advantage of that opportunity that often correlate with successful on-the-job performance. A former labor lawyer helped me understand this phenomenon based on his experience defending employment discrimination lawsuits. As he put it, those given the chance to succeed are in fact most likely to succeed. What we often mean by merit, he said, is the same thing as opportunity: those who are given the opportunity to go to Harvard do better in life than those who are denied that opportunity, and those who are hungry for that opportunity succeed more often than those for whom the opportunity was taken for granted. Incremental differences on one-size-fits-all paper-and-pencil tests may not be adequate to tell us to whom we should give that opportunity.[18]

Our first conclusion, therefore, is that merit, meaning the capacity to do the job of lawyer, is not predicted or determined by conventional standardized tests. Like the Harvard study of three classes of alumni, our study of women law students reveals the limitations of seeking to predict performance based on a single instrument or a one-size-fits-all approach to ranking.

Second, our study reveals that sameness is not necessarily fairness. Even when we think we are treating people as equals, we may in fact be treating some differently. What looks the same if you are generalizing from your own experience may be construed differently by others: sameness as a uniform standard assumes that one can generalize from the perspective or intent of the person setting that standard.

Our data on women at Penn Law School suggest that while the

school may be treating all students the same, it may not be treating all students equitably. Some students may not be participating as much, learning as much, or feeling as competent when we insist on teaching them all by the same methods and all in a hierarchical, adversarial, formalistic way. Sameness may not be fairness in this context.

For example, when we asked students in a 1991 seminar and then again in a 1992 seminar why men and women responding to Ann's survey chose different qualities as being important in a professor—with the men in the aggregate valuing "expresses ideas clearly" and the women choosing instead "treats students with respect"—they responded that men are already treated with respect and therefore do not value that quality as much. But an alternative explanation, offered by a female colleague, is that many women need friendliness cues more than men—that men, either because of the culture of law school or because of the culture of American society, feel entitled to ask questions and approach faculty, whereas women *and many people of color* wait for a signal first that it is "safe" to approach. Thus the professors may be treating both men and women, whites and people of color, "the same," but the effect of that treatment is very different depending on how it is perceived and received.

Our study shows that certain students—including many but not all women and probably some men—bring a different perspective to the role of lawyering. As mentioned above, for example, many more women than men came to law school to do public interest or public service work. This difference paralleled the difference we found in class participation.

Female law students were significantly more likely than male law students to report that they "never" or "only occasionally" asked questions or volunteered answers in class. The women students who responded to our survey reported that men ask more questions, volunteer more often, enjoy greater peer tolerance of their remarks, receive more attention from faculty during classes, get called on more frequently, and receive more post-class "follow-up" than women. Similarly, a recent study of law school teaching at eight different law schools across the country found that male students speak disproportionately more in all classes taught by men, and that gender disparities are more apparent in the elite schools regardless of the gender of the professor. As Catherine Krupnick found in her study of twenty-four Harvard classrooms, professors allowed those with the quickest response time to dominate class-room discussion.[19]

One of the reasons for this differential level of participation may be that the very large, traditional law school classroom does not create a learning space for those students—many of them women—who learn better through collaborative and nonadversarial methods. The requirement to perform in a particular way in law school establishes the harshest and most adversarial version of the Socratic method as the benchmark for success. One commentator has described the stereotypical Socratic approach at its worst as learning how to ask rude questions. Most people ask questions because they want to know the answer; lawyers are trained never to ask questions unless they already know the answer.

In training students to think of the process of asking and an-swering questions as an opportunity to put someone on the spot, to demonstrate how little that person knows, or to identify important hidden assumptions, conversation is valued for its adversarial style. It is perceived as a fight to prevail, not a method of inquiry. To the extent this occurs, the technique of Socratic teaching—in which law professors train students to "think like lawyers" by asking indi-vidual students to answer a stream of questions in front of their peers, often "cold calling" on students who are not identified in ad-vance—looks to many women like ritualized combat. Students who do well often do so because they see this version of the Socratic method as a game, and as in all games, they play to win.

Many men told us that this is in fact the way they see law school participation, as an exchange of verbal retorts. You win when you silence your opponent. You also win when you are the first to raise your hand. So some students—mostly men—seeking to score, raise their hands to ask questions without yet organizing their ideas. They take up a lot of "air time" as everyone gets to hear them think aloud. They learn the important skill of presenting ideas to an audience, and because they are first, they help set the agenda. But others—including many women—are put off by the gamesman-ship and simply withdraw or seek to participate on different terms.

Many of the women who responded to Ann's survey reported that they wanted to participate or volunteer answers but only if these seemed truly relevant. They didn't worry about being the first to raise their hands in class; they didn't want to speak unless they were certain they had something to say. They wanted to participate in a way that built on or connected to what someone else was saying.

In my own experience, women students like these are eager to learn by listening first to what other students say. So as they listen, they often edit their remarks before raising their hands. Some spend so much time outlining what they want to say that it's as if they're writing haiku poems. By the time they're called on, their comments are so concise, so pithy, that they may be brilliant but don't register or are no longer relevant because the class has moved on.

These women are not there to silence others or to watch others score. Like those that NBC Sports reportedly wanted to attract to the audience for the 1996 Summer Olympics, they are not drawn to the drama of identifying winners and losers through confrontation. Dick Ebersol explained his network's strategy for attracting a large number of female viewers: "Men will sit through the Olympics for almost anything, as long as they get to see some winners and losers. Women tend to approach this differently. They want to know who the athletes are, how they got there, what sacrifices they've made. They want an attachment, a rooting interest."[20] NBC's research had shown that women want to understand the personal identities of the participants in the Olympic sporting events,[21] that they care more about understanding the background leading up to an event than they do about the results.[22] NBC television coverage had its highest ratings among women viewers when it presented the athletes in a personal context. Similarly, many female law students prefer to know the human context in which legal rules develop and apply.

Looking at the dynamic of class participation may give us an insight into how some women of all colors learn.[23] Like Uri Treisman's African-American math students, they often learn better in informal peer groups that integrate social and academic experiences, not only in terms of learning a body of information, but also in terms of developing leadership skills. Many prefer a more cooperative rather than a competitive environment. Like the viewers NBC hoped to attract for the 1996 Summer Olympics, they want to learn the stories behind the cases. They participate only after listening to what others are saying. They see conversation as a way of collaborating to synthesize information rather than competing to perform or to win.

Skeptics may conclude that those women who are reluctant class participants in law school are basically not cut out to be good lawyers, because we all know that lawyers are ruthlessly competitive and individualistic. Lawyers are aggressive advocates; lawyers are performers. But is that the only way, or even the best way, to be a good lawyer?

The third lesson to be learned from our study is that bringing new voices into the law school classroom can provide an occasion to rethink what it means to be a good lawyer. Women who disengage from intimidating Socratic exchanges are not asking for special preferences; their experience instead shows how the normal operation of some existing educational policies are themselves dysfunctional, not just unfair. For example, the challenge to the LSAT as *the* entry-level test for law school implicit in our study is not that the test is culturally biased against blacks, Latinos, and women of all colors in favor of upper-income white men, but that the test itself is simply an inadequate measure of future job performance. The test may measure the ability to think quickly and to make strategic decisions with less than perfect information, but it does not measure the full range of skills needed to be a good lawyer.

After all, lawyers are basically problem solvers.[24] UCLA law professor Jerry Lopez's essay "Lay Lawyering" begins, "Lawyering means problem-solving. Problem-solving involves perceiving that the world we would like varies from the world as it is and trying to move the world in the desired direction."[25] Problem solving is the "fundamental lawyering skill" listed first among those skills the American Bar Association's MacCrate Report task force deems important.[26]

But not all problems can be solved through quick thinking or aggressive questioning. Not all problems belong in court. Not all problems lend themselves to litigation. Often lawyers work as members of teams representing large organizations in multiparty transactions or disputes and only rarely go to court. The lawyer as aggressive litigator representing a single client may be outmoded in terms of what most lawyers actually do, and this paradigm may be dysfunctional in terms of "the collection of competencies" law-yers need to possess in order to do their jobs well.[27] Professor Carrie Menkel-Meadow identifies from the contemporary clini-cal literature studies defining the central work of the lawyer as "decision-maker, advisor, fact developer, advocate, friend, investi-gator, and organizer."[28] Being first to answer a question in class—playing the game, "winning" as if lawyering were tennis—is not one of the most important skills. It is a useful skill in some, but not all, situations.

Indeed, one of my colleagues who conducts a class in negotiation reports that those students who function cooperatively, who put all their information out on the table in advance, are more likely to ar-rive at the optimal solution—one which satisfies both sides—than are those who approach problems in a competitive, adversarial manner.

Conventional approaches to legal education value those who think fast in a highly structured, performance-on-display atmo-sphere. The competition is important because for some students it encourages individual initiative. Yet for many—including women and other traditional outsiders—initiative is suppressed or dis-couraged when their only opportunity to excel requires individual competition in a highly adversarial relationship.

This does not mean that these individuals do not learn or cannot become excellent lawyers. In real-life settings where their perspec-tive is valued, they not only display initiative but provide needed balance and framing to solve complicated, twenty-first-century legal problems. They may in fact be Peter Drucker's knowledge workers: people who can share information, collaborate with a team, utilize diverse perspectives to innovate.

For example, in a finding that surprised researchers who de-signed a study to identify leadership abilities in the corporate world, women senior managers were stronger than their male counterparts at producing high-quality work, generating ideas, problem solving, and planning. Women, however, often did not get credit for their skills because they were not as good at self-promotion as were men.[29] Anecdotal evidence suggests that by widely dispersing true authority and listening to innovative ideas from their own employees, female outsiders can transform tradi-tional companies to improve productivity.[30]

Indeed, if law schools promote an environment in which alternative perspectives and approaches to learning are not supported, they may be denying the legal profession and its clients the advantages of creative tension, of solving problems by synthesizing information from diverse sources. All lawyers may then be denied the training they need to exercise independent judgment by accommodating competing visions and approaches.

In particular, women who focus on listening, who function cooperatively, who are open to "new ideas and new information" can bring a fresh perspective to a profession which is suffering in public esteem. In our study, we also heard from many students of color who expressed a deep sense of community responsibility. Listening to their voices could bring a sense of much-needed public accountability to a profession that, along with politicians and journalists, the American public loves to hate.

All lawyers can give better advice to clients if they have listened more carefully to what the client really defines as the nature of his or her problem.[31] Indeed, people who listen, people who have respect for their clients in human terms, not just monetary terms, are in a position to give a range of advice. Lawyers—men *and* women—who are trained to integrate and synthesize knowledge and information from different sources can manage crises and provide damage control because they can prioritize issues, look at problems from different sides, and apply legal principles to different factual circumstances. These are qualities that go beyond the courtroom, and may in fact be undervalued if they are not called upon until the issues polarize and litigation is the only resort.

*   *   *

If one-size-fits-all tests do not predict professional competence except at the very extremes, if treating people the same does not necessarily mean we are treating them fairly, if using a single test or a single approach to learning means some do not learn at all and others do not learn all that they need to know, then maybe it is time to use the information from the margin to rethink the whole. Maybe it is time to rethink the criteria we use to distribute opportunities and rewards in light of the nature of the jobs we need lawyers to do.

The lesson of our study is that we need a tough but broad-minded critique of so-called neutral standards for admissions, evaluation, and selection. I must emphasize here that we are not talking about lowering standards. To repeat, we are not advocating lower standards. Nor are we talking about shrinking from a commitment to excellence. This is about adapting standards to fit a changing and changed environment. This is about adaptive work in which people are challenged to tackle tough problems, to engage with each other to cooperate and to respond to collective problems with excellent solutions that represent our collective thinking.

Opportunities for lawyers are shrinking. Yet, my colleague Susan Sturm, whose work has inspired so many of the ideas in this chapter, proposes an adaptive critique. In her provocative essay, *From Gladiators to Problem-Solvers*, she argues that we need to connect the issue of women lawyers challenging uniform rules to a conversation about the ways in which economic decisions such as corporate downsizing, globalization, and increasing reliance on new technologies are changing our workplace. We need to link the issue of revitalizing our economy to the changing demographics of our workforce. We need to talk about whether conventional standards—those "testocratic" rules that so many of us are committed to defending—may undermine our ability to meet these new challenges.

Indeed, despite its dangers, the tendency to prefer single rules that rank or sort people is not limited to law schools or educational environments. For example, New York City once used a height requirement pegged to tall men to select police officers. This discriminated against women, Asian men, some Latino men, and short white men. It also defined the job of police officer as something only tall people are capable of doing, and normalized a particular type of officer—tough, brawny, macho.

But when standards changed and more women became cops, it was discovered that often they were actually better able to keep the peace than their male counterparts in some situations. In certain New York City housing projects, for example, black and Puerto Rican women cops from the surrounding community mentored rather than confronted young teenage boys, offering them respect, and the young men, grateful for the attention of adults, checked their own behavior.[32] And women of all colors were found to be better at defusing domestic violence situations. Furthermore, when the Los Angeles Police Department wanted to do something about the problem of police abuse, the Christopher Commission Report told the city to *hire more women*. The commission found that women were prepared to use force when necessary, but rely less on violence and more on verbal skills in handling conflict; the report concluded that current approaches to policing underemphasize interpersonal skills, sensitivity, politeness, and the ability to communicate.[33]

Those who insist upon a single standard of "ranking" for all lawyers or all police officers may unwittingly institutionalize value preferences that promote a particular group's chances for success *and* deny all of us the benefit of adaptive work, meaning new forms and innovative ways of doing old jobs. In New York City, height thresholds for police officers were arbitrary, exclusionary, and normalizing of a single, distorted view of the actual police function. They were arbitrary because no one correlated being a certain height to being a good cop; the standard was based on an idealized image that was not validated by the duties of housing authority police officers. They were exclusionary because they limited opportunities for police work to a fixed category, tall males; women, Asian men, Latino men, and short white males were all denied the opportunity to be police officers. This limited the chance for a police force to reflect the diversity of its population.

The challenge to the height requirement was a signal of institutional failure. More importantly, however, it became a catalyst for institutional innovation. It turns out that diversifying the repertoire of skills and approaches to policing benefits everyone. Including women and people of color offers us their insight and an opportunity.[34] They demonstrated that cops can utilize others' skills in a team. They showed us that our communities are safer when people in law enforcement are adept at de-escalating potentially violent confrontations, using their skills and temperament to keep the peace in new as well as traditional ways.[35]

To think of this issue in another way, consider the standard podium, in which the microphone and platform are fixed to accommodate the average speaker. For most people, the podium will work, more or less. But for very tall or very short people, and especially for people in wheelchairs, it's dysfunctional. Short speakers stand on a box to adjust their height; tall speakers simply bend down, hunch their shoulders, and try to shrink themselves to fit. The fixed platform represents a single solution to a complex problem, one in which those who do not fit the norm must make adjustments, or even be excluded.

Why not rethink "the norm"? Why not get an adjustable lectern and a microphone that moves to fit the height of the speaker? Why not devise an adaptive solution that does not presume the existence of a single right answer, a single set height for all speakers?

The point is not that only women can be cops or that we don't want aggressive, individualistic men in some situations. Nor is the point that all women are short or polite, or that all men are tall or rude. The point is that no single rule predicts success and no single criterion defines the job. If we understand this, we can learn to use the experience of women who gain access to previously male-dominated professions, jobs, or podiums as a window, not a wedge. If we in the legal profession abandon certain one-size-fits-all rules we can create opportunities for everyone who can do the job, for people who can do the job differently and maybe even better, and for people who because of their creativity, motivation, and ability to work in teams will make America better able to confront the challenges of the next century.

Taking seriously the voices of women and other underrepresented outsiders is necessary to open our minds to the ways in which a single-minded focus on so-called objective criteria skews the results of our selection process and denies opportunity to many potentially excellent candidates. This is not about substituting a set of subjective criteria for a flawed set of objective criteria. It is not about rigid numerical quotas. This is about the ways in which a commitment to diversity and innovation can help us better understand and fulfill our commitment to genuine merit.

It is about anticipating backward from job performance to determine what constitutes merit. For example, there is a movement among high school and college teachers to work together on "planning backward" from freshman year of college to what ninth-graders need to know, based on where high school teachers want them to go and where college faculty need them to be. Can we imagine a comparable strategy by which law faculty, law firms, public interest law organizations, and graduates could "strategize backward" to identify what skills, talents, angles of vision need to be sharpened, invented, or unearthed by law school students prior to graduation?

In sum, we posit that merit should be judged in terms of performance on the job, not performance on a test predicting performance on the job. We believe that fairness is treating everyone equitably, not necessarily treating them the same. Finally, we conclude that diversity is our future, but only if we go beyond the conventional practice of using women or people of color as an add-on to an unchanged set of practices and traditions. True diversity promotes merit because bringing in new people who have traditionally been left out is a way to enrich our experience, to redefine the job, to solve the problem better *for all of us.*

The diversity we describe is not "add women and stir." The problem with that approach is that it offers opportunities to too few deserving candidates—and leaves out many who have initiative, who have ability but do not test well in advance, or whose ability to not only do the job as is but to do it better does not "test" at all when they feel underutilized or excluded.[36] It often marginalizes those very individuals who are its beneficiaries because it does nothing to articulate the failures of conventional standards to embody important institutional or societal values. It fails to demystify the way in which claims of the testocracy are incomplete truths: that test scores tell us something about potential candidates but not necessarily what we want to know. Too often, they tell us more about a candidate's parents than about the candidate's future. They may also fail to tell us all that we want to know about the job itself: they may assume only one way of doing the job when as a society we need multiple skills to do the job well.

The challenge, then, is not to invent new victims or new scapegoats but to mobilize America for the future. Perhaps it is finally time to move from the nineteenth-century aristocratic concept of merit (the old boys' network), and from the twentieth-century testocratic concept of merit (the one-size-fits-all paper-and-pencil standardized test) to a more democratic, egalitarian concept for the twenty-first century. What would it take to ensure that all of us can succeed at getting the job done, the problem solved, and the future more secure? The standards by which we judge merit should not be based on who you know or who your parents were. They should reflect the broad diversity of people and skills that are needed to adapt to a changing, complex world.

We may not yet know the answer. There probably is no single answer. But we do at least know the question. Before we proceed, we must at least be prepared to answer the following: What are we using one-size-fits-all standards to do? Only when we know exactly what our standards are designed to produce can we find a way to ensure that they incorporate the needs and concerns of all of those who are affected by them.

*   *   *

What can we learn from the experience of those who have been excluded that may help all of us do our job better? In the second chapter in this volume, the study entitled "Becoming Gentlemen: Women's Experiences at One Ivy League Law School," we argue that the saga of women provides law schools and other male-dominated institutions a chance to reinvent themselves to benefit *and inspire* women and men, white students and students of color, black women law professors and law professors of all colors. The experience of the women we studied offers an opportunity to learn, not lament. These women are both survivors of their own dissatisfaction and teachers of an important lesson. We can learn the importance of rethinking the conventional, one-size-fits-all pedagogical procedures that law schools use to train and rank everyone.

The third essay, "Models and Mentors," uses autobiographical material to ask and answer a related question: What can we learn from women of color in law school?

I begin by recounting my own experience of being invisible as one of only two or three women students in a "Business Units 1" class at Yale Law School in 1974. This essay was first presented at a symposium of black women law professors offering our views about our professional roles. We wrote short personal statements "to increase awareness of the significance of our personal experiences to our work." We sought to find our voices and to help other women and people of color find theirs.

We were particularly intrigued by the call for more black women law professors to be role models. I take issue with that term, preferring the concept of mentoring. I argue that the opportunity to succeed must be reinforced by institutionalized mentoring—guidance on the informal rules for getting ahead—and on-the-job training.[37]

Who succeeds at learning the job once given a chance is partially a function of mentoring and communication skills. And we tend to mentor those we know or those who remind us of who we once were.[38]

On the occasion of Robert MacNeil's retirement from *The Mac-Neil/Lehrer News Hour* on PBS, for example, Jim Lehrer gave an interview on NPR. He was asked whether he ever went back to listen to the early tapes of the broadcast. Lehrer said no, he was too embarrassed. He didn't know what he was doing then; he followed a scripted seven-question format, which did not involve listening to and engaging with his subjects. He learned how to conduct a good interview over time, as he watched and learned from others who were doing the job better.[39] In other words, his improved performance correlated with on-the-job training and mentoring.

In trying to convert the demands for more black women role models into an exploration of the role of mentors, I have also tried to show how an outsider perspective can enrich the experience of all students. For many students, a teaching style that legitimizes alternative forms of participation, respects all participation, and broadens the educational dialogue makes them better advocates by deepening their knowledge of the world around them as well as enhancing their understanding of the implications of their claims.

My own experience suggests the importance of opening up a static system to create innovative approaches that will benefit everyone. I believe in a commitment to inclusiveness not just as an outcome but as a process in which we acknowledge the continuing significance of group exclusion and question the fundamental fairness of existing ways of distributing opportunity. As Michelle Fine reminds me, by learning from the margins, we may all discover that multiple perspectives in our classrooms make them smarter places, while multiple consciousness in our heads can make us smart in different ways (even if it does sometimes give us a headache).

With this book, we hope to use the perspective of adaptive work to begin a conversation about women and legal education in which the experience of those who have previously been excluded becomes a window on a much larger set of questions about merit, fairness, and the kind of society in which we want to raise our children.

I, for one, am optimistic about the results of such a conversation. I am optimistic about the future. I am optimistic about the future because of the lessons I have learned from raising a nine-year-old son.

With Niko's permission, I offer some excerpts from his second-grade journal, written when he was seven. In response to a question about his family, Niko writes, "My sister is in college. My mom works a lot, and my dad often cooks. Often my dad has fun with me." His teacher then asks him to explain what his mother does: "My mom teach's at Penn law school. I think its boring. Also, I think its fun. I think its boring because you usually sit at your computer with no games. I think its fun because you get to teach and your the boss. And I love my family." In response to the request "Name the cozy spots in your house," Niko writes: "One spot is the T.V. room. One spot also is my bed. Another spot is the basement. Another spot is the kitchen. I like these spots because my family is in them with me. But my dad is with me most."

So Niko lets me know he knows that I am often not home as much as I would be if ours were a more traditional family. He also lets me know he is still a *boy* who thinks "games are fun" and that being "the boss" is important. But his particular family dynamic helps him to take some unconventional positions. For example, in a group discussion, one of his second-grade classmates described what his mother does. "My mother is vice-president at a bank," the young boy said with obvious pride. Niko listened attentively and then blurted out, "Why isn't she *president?*" Why isn't *she* president?

So I am optimistic that in a future with young men raised to do their own adaptive work, they will be open to rethinking traditional expectations about what is normal, what is fair, and what will work for men *and* women, whites and people of color, short folks and tall.

And what might we learn in rethinking the possible responses to my son's question: Why isn't *she* president?

A first possible response (among many) is that she is not president of the bank because she does not possess the capacity to do the job of president as presently defined. A second is that she cannot make important contributions to the bank's management team as its leader even in a reorganized workplace. The first answer focuses on her inadequacies to do the present job. The second says she cannot help the bank adapt to the changing demands of the economy and the changing demographics of the workplace (according to the

Workforce 2000 Report, 65% of new entrants into the workforce will soon be women and minorities); presumably, the bank's board of directors would have looked at each applicant's ability to maximize the contributions of all members of an increasingly diverse workforce.

Unfortunately, in the conventional debate about standards and qualifications, too often we don't get to consider either of these responses. We don't look at the actual skills needed to be a bank president and work backward to develop appropriate selection criteria. Nor do we have in mind a dynamic conception of the changing nature of the bank president's work or the bank's workforce. Instead we tend to focus on two other issues. We may be told, "She doesn't get to compete for the job because she doesn't know the right people, doesn't play golf, didn't join the right clubs"—that is, *she* is not a *he*. This answer assumes that people get to "the top" based on whom they know, not what they know. To be a bank president, she, like the 95% of senior executives who are white males, must first become a "gentleman."

Alternatively, we may be told that she isn't president because the bank gave a test to its employees and she did not get the highest score. Those who defend the fairness of the test usually emphasize the efficiency and integrity that comes with objective, uniform criteria. But these same observers do not always acknowledge the under-inclusive, subjective, and arbitrary aspects of these supposedly neutral or objective criteria. Nor do they assure us that success, however we define it, correlates with playing by a single set of rules. They proceed to defend the use of a single yardstick to evaluate a complex reality, all the while acknowledging the role of multiple kinds of intelligence, skills, and motivation. They don't question whether those who succeed are the most qualified to do the job as it actually needs to be done. They emphasize instead the importance of certainty that comes with a one-size-fits-all set of uniform criteria.

In this book, we try to show that a genuine commitment to inclusion can become the basis for rethinking how we distribute opportunities starting from job needs and moving backward to new ways of assessing job applicants, differentiating among a band of qualified people in ways that ensure that all applicants believe they have a fair chance of competing, and thinking about apprenticeship programs and school-to-work internships as ways of assessing skills in context.

Listening to the voices of those on the margin may help us follow President Clinton's admonition to build "a society in which everyone has a chance to win together." Studying carefully the experience of outsiders can help us to begin questioning our conventional approaches to other aspects of our society, not just law or government. By using diverse problem-solving approaches we will meet the challenges of the twenty-first century together.

We can upsize the pool of genuinely qualified candidates and downsize the one-size-fits-all mentality. We can move forward in such a way that all who participate must concede that the system is fair. This is about developing a good twenty-first-century answer to the question of how to move beyond preconceptions about role allocations and assumptions about what is normal. This is about having a functional, inclusive, and genuinely meritocratic answer for the child who asks, "WHY ISN'T *SHE* PRESIDENT?"

❧ II ❧

Becoming Gentlemen:
Women's Experiences at One
Ivy League Law School

LANI GUINIER, MICHELLE FINE, & JANE BALIN
with Ann Bartow & Deborah Lee Stachel

*Am I to be cursed forever with becoming
somebody else on the way to myself?*

—Audre Lorde, "Change of Season"

*That's right. I used to be very driven, competitive.
Then I started to realize that all my effort was getting me nowhere.
I just stopped trying; just stopped caring. I am scarred forever.*

—Female law student, University of Pennsylvania

INTRODUCTION

*I*N THIS CHAPTER we describe preliminary research by and about women law students at the University of Pennsylvania Law School—a typical, if elite, law school stratified deeply along gender lines.[1] Our database draws from students enrolled at the law school between 1987 and 1992, and includes academic performance data on 981 students, self-reported survey data from 366 students, written narratives from 104 students, and group-level interview data from approximately 80 female and male students.[2] From these data we conclude that the law school experience of women in the aggregate differs markedly from that of their male peers.[3]

First, we find strong academic differences between graduating men and women. Despite identical entry-level credentials, this performance differential between men and women is created in the first year of law school and maintained over the next three years.[4] By the end of their first year in law school, men are *three times more likely* than women to be in the top 10% of their law school class.[5]

Second, we find strong attitudinal differences between women and men in year one, with a striking homogenization by year three.[6] The first-year women we studied are far more critical than their first-year male peers of the social status quo, of legal education, and of themselves as students.[7] Third-year female students, however, are less critical than their third-year male colleagues, and far less critical than their first-year female counterparts.[8] A disproportionate number of the women we studied enter law school with a commitment to public interest law, ready to fight for social justice. But their third-year female counterparts leave law school with corporate ambitions and some indications of mental health distress.[9]

Third, many women are alienated by the way the Socratic method is used in large classroom instruction, which is the dominant pedagogy for almost *all* first-year instruction.[10] Women self-report much lower rates of class participation than do men for all three years of law school.[11] Our data suggest that many women do not "engage" with a methodology that makes them feel strange, alienated, and "delegitimated."[12] These women describe a dynamic in which they feel that their voices were "stolen" from them during the first year. Some complain that they can no longer recognize their former selves, which have become submerged:[13]

> Law school is the most bizarre place I have ever been. . . . [First year] was like a frightening out-of-body experience. Lots of women agree with me. I have no words to say what I feel. My voice from that year is gone.

Another young woman added, "For me the damage is done; *it's in me*. I will never be the same. I feel so defeated."[14]

Even those women who do well academically report a higher degree of alienation from the law school than their male counterparts, based in part on complaints that "women's sexuality becomes a focus for keeping [women] in their place." For these women, learning to think like a lawyer means learning to think and act like a man. As one male professor told a first-year class, "To be a good lawyer, behave like a gentleman."[15] Hence our title.

Finally, we document substantial material consequences for those women who exit the law school after sustaining what they describe as a crisis of identity, and, we would add, a deflation of credentials. These women graduate with less competitive academic credentials, are not represented equally within the law school's academic and social hierarchies, and are apparently less competitive in securing prestigious and/or desirable jobs after graduation than their male peers.[16]

We propose three related hypotheses to explain our primary empirical finding, which is that men outperform women at the University of Pennsylvania Law School. Our research leads us to conclude that (1) many women *feel* excluded from the formal educational structure of the law school; (2) many women *are* excluded from the informal educational environment; and (3) some women are individually affected by the gendered stratification within the school, in terms of potentially adverse psychological consequences and more limited employment opportunities.

We believe that our data documenting the differing experiences of male and female law students offer an opportunity to reconsider the educational project of law school. Although some have said in response to our data that perhaps most women are not well suited to law school or should simply learn to adapt better to its rigors, we are inclined to believe that it is law school—not the women— that should change.[17] Indeed, changes to the existing structure of the law school might improve the quality of legal education for all students.

This study reports our empirical findings, assesses them in the context of studies of women at other law schools, and suggests several ways to place our findings within the ongoing debate about individual assimilation into hostile, elite, and previously all-male organizations. Further, our study indicates directions for future research and identifies the potential for transforming legal education, for changing its methods and its assumptions about hierarchy in order to better train and support the needs of *all* students.

1. THREE WINDOWS INTO THE LAW SCHOOL

A. *Methodologies*

In April 1990, Ann Bartow, then a third-year law student at the University of Pennsylvania Law School, surveyed the school's full population of 712 students about their views of gender and the law school experience.[18] Questionnaires were placed in the mail folders of every first-, second-, and third-year student. Of the 366 students who responded, 174, or 47.5%, identified themselves as female (compared to 41% then enrolled at the law school), and the remaining 192, or 52.5%, identified themselves as male. The responses of female and male Penn law students were compared across the first, second, and third years of law school and used to investigate anecdotal observations that had been offered by several female law students about stigmatization, harassment, and general malaise related to their gender.[19]

The Bartow Survey consists of a multiple-choice questionnaire and one open-ended question designed to elicit narrative responses (see Appendixes A and B, at the end of this chapter). One hundred and four of the 366 respondents answered the open-ended question. The data, analyzed by gender and year in law school, revealed significantly gendered attitudes and beliefs among the respondents, who constituted 51% of the men and women enrolled in 1990.

Intrigued by the initial results, we set up a multiple-method research design to assess the comparative status of women and men when they enter, as they participate in, and when they leave law school. Our three-part research design investigated gender-related differences in levels of academic performance, law student attitudes toward career goals, and general satisfaction with law school experiences.

The Bartow cross-sectional survey of 366 law students formed the initial database, one that was not longitudinal and was affected by a selectivity bias.[20] The Bartow Survey captures, however, the attitudes and experiences of a little over half (366 out of 712) of the men and women enrolled at the law school in 1990. Discovering significantly gendered attitudes and beliefs, we then sought to analyze student performance data as well.

Our second database comprised a quantitative cohort analysis of the academic performance of 981 students at the law school.[21] This database was longitudinal and was designed to determine the relationship, if any, along gender lines between incoming credentials and a law student's academic performance. The second database began in 1990 as an archival cohort study of the 712 students then enrolled in the law school. With the full cooperation of Colin Diver, Dean of the University of Pennsylvania Law School, we subsequently analyzed performance data for all students enrolled during the academic year ending June 1991, in order to confirm our initial findings. As a result, we collected and analyzed performance data for a total of 981 students, 712 of whom were enrolled at the time of the 1990 Bartow Survey, and 366 of whom submitted responses to her survey. We have the full academic performance data for the classes of 1990 and 1991, the first two years of law school for the class of 1992, and the first year of law school for the class of 1993.

The law school furnished us with anonymous demographic data for each of the 981 students, including gender, race, undergraduate grade point average (GPA), Law School Admission Test (LSAT) score, undergraduate institution, undergraduate rank, and law school GPA for each year in law school. We did not receive information about size of individual law classes, gender of the professor, or type of examination. We did not examine, therefore, possible correlations between these variables and student performance by gender. These areas of study may prove fruitful for future research.

Finally, in order to generate more detailed understandings of the gendered experiences suggested by the quantitative survey and academic performance data, we created a third, qualitative database. Qualitative data have become central to the work of social scientists, enabling them to produce more context-specific explanations of social life by collecting evidence on the perspectives and understandings of research informants.[22] Our qualitative data include the 104 narrative responses to the open-ended question about student experiences of gender discrimination in the Bartow Survey,[23] focus-group data collected from twenty-seven students (including white students and students of color, both male and female),[24] our observation of and participation with two classes of a critical perspectives seminar,[25] a meeting with the Women's Law Group,[26] and several meetings with law school faculty.[27]

Each of the three databases provides a different window onto the students' gendered experience of law school. The academic performance data represent the entire population of students enrolled between 1990 and 1992. It is a definitive statement reflecting the disparity in grades between men and women during the period of our research.

The narrative responses offer qualitative data that are reliable, meaning that the instrument for collecting the data is likely to generate the same response over several observations taken in the same time period.[28] They are also valid, meaning that the categories of analysis used by the researchers are the same categories that the subjects employ.[29] The focus groups and responses to the presentation of our data were neither randomly selected nor necessarily representative. They are substantively valid, but not necessarily generalizable. We use these qualitative data to generate hypotheses explaining the more reliable quantitative data.[30]

By triangulating our databases—that is, moving back and forth among the three sets of data collected during our research—we have developed a number of observations regarding the divergent experiences of many men and women at the University of Pennsylvania Law School. Our multi-method design seeks to contextualize and explain our primary empirical finding: Given traditional academic predictors, why do equally qualified women at the University of Pennsylvania Law School underperform, over time, compared to their male counterparts?

B. *Related Research*

We designed our study to compensate for some of the untested assumptions in the literature. Although other studies found lower rates of classroom participation among women law students,[31] no one had systematically documented the extent of gendered difference; nor had anyone researched the academic and emotional costs paid by women for their "different" or "dominated" experiences.[32] Our study is the first that attempts to weave a full analysis out of self-reported survey data, actual academic performance data, and open-ended narrative responses.

Early surveys of law students generally failed to examine the experience of legal education critically.[33] The original studies of women's experiences focused narrowly on women's entry into[34] and motivation for going to[35] law school, how women adapted to law school and professional success,[36] and what types of practice women pursued after graduation.[37] When women were novel in the field of law,[38] researchers were asking more simple questions: Were women too "feminine" to succeed in a "masculine" field? Could they adequately adapt to and incorporate the necessary attributes (that is, male styles) of professional conduct?[39] These researchers wanted to know if women could "fit" into law school. The structure and practices of the school were not considered problematic; the only interesting question was could women "make it"?

The more recent studies we reviewed tended to contemplate "the gender question" as a feature of the law school as an institution.[40] More concerned with how male and female students experience law schools, these projects analyze gender by classroom performance and degree of social alienation. Many have particularly focused, for instance, on women's silence in the classroom.[41]

These more recent studies have been undertaken primarily by women law students and/or legal professionals, and have been influenced by the women's movement and feminist legal theory. The law school experience—especially that of being silenced in the classroom—provoked some women to search for broader understandings of what others termed "personal problems." It was this phenomenon that originally motivated Bartow's 1990 study at Penn.[42] Carol Gilligan's early writings on women's "different voices"[43] had a profound influence on these works,[44] as did the writings of Catharine MacKinnon on domination and identity formation,[45] and Mari Matsuda's theories about the multiple consciousness of outsiders.[46] Studies at both Berkeley and Yale law schools drew heavily from Professor Matsuda's suggestion that outsiders experience their presence within mainstream institutions as a forum for both assimilation and resistance.[47]

Students at Stanford Law School were especially interested in testing Gilligan's proposition that men and women employ distinct types of moral reasoning when confronted with legal problems, as well as in examining how female and male law students experience law school and think about the law and their lifestyles.[48] Their study found only slight differences between men's and women's responses to two of the three hypotheticals pertaining to moral reasoning.[49] Although the differences were "in the predicted direction," these disparities reached a statistical significance inconsistently, and for only a few questions per hypothetical.[50] The Stanford survey concluded that "few gender differences [are found] among [law] students" in their reactions to these hypotheticals, and that the students therefore displayed few differences in moral reasoning.[51]

This finding of few differences may reflect the influence of legal education on the moral reasoning of both men and women.[52] It may also be attributable to the design of the survey[53] and the distinctive environment of Stanford.[54] Other studies of gender in law school conclude that women's experience as "outsiders" differs from the experience of men,[55] causing them to formulate a more extensive critique of the educational enterprise.[56]

More typical is a study of Berkeley law students that began with the presumption that men and women experience law school differently, and that these differences disadvantage women.[57] The authors of the study assumed that some women do not feel good about themselves despite performing as well as men;[58] thus the primary objective of the survey questions was to test self-esteem.[59] Many women students expressed intense feelings of pain, frustration, and isolation.[60] The vast majority of survey responses split along gender lines,[61] most noticeably on those questions regarding participation in class.[62]

In our view, each of these prior studies contained important methodological flaws. For example, unlike the designers of the Berkeley study, which had not been published when we began our work, we did not begin our research assuming that men and women experience law school differently. Indeed, we initiated the Bartow Survey to investigate this very claim. Unlike the researchers who did the Stanford study, we did not assume that gendered differences could be best captured in answers to hypotheticals about moral reasoning. Our survey did not ask about hypothetical situations. We developed instead a number of focus groups in which women and men were invited to reflect on their perceptions of their actual law school experiences.[63] In contrast to the Stanford survey, we also included in the written survey an open-ended question for narrative responses.

From Banks's pioneering attempt to document women's silence in the classroom to the more full-bodied examination of the law school experience of outsiders at Berkeley, all studies of female law students have been based primarily on self-reported data.[64] Unlike the authors of these studies, we did not limit ourselves to self-reported data, nor did we assume that men and women achieve similar levels of academic performance. With the support of the dean, we received unlimited access to four cohorts of anonymous academic performance data and designed a study to assess actual performance by following three separate classes of law students throughout much of their law school careers.[65] Our research thus builds on and extends the methodologies and findings of prior studies.

2. ON GENDER

A. *Quantitative Data on Academic Performance*

Third-year woman: I changed so much. I used to be a much more compassionate person, much more tolerant of different choices, in terms of lifestyle, in terms of personality. I just feel like law school has put huge blinders on my eyes.

Third-year woman: I came in here a very bright person, we all came in here very bright people, but what I lost while I was here, I lost the ability and the interest to really think about things, to think critically, to explore all of the avenues that were around.

Following our surprising survey results, we investigated academic performance to determine whether differences in the accumulated grades and credentials earned by men and women up to the point that they leave law school are explained by differences in entry-level credentials.[66] From these analyses, detailed below, we conclude that there is indeed a gendered academic experience. But the differences we identify are not predicted by those entry-level credentials on which the law school bases admission decisions. On the one hand, our data indicate that the quantitative entry-level credentials the law school employs to determine admissions, particularly the LSAT, explain very little about *men's or women's* performance once they have entered law school. On the other hand, women and men begin Penn Law School with equally stellar credentials. Holding incoming statistics constant, however, women graduate with significantly less distinguished professional credentials.

TABLE 1

MEAN STATISTICS FOR INCOMING STUDENTS

| | College GPA | | | Rank in College | | |
	N	Mean	σ	N	Mean	σ
Men	542	3.49	.31	544	78.44	20.35
Women	408	3.52	.28	409	80.13	18.45
		p=.143			p=.188	

| | LSAT | | | Lonsdorf Index | | |
	N	Mean	σ	N	Mean	σ
Men	544	40.98	4.16	543	4.73	.370
Women	413	40.87	4.09	408	4.74	.367
		p=.677			p=.685	

TABLE 2

MEAN LAW SCHOOL GPAs[68]

| | First-Year GPA (GPA1) | | | Second-Year GPA (GPA2) | | | Third-Year GPA (GPA3) | | |
	N	Mean	σ	N	Mean	σ	N	Mean	σ
Men	532	0.932	.524	397	1.005	.456	382	1.047	.425
Women	397	0.771	.475	303	0.853	.429	294	0.923	.416
		p=.000			p=.000			p=.000	

Both men and women come to the law school with very impressive, and quite comparable, records based on undergraduate GPA and rank in class, LSAT, Lonsdorf Index,[67] and undergraduate institution (see table 1). On two of the admission criteria, the women actually present incrementally stronger records. The men, on average, achieve a 3.49 undergraduate GPA, whereas women attain a 3.52. Men, on average, enter with an undergraduate class rank of 78.44, and women with 80.13. On a scale from one to forty-eight, the men's mean LSAT is 40.98, and the women's is 40.87. Finally, the men's average Lonsdorf Index is 4.73; the average for the women is 4.74. None of these differences is significant at the .05 level.

FIGURE 1

MEAN GPAs FOR LAW STUDENTS

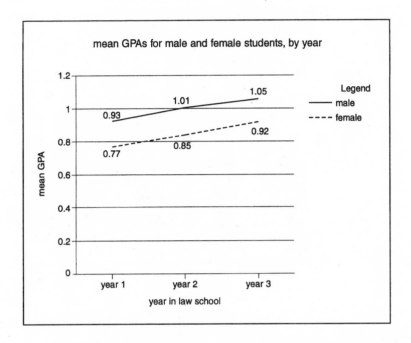

mean GPAs for male and female students, by year

Tracking law school GPAs for men and women across years one, two, and three reveals that despite equivalent entry profiles, there is a solid and stable gender difference in performance, sustained over time (see table 2). Although men and women enter with virtually equivalent statistics, men receive, on average, significantly better grades by the end of year one. Further, they maintain this advantage through graduation;[69] that is, the gender difference for mean GPA is stable across the three years in the law school (see figure 1). In terms of rank and GPA, first- and second-year men are 1.6 times more likely to be in the top fiftieth percentile of the class than are women. Third-year men are 1.5 times more likely to be in the top fiftieth percentile.[70] Our data show that 53.8% of the first-year male law students are the top fiftieth percentile of their class, compared to 42.8% of the first-year women (see figure 2).

If we look at an even more stringent measure of success—being

FIGURE 2[71]

PERCENT OF STUDENTS IN TOP FIFTIETH PERCENTILE OF CLASS

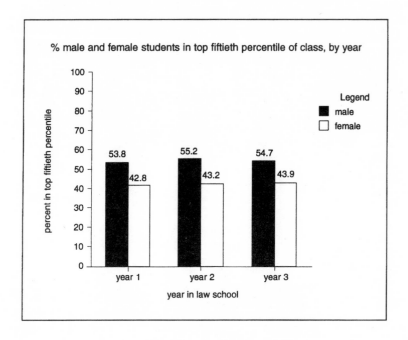

% male and female students in top fiftieth percentile of class, by year

in the top 10% of the class—we find that in the first year men are almost three times more likely than women to reach the top 10%; in the second and third years, men are two times more likely to do so (see figure 3). To summarize, our data document that women and men enter Penn Law School with comparable credentials,[72] but, in a pattern established firmly in the first year and maintained thereafter, women receive relatively lower grades, achieve lower class ranks, and earn fewer honors than do men.[73]

Clearly, women's entry-level statistics tell us little about their actual performance at the law school, but it is important to note that this is also true of men's entry-level statistics, particularly LSAT scores. We looked at how well LSAT scores explain the law school performance of both men and women; we found that the LSAT explains at most 21% of the difference in all student grades by the third year of law school and even less for the first two years. Fur-

FIGURE 3

PERCENT OF STUDENTS IN TOP TENTH PERCENTILE OF CLASS

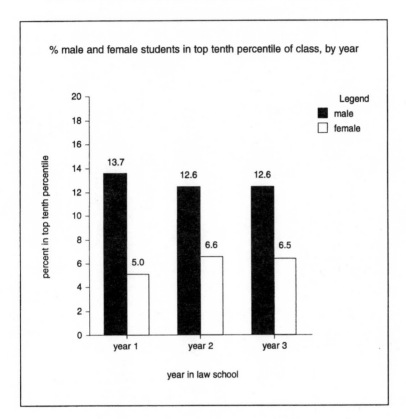

thermore, we found that the impact of LSAT decreased when we added race and gender to the equation. In other words, the impact of LSAT on law school grades in the bivariate regressions is masking the separate impact of race and gender on law school performance.[74]

Figure 4 is a pictorial account of the weak relationship between LSAT and law school GPAs. (We illustrate first-year GPA here because we have the most complete data for that cohort.) As LSAT increases (illustrated on the horizontal axis), first year GPA increases on the vertical axis. However, this relationship is almost random for

FIGURE 4

RELATIONSHIP BETWEEN LSATS
AND FIRST-YEAR LAW SCHOOL GPA

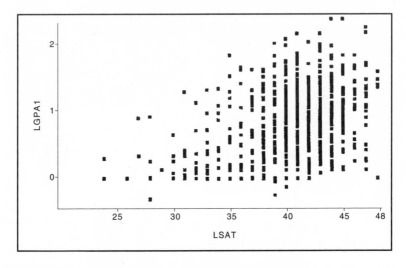

RELATIONSHIP BETWEEN LSATS OVER 35
AND FIRST-YEAR LAW SCHOOL GPA

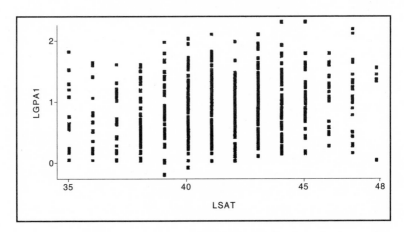

Table 3

Men and Women Selected for Various Honors, by Class[75]

	Class of 1990		Class of 1991		Class of 1992	
	Men	Women	Men	Women	Men	Women
Order of the Coif	19	5	16	7	21	7
Law Review Member						
(Non-Board)	25	3	16	12	21	11
Law Review Board	13	2	11	4	11	4
Moot Court Finalist	7	0	4	2	7	1
Moot Court Board	12	4	11	1	10	2
Faculty-Chosen						
Graduation Awards[76]	12	8	11	8	15	6

those who score over 35 on the LSAT, including those with the very highest LSAT scores. In other words, there appears to be a threshold beyond which LSATs *just don't matter* in terms of predicting law school performance for both men and women. Furthermore, some students with an LSAT of 30 do as well in law school as others with perfect (48) or near-perfect scores.

In addition to earning disproportionately low class ranks, women law students are underrepresented in the law school's prestigious positions and extracurricular activities. Over the three years of our study—from 1990 to 1992—women were underrepresented in the Order of the Coif,[77] the graduation awards given by the faculty, the *Law Review* membership and board, and the moot court competitions and board.

Part of this disparity (displayed in table 3) is due to the grade differential just described. Many honors are distributed, in whole or in part, on the basis of academic performance. For example, selection for membership on the *University of Pennsylvania Law Review* is based partially on first-year grades, and thus women, despite applying at rates proportionate to their numbers in the school, are less likely to be selected than men.[78] Graduating as a member of the Order of the Coif requires a student to be ranked in the top decile; in 1991 and 1992, men were almost twice as likely to be selected for the Order of the Coif as were women, and in 1990, men were more than twice as likely to be selected.[79]

Underrepresentation in other areas may be related to the fact that some honors are awarded on the basis of subjective judgments made by faculty and, at times, student peers who may have imported and/or internalized the academic hierarchy established during the first year.[80] For example, in 1990, each of the three student-run publications (*Law Review, Comparative Labor Law Journal,* and *Journal of International Business Law*) was headed by a male editor-in-chief.[81] Women also serve less frequently than men as editorial board members on the *Law Review.*[82] Additionally, women are rarely selected as finalists in the moot court competitions or to be members of the moot court board.[83]

When Ann Bartow first approached Professor Guinier in January 1990 about doing a video documentary about the experience of women law students, she related a story that resonates with these data. Bartow reported that some of her male colleagues at the law school chose their upper-level classes based on the number of women enrolled. Women were perceived as "Q-absorbing" buffers, with Q ("qualified") being the lowest passing grade on formal and informal grading curves.[84] These men assumed that their own chances of receiving a grade higher than Q increased as the number of women enrolled in the class increased, because the women would absorb a disproportionate number of the "qualified" grades, even with "blind" grading. They sarcastically referred to large groups of women in a class as the "Q quotient." At the time Bartow related this story, she was using it as an example of male stereotyping. What she did not articulate, but her male colleagues intuitively realized, was that the gendered performance differential we found was already known on some level (even as it was being created) within the law school community.

B. *Quantitative Data from the Bartow Survey*

Male student: I tend to find [professors] more accessible outside of class than I do in class actually. Yes, I do have—yes, I do talk to professors outside of the classroom. And I do have relationships with them, but it's divided up into different groups, though. I talk to a lot of professors outside of class.

Third-year woman: A lot of it I guess has to do with the professors, I think. For some reason, the atmosphere, the law school atmosphere at Penn doesn't really engender, um, that type of, um, communication where I feel I can approach a professor and we can develop some kind of a relationship. For instance, like I mentioned before, I'm interested in criminal law. Now [Professor X] is the type of person where if you have a question, you'll get an answer and he'll answer but he's not really a person you can hold a conversation with—just talk about, like, just day-to-day things. . . . He does, divert his eyes—like, . . . he averts his eyes, instead of giving, like, eye contact and, you know, holding a conversation if he sees you in the hallway. So I felt uncomfortable with that, so I just dropped that. . . . As far as the other professors, now—without mentioning names—there were times when I did feel uncomfortable when I went into their offices.

Third-year woman: I rarely speak to professors. Um, I am more likely to speak to professors of color or women or those teaching, like I said, the courses that I'm interested in that involve people and I can, you know, discuss people's issues. I can't imagine going up to a professor and talking about security regulations after class. It doesn't interest me enough. . . . But then again I don't think most of them are approachable. A lot of them are aloof, a lot of them act busy.

Third-year woman: I have very few interactions with any law professors. I don't even like to—I don't usually even go to talk to them when I have questions. I usually figure it out myself or ask somebody else.

The 1990 Bartow Survey was designed to track male and female law students' attitudes and experiences in law school. The data demonstrate that female law students are significantly more likely than male law students to report that they "never" or "only occasionally" ask questions or volunteer answers in class.[85] Women, more than men, report that men ask more questions, volunteer more often, enjoy greater peer tolerance of their remarks, receive more attention from faculty during classes, get called on more frequently, and receive more post-class "follow-up" than women.[86] All of these differences reached a level ($p = .05$) of statistical significance.

We were also interested in understanding how women and men students view the "fairness" of female and male faculty. With regard to perceived male faculty bias, gender differences are most apparent. In year one, women are four times more likely than men to say that male professors favor male students; by year three, the discrepancy remains. Most interestingly, 14% of first-year women versus 6% of first-year men indicate that only female faculty treat students equally. This discrepancy in perceptions continues through year three. In addition, male students are dramatically more likely to rate female faculty as favoring female students. It is important, however, to remember that faculty alone do not create the climate in the classroom. As we will discuss further, many women in our study expressed great concern with the attitudes, behavior, and intolerant remarks of male peers uninterrupted by faculty and/or other students.[87]

Perhaps because of their differing rates of participation, women and men also seek distinct qualities in law professors. Students were asked to name the three qualities they admired most in a law school professor. The men and women both chose "knowledge of subject matter" and "enthusiasm for teaching" as their top two qualities. Ninety-three percent of the women, however, selected "treats students with respect" as their third most admired quality,[88] whereas 82% of men selected "expresses ideas clearly."[89] We also observed gender-based responses that differed significantly with respect to qualities such as a professor's "openness to questions outside class" (valued by 69% of women, 55% of men) and "friendly with students" (valued by 65% of women, 56% of men).[90]

Across years, male students appear to be far more comfortable speaking with faculty of either gender than female students.[91] When asked, "How comfortable are you in interactions occurring outside of class with professors of the same or opposite sex?" 60% of the men, compared to 40% of the women, reported that they felt "very comfortable."[92] Men, in group interviews, confirmed their substantially greater degree of comfort with faculty. In contrast, many women indicated their inability either to approach faculty or, once engaged in conversation, to sustain a useful interaction. Several women in follow-up interviews expressed frustration at what they perceived to be aloofness on the part of the faculty.

The rates of participation reported by women as first-year students and as third-year students differ only to the extent that they reflect a transition from women never asking questions to asking questions infrequently. Women's level of satisfaction with this relatively stable rate of nonparticipation, however, increased over time. To the question, "Are you comfortable with your level of voluntary participation in class?" we see dramatic gender differences for year one (28% of the women responded "yes" versus 68% of the men).[93]

By year three, however, 64% of the women respond that they are now comfortable with their essentially unchanged level of participation, as do 72% of the men.[94]

In sum, women and men report significantly different assessments of their own classroom performance and perceptions of gender bias in the classroom. Also interesting, however, are the highly significant differences between the responses of the first-year women and all other categories of students. First-year female students, more than all other groups, report that men are called on more often than women[95] and receive more time and more follow-up in class,[96] that the gender of students affects class experience,[97] and that sexist comments are permitted under the informal "house rules" of the law school.[98] The concerns expressed by first-year women about male dominance in the classroom and failure to use gender-neutral language, as well as their perception that sexist comments are permitted, are not identified as problems by third-year female respondents.[99] After three years at the law school, either women seem to tolerate displays of what they, as first-year students, interpreted as offensive incidents of sexism, or, in fact, the frequency of such incidents diminishes.[100] "I am more willing to tolerate sexist comments or to assume they are jokes rather than offenses," said one third-year woman (who worries that school has changed her because she now feels more ambivalent about what constitutes sexism).

A dramatic difference between the positions of first- and third-year women is also reflected in responses to questions about career aspirations. Many more women than men come to the law school expressing a commitment to public interest law. A quarter of the first-year women, compared to 7% of the first-year men, indicated that they expected a job in public interest law.[101]

In response to the question, "What kind of law do you expect to practice?" first- and third-year men consistently expressed minimal interest in public interest work (see table 4). In contrast, the first-year women were at least three times more likely than men to express interest in public interest law. Third-year women's level of interest, however, was nearly as low as that of first- and third-year men. Whereas 25% to 33% of the first-year women planned to practice some form of public interest law, only 8% to 10% of the third-year women expressed such intentions.[102] This suggests that, over

TABLE 4

EXPECTED AREA OF PRACTICE
(percentage of group)
(columns may exceed 100% because multiple selections permitted)

	First-Year Women	Third-Year Women	First-Year Men	Third-Year Men
Corporation	33	28	56	41
Labor	28	6	10	10
Litigation	28	38	46	44
Public Interest	33	10	8	5
Estate	23	18	23	18
Bankruptcy	11	18	10	17

three years at the law school, women students come to sound more like their male classmates, and significantly less like their first-year "selves."[103] One could conclude that women become more "like men" over time in this particular law school, at least in terms of their reported attitudes toward gender, sexism, and career goals. Yet women's academic performance over time does not mirror that of men. As we have described, a disproportionate number of women —including those who move away from an interest in public interest law or drop their initial social critique—also graduate with significantly less impressive credentials than those of their male counterparts. Attitudinally they become closer to men; academically they move apart.[104]

C. *Narrative Data*

Second-year woman: In general in the classroom, some men tend to be somewhat condescending and didactic when they volunteer answers.

Another woman: I think that the comments that women make in class are not always taken seriously before the point is even made, because people make the assumption that the women may be taking the liberal, "sensitive" position—and these positions are not always given the credit and attention that they deserve.

After crafting a preliminary summary of the data from the Bartow Survey, in the spring of 1991 and 1992 we asked two groups of self-selected law students in a "Race and Gender" seminar to reflect on their experiences as first-, second-, and third-year law students. Each group of approximately eighteen to twenty-three students was diverse with respect to age, gender, and race/ethnicity.[105] A different group of approximately ten first-, second-, and third-year female students who were members of the Women's Law Group also responded to the data at a specially convened meeting.[106] Further, we conducted in-depth interviews with twenty-seven additional students who were selected to represent a better cross-section of law school opinion. Those interviewed included editors of the *Law Review*, students in the top 10% of their class, instructors of first-year legal writing sections, and separate groups of white, African-American, Latino, and Asian-American students.[107] We also analyzed the 104 responses to the open-ended question on the Bartow Survey.

We acknowledge that the students who volunteered to participate in our group interviews were unusually motivated to tell their stories; although the composition of these focus groups was representative by gender, year in law school, involvement in law school activities and journals, and class rank, the students we interviewed were arguably among the more alienated members of the school population. Similarly, those students who chose to respond to the open-ended questions in the Bartow Survey may not have been typical of the entire student body.

We nevertheless believe that the stories we report in this section are important for several reasons. First, they come from students who excel academically, those in the middle range, and those who do not excel in law school. Second, the comments of individual students in group discussions echo the responses to the open-ended narrative question in the 1990 Bartow Survey, which came from over 50% of the student population in that same year and were received at a rate proportionate to the gender distribution in the survey as a whole. Third, in addition to reinforcing quantitative data collected independently, these statements give context to our other empirical findings.

As in the survey, the women students we interviewed almost universally expressed stronger and more passionate feelings of alienation and outrage than the male students we interviewed, even when we control for year in law school and rank in class.

We observe the following about students' perspectives of their law school experience: many women express high levels of alienation; the law school experience, which is designed to establish an academic hierarchy, in turn generates gendered and racial alienation; and many men at the law school deny the gendered origins and effects, and the institutional impact of this hierarchy.

In particular, almost all the women we interviewed described their first-year experience as a radical, painful, or repressive experience, "one that I will never forget." Several women reported their voices were "stolen" from them in the first year. Some of the women who felt alienated did very well academically, yet they did not recognize their former selves, which they perceived as submerged in the pursuit of succeeding as a "social male." One woman said she felt silenced by what she termed "a group of frat boys who call you man-hating lesbian, or feminist—as though those are bad—if you are too outspoken." Other women reported suffering from hissing, public humiliation, and gossip simply for speaking aloud in class.[108] They expressed profound alienation from the law school, the educational process, and, most disturbing, from themselves, or who they used to be.

> *Female student:* I try to block out the entire experience. I won't take pictures, talk on tapes; I hope to forget this whole thing as soon as I'm gone. I hope to skip that space in time.
> *Female student:* Whatever ideals we came in with, they get bashed out of us.
> *Male student:* The first year is like basic training. They need to mold you.
> *Female student:* There are so few safe spaces for women in this law school.

These women often internalize their difficulties, seek counseling more frequently than the men, and look to other women for support. This is illustrated by an interaction we observed between male and female students in 1991.

> *Male student:* After my first year I realized that I was making a mountain out of a molehill.
> *Female student:* But you're not listening to what [the previous speaker] said. She said, "It entirely shook my faith in myself. I will never recover." Some of us just sunk deeper and deeper in a mire, and just keep sinking lower and lower.
> *Female student:* I came here with something to prove and at that moment [in first year] I lost all my drive. Talk about a light switch—it went off. It just shook my faith, all my self-esteem.

The women, as opposed to the men participating in this and the previous exchange, attributed their academic difficulties to themselves. As one woman explained,

> When we get bad grades, we just think we're stupid. You guys get over it! Men suppress their feelings, so it doesn't take a toll. I used to never cry; last year [as a first-year student] I cried every week. Guys think law school is hard, and we just think we're stupid.

In response to a series of mental health inquiries in the survey, we found that although men and women report no differences with respect to involvement in fights or the use of alcohol or drugs, women are significantly more likely to report eating disorders, sleeping difficulties, crying, and symptoms of depression or anxiety. Whereas 68% of the men reported that they never cried during law school (compared to 15% of the women), 35% of the women reported that they cried at least once a month (compared to only 4% of the men). Women were five times more likely to seek professional help for law school concerns, with rates of 15.5% for the women, compared to 3.6% for the men.[109]

Other women seek support from each other. Several women described a pact they had made during their first year to follow up on the comments of any woman who spoke in order to minimize their experience of isolation.[110] For them, supporting other women became a crucial precondition to the learning process, indicating how far they had to go even to begin to learn in this environment. This informal attempt at support and solidarity may have helped to combat some of the alienation that these women felt, but it was a temporary solution that did not address the cause of their alienation.[111]

Furthermore, we are inclined to see this "gendered effect" as implicating the institutional design of the law school experience, rather than personal qualities of individual female or male students. The pedagogical structure of the first year—large classes, often constrained by limits on student participation, fierce competition, a mandatory grading curve, and few women faculty—produces alienation and a gender-stratified hierarchy.

> *Third-year woman:* I really resent being an instrument for many —and I think it is true for many, not all of the professors—for a professor's lecture. I really resent feeling like after I am laying out all of this money and putting myself under a pretty unpleasant pro-

cess, that on top of this, I should be forced to participate. . . . I took this "Critical Perspective" class and I couldn't shut up. It was interesting and something was going on that was interesting. We are all teaching it ourselves. I had been worried until I took this class that maybe I had lost my ability to like think and participate in class the first year. It's not that. I just don't find most of the classroom experiences here to be particularly valuable.

Third-year woman: Just look at the way many professors here conduct their classes. They call on men predominantly. I sat in classes and had not heard a single female voice and we sort of— one year we did a study of that, an informal thing amongst ourselves. . . . I think if you look at the people in our class who have formed relationships with professors, they are very much the same men who all of us despise in class. The ones who feel they can monopolize the class time, the ones who rush up after class and make sure that other people can't ask the professor a question because they have something very long to say.

Indeed, some variation of the Socratic method is almost universally used in first-year courses at Penn,[112] thereby exposing all students to the law school's model of how lawyers "are."[113] Many women report, however, that when speaking feels like a performance they respond with silence rather than participation, especially when the Socratic method is employed to intimidate or to establish a hierarchy within large classes. This pressure is especially problematic for students who perceive that they are expected to "perform" as spokespersons for their racial or gender group.[114]

Several women who were intimidated or not engaged by Socratic-style questioning in large first-year classrooms stated matter-of-factly that they could not learn in such an environment. One admitted that she even had a principle of law named after her, which she was called upon weekly to restate; in the large classroom atmosphere, she would repeat the principle by rote. Two years later, she reported that at the time she did not understand the principle, nor could she now explain to her listeners what it meant. A few men also reported discomfort with the Socratic style, although they seemed less likely to internalize the discomfort.[115]

The hierarchy within a large first-year Socratic class also includes a hierarchy of perspectives. Those who most identify with the institution, its faculty, its texts, and its individualistic perspectives experience little dissonance in the first year.[116] Others—students who bring with them a lesser sense of personal entitlement and an ambivalent identification with the institution; who resist competitive adversarial relationships; who do not see themselves represented on the faculty; who vacillate on the emotionally detached, "objective" perspectives inscribed as "law"; or who identify with the lives of persons who suffer from existing political arrangements—these students experience much dissonance.

> *Third-year white woman:* I think that maybe in view of the whole Rodney King thing that we need to keep in mind that it's not just issues of race and it's not just issues of gender. Issues of class, really, you never discuss them. You never discuss them, unless it's a course devoted to speaking about welfare or the underclass, you never talk about the difference in perspective, not in criminal law and not in constitutional law, unless somebody brings it up and it is so unlikely because we are all reduced to that white-male and middle-class perspective.
>
> *First-year Latina:* Likewise, I think that there is a lot of discrediting on the side of the white students. I don't know, maybe it's a paranoia, or [I] wonder how people are perceiving me. I guess the sense that, perhaps, people won't listen to me as much as if I was a white person saying it. I think when they listen to me, they say "of course she is going to say that because she is speaking for her own self-interest" and as a result, I don't feel our feelings are ticking as individuals.
>
> *Two first-year black women:* I think that still most people do not understand that African-Americans are still struggling or why they are struggling. To me it's incredible because it's like blindness and I listen to some of the comments in class and I realize that I am coming from an entirely different world in that perspective than most people, just because I'm more aware of history and the law and things like that, as it relates to black people.
>
> I think that part of it has to do with the fact that [the] perception of white students is that they are going to be lawyers. They can be whatever kind of lawyers they want to be. They don't have to represent all black people as mentioned earlier. Some of us have changed our career paths because it is necessary to help people in our community as opposed to being able to go out there and just do whatever it is for you and I think that perception is somewhat different from the whole administration's idea. I don't know, it seems to gear you towards what you kind of need to do and make you feel like no one else is going to do it so you need to. It is sort of like a heavier burden on us, as black students, that we have to consider the community as well as ourselves and we can't just have a free and easy life as a law student.

A disproportionate number of women of all racial and ethnic groups, and men of color also experience alienation in that they enter law school with a zeal for public interest work, but end by having opted for corporate or other private sector employment. Our data suggest that there is an academic cost, and perhaps a mental health cost, to discarding passions, politics, emotions, and community-based identities that were once central to a student's identity.[117] In their narratives, for example, some men of color and women indicate that law school is a moment in adult socialization in which their political and professional identities become "zippered"—with legal perspectives internalized as neutral professionalism. Many express deep feelings of alienation from their backgrounds, passions, and communities.

Laced throughout the interviews with both white women and, to a greater degree, women of color, we hear the desire to reinsert culture, race, politics, and "emotions" back into legal interpretations. Many students explain that the law is structured in ways that value only individuals, not communities.

> *First-year black woman:* I changed since I wanted to come here to get into the corporate law stream. After I have seen the injustices, I have decided to change my career goals. My people need representation. . . . I want to help those people who have helped me to get to where I am.

These students want to be able to move from the perspective of the elite to that of the victim, to pivot their vantage and interpretations in ways that might disrupt precedent, rather than merely accept the "logic" of what has "neutrally" been decided before.

> *Third-year white woman:* I feel that [compassion] is something that is eradicated in law school. This notion that we can present things as though, like the law, it's a self-contained unit, it's a sphere that we can look down upon as though we were astronauts that can look down on the earth. The whole idea that these things are neutral and that a neutral outcome results just eliminates any notion of compassion because professors sort of play on that, "Oh, you feel sorry for these people. Oh, well that's too bad. Oh, well the law says, *X*." We are really taught that compassion is a bad thing.
>
> *Third-year white woman* (responding to above comment): I think that what you just said is so accurate, this notion that there is a neutral presentation of the law and that any concerns that may affect the real world are therefore not neutral. As though not mentioning these concerns is neutral as opposed to a political choice.

The disjunction between some women's concerns for community and the law school's emphasis on individualism creates a dissonance for these students that results, at best, in a bicultural consciousness.[118]

Although one man indicates that the point of law school is to "play the game," another worries that the press for objectivity in his three years of law school has forced him to remove his mind from his Latino body and emotions:

> The one thing bad about the way I argue now is that I think it's a little bit less passionately. I've been taught [here] that emotion in an argument is a minus and in my culture emotion in an argument is a plus. And here whenever you present an emotional side of an argument—which I think is just as valid as many other arguments—you know, about the abortion issue. You know, how a woman feels about having to have a baby—and I mean why isn't that any more legitimate than endless arguments about the constitutional right to privacy? I don't think one really should take precedence over the other. And I think it's instilled in you that if you make an emotional argument then it's wrong.

With remarkable consistency, students indicate that law school taught them to be "less emotional," "more objective," and to "put away . . . passions."[119] For some, this demand to suppress feelings is considered an enormous accomplishment; for others, it is considered a defeat. Second only to the skills of "objectivity," students report that over time they have learned to stop caring about others and have become more conservative. Some men indicate they have grown more aggressive and abrasive over their three years in law school; some women see themselves as more "humble" and "nitpicking." One woman concluded her interview by saying, "Here [at the law school], it's okay to be intolerant."

The competitive, hierarchical format of the law school's dominant pedagogy is also sometimes used by peers to put down women. Many women who complained that their voices are pushed back and down, suffocated early on by hostile first-year classmates, described how those women who did speak out felt humiliated by male, and some female, contemporaries who silenced those who publicly dared *not* to "act like gentlemen." Ideas about women's sexuality, for example, became a basis for ridiculing individual women, especially those who spoke out in class.[120] These putdowns may occur in informal networks that exist outside the classroom, but they are normalized by and may reproduce behavior that is performed within the classroom.

> *Female student:* Women's sexuality becomes the focus for keeping us in our place. If someone was rumored to be a woman who speaks too much, she was a lesbian.[121] That is, women don't speak partially because our sexuality becomes implicated as soon as we act "too much like men" for their liking. . . . Now, I'm in a room with 120 frat boys, a mass of faces that say nothing when you speak. No feedback from professors. No one cares what you did, and who you were, people hiss, laugh, and there is rarely an interruption of that from other students or professors. We need to change class size and how classes are taught so that men and women can speak publicly, and not self-consciously, in front of others.
>
> *Another female student:* After I discovered I was being called a feminazi dyke, I never spoke in class again.

The classroom pecking order is also observed outside the formal classroom setting. Women indicate that "student organizations and activities" are significantly more important to them, relative to men. They report that they spend more time with law students who are female, and they are more likely to study with peers. Nevertheless, although women appear to participate in social groups and student groups more than men, women are not perceived as holding leadership positions at equivalent rates.[122] The data suggest that a plurality of students see an equal distribution of leadership positions, but more than one-third of women students perceive men as holding a disproportionate share of those leadership positions.

In an attempt to "explain away" the gender and institutional implications of the data, many men, both students and faculty, resort to alternative explanations which identify a source unrelated to gender or the school for the differences we found.[123] For example, they proffered age, undergraduate major, and even (men's greater) participation in varsity sports in college as possible explanations for the differential between women's and men's performance as measured by grades in law school. We found no statistically significant difference between women and men in these categories. Women and men at Penn Law School are roughly the same age and have majored in similar fields as undergraduates.[124] The point, however, is not whether these alternative explanations are worth

Table 5[131]

Distribution of Narrative Responses

	First-Year Women	Second-Year Women	Third-Year Women	First-Year Men	Second-Year Men	Third-Year Men
Survey biased	0	1	0	2	2	0
Gender tensions	18	19	5	4	5	3
No bias here	0	0	0	1	2	0
Women are paranoid	2	0	1	7	4	6
Reverse discrimination by women faculty	0	0	0	2	3	6
Sensitive profs & peers	1	0	4	2	1	0
Other	0	0	1	2	0	0
Total responses	21	20	11	20	17	15

pursuing.[125] The point is that many men immediately generated hypotheses that located the problem outside of gender and outside of the law school.[126]

> *Male student:* I think that the women are saying it is a problem because they are straight from undergraduate school. I came to school when I was experienced, had a family, and school wasn't all that I was living for. Probably you should check for an age or experience comparison.[127]
>
> *Male professor:* Men students probably come from the "hard sciences" which better prepare them for the rigors of law school.[128]

We explored these intuitions and found that when controlling for incoming demographics, gender alone predicted third-year law school class rank.[129]

Many men (and some women) are uncomfortable with the attention paid to gender,[130] as is evident in the responses to the 1990 open-ended survey question (see table 5). Many men were offended simply by being asked about gender.

As with the academic performance data, the survey narratives reveal a distinct gender effect that continues through each year of law school. First-, second-, and third-year men, in their responses to our open-ended questions, describe women students who are concerned with gender as "paranoid," "overly sensitive," and "intimidat[ed by] conversation."

Men of all classes frequently criticized the survey methods,[132] feminist students,[133] and women faculty, and reported reverse discrimination.[134] One young man stated:

> There have been many instances of women professors alienating male law students by showing clear favoritism to women law students. Many would argue that this treatment is necessary to *bend the stick to the center* based on perceived sexism in the schools, whether institutional or otherwise.

In contrast, women students were more likely to use the open-ended space to express concerns with sexist language and assumptions of professors and peers, especially peers.[135] Several women, but only one man, worried about the trivialization, in classes on criminal law, of women as victims of the crime of rape.[136] Women, but no men, reported that they felt ignored or opposed by faculty and peers in class.[137] Further, several women, but again no men, reported moderate to severe forms of harassment from male students.[138] These women were distressed that many of their peers claimed that discrimination is a "thing of the past."[139]

First-year women students report the most discomfort. They describe gender tensions, hostilities, and male faculty and/or students "not taking women very seriously." Nevertheless, although a full 78% of first-year women report sexist incidents in their comments section, only 41% of third-year women do the same. By year three, 33% of women students consider professors and peers at the law school "quite sensitive" to issues of gender. As one second-year woman observed, "Not all women are feminists and not all women agree. . . . It is very uncomfortable for me that sex is such a big issue in the classroom and the law school community." A few second- and third-year women students express similar resentment "when other women make a big deal about sex-related issues in class." Third-year women report an increased tolerance and decreased awareness of gender bias, while the responses of the men remain stable from their first to third years. By their third year, women are far less concerned with gender tensions and more likely to report that faculty and peers are "sensitive" to issues of gender.[140]

3. ANALYSIS AND RECOMMENDATIONS

From our data, we conclude that this institution may be typical but is nevertheless a hostile learning environment for a disproportionate number of its female students. Our data document that the women at this law school graduate with weaker academic credentials than do the men. The disparate quality of women's accumulated credentials interacts with higher levels of alienation and lower self-esteem for many women, even those who do well academically.

We reiterate, however, two important limiting caveats. First, our research does not suggest that every female law student feels alienated, fails to succeed academically, or brings a social justice critique to her legal education. Many University of Pennsylvania women do "become gentlemen" at least to the extent that they "aspire to ascend the status hierarchy without necessarily confronting its normative condition along the way."[141] We do not claim to describe the experience of each and every woman attending the University of Pennsylvania Law School. Nor does our research suggest that all men do well or that no men feel alienated.

Second, the problems many women experience at the University of Pennsylvania Law School are not unique to this school.[142] We identify problems at the site of our research, but we do not claim those problems are peculiar to—or completely defined by—this one institution, its faculty, its student body, or its administration;[143] indeed, we have been actively encouraged by the administration, and in particular by Dean Diver, to pursue this research. In addition, we do not deny that the sources of responsibility for many gendered differences may be outside of this law school, which does not exist independent of national norms and long-standing traditions governing legal education and legal practice; the faculty and administration of this law school strive to conform to their perception of the norms and conventions of peer institutions.[144]

In sum, references to women as a group mean a disproportionate number of women relative to their absolute numbers and to the responses of comparable numbers of men. References to the University of Pennsylvania Law School reflect the fact that this law school is the focus of our study, yet it may not be the sole structural "source" or locus of the problem. With these important limitations, we propose three explanations of our findings. In our view, each of these claims deserves further study as part of a serious reevaluation of the formal and informal organization of law school education.

A. *Alienation and Academic Performance Within the Formal Structure of the Institution*

"Becoming gentlemen" appears to exact an academic cost for many women, and, as the narratives suggest, for some men of color. Women's enfeebled participation within the formal structure of legal education occurs simultaneously with their less successful performance on the anonymously graded examinations from which law school grades are derived. In other words, low levels of class participation in the formal, structured pedagogy correlate with weak performance within the formal, structured evaluation system.[145]

There is also a psychological dimension to women's relatively weak academic performance. Along with a formal link between classroom participation and examination success, we suspect that there exists a psychological link between self-confidence, alienation, and academic performance. Students who are alienated by the system's formal classroom methodology, hierarchy, and large class size are arguably not psychologically prepared to succeed on the formal examinations.[146] Those who doubt themselves or doubt whether they belong in the law school do not perform as well.[147]

Many students, especially many women, have simply not been socialized to thrive in the type of ritualized combat that comprises much of the legal educational method.[148] The theory of legal education assumes that learning is accomplished by self-teaching and that a certain level of stress or anxiety is a necessary precondition to initiate the learning process.[149] But many women claim that neither their initiative nor their problem-solving abilities are engaged in an intimidating learning environment.[150] The performance aspect of a large Socratic classroom disables some women from performing up to their potential, especially when this teaching method is used to intimidate. If no comparably significant formal learning experiences are provided, first-year women in particular are most likely to be affected, but these phenomena also adversely affect some men; indeed, it has been said that elite law

schools may prepare their top male students "to become law professors but fail to prepare the rest of their students to become practicing lawyers."[151]

From the reactions of their professors and the responses to their
performance in all areas of the institution, some female students
learn that they cannot thrive well in the law school environment.
For example, the perception is widespread that within the classroom, white men are encouraged and allowed to speak more often
than women of all colors and men of color, for longer periods of
time, and with greater positive feedback from professors and
peers.[152] When women fail to receive the same level of positive response from faculty, many experience a blow to their self-esteem.
Our data suggest that some women internalize the absence of positive feedback, even when the professor's aloofness reaches across
gender lines,[153] and some come to believe that they have little to
contribute, becoming further alienated from the law school and the
process of legal education. Others refuse to engage in discussion
and opt for a strong stance of silence[154] because they find the law
school's adversarial nature, its focus on argumentation, and its emphasis on abstract as opposed to contextual reasoning to be unap-
pealing. Their method of resistance may be to disengage. Even if
this is the case, our data suggest there may be an academic price to
pay for such a stance.[155]

It is important to recognize that peer relations further reinforce
women's silence via "hazing" imposed on women by white males.
Students describe hazing as taking the form of "laughing at what I
said" or "lesbian-baiting."[156] Apparently, merely being called a feminist[157] is sometimes considered sufficiently insulting to silence
women who try to challenge prevailing interpretations of legal
texts.[158]

Many women complain that their male peers discourage
women's participation by making disparaging comments; women
further express concern that faculty do not intervene.[159] Whether
self-esteem suffers from direct or indirect comparisons, the psychological literature suggests that low self-esteem adversely affects academic performance,[160] usually where negative stereotypes
of women are created and reinforced by men—as in Bartow's "Q"
quotient anecdote.[161]

For those whose reaction is not to "fight back," their first contact with the law school environment may be one of defeat. If they have accepted the norms of the institution, these students come to believe that their place within the hierarchy is, deservedly, at the bottom. We believe that this element of socialization to one's "place" in the hierarchy helps to ensure the success of male students at the expense of women. The student culture itself reinforces the low status of many women who fear they cannot measure up because they are just not as good at "playing the game" as their male peers. For these women, the moment they speak out to challenge what they perceive as sexist assumptions or offensive language, they may jeopardize the level at which they are taken seriously. To retain status they must often feign indifference and, as one woman reported, feel complimented when rewarded by male peers for being "such a guy." In other words, women cannot discuss issues of concern to "women" without feeling stigmatized and diminished.[162] And many faculty seem to do little to create safe, accessible, democratic spaces within their classrooms.

For many women, therefore, the first year of law school is experienced as the construction of the law school hierarchy; for them it is the most emotionally draining and intellectually debilitating year. The quantitative data suggest that gendered academic differentials are cemented in the first year and sustained over time. Within that one year, white men rise to the top, but women scatter downward, and this stratification continues throughout the next two years. Even when LSAT score, undergraduate GPA, and undergraduate class rank are held constant, gender and race interact to play a significant role in predicting third-year class rank in law school.

One's place in the law school hierarchy is orchestrated by a mandatory grading curve, large Socratic classrooms, skewed presentations of professional identity,[163] and fierce competition brewing uninterrupted within peer culture.[164] The Socratic classroom itself becomes the idealized representation of a system of legal education in which there are few winners and many losers.[165]

Those most comfortable at the top of the hierarchy secure virtual monopoly access to good grades and high rank. Women who do not participate in large Socratic classes may suffer directly if timed examinations do in fact test either the enhanced learning that participation presumably produces or the emphasis on quick, strategic issue-spotting that aggressive forms of the Socratic dialogue reward. In part because social comparison is an important part of self-esteem, women's self-esteem may also suffer indirectly if they internalize their alienation or are intimidated into silence.[166] Such silence may become evidence to these women that they are not as smart or clever as their more vocal male peers.[167]

Although some justify hierarchy as separating "the men from the boys,"[168] many of our respondents perceive the process as legitimating the separation of "the white men from the white women and people of color." Some might suggest that the law school "merely 'reproduce[s]' gender hierarchies through the transmission of male-oriented values."[169] We suggest instead, or in addition, that the law school provides "a context through which gender identity and experience is 'constituted' in relation to a student's biography and interactions within school."[170] We believe that on some level the school creates the categories that it then presumes to be sifting. We call this the process of "legitimation."[171] Those who identify with the norms and goals of the institution feel entitled to exploit faculty and peer resources. They perform accordingly and are legitimated through institutional rewards. In turn, the institution is legitimated in its selection criteria by the very fact that there are always those who meet these criteria.

This process affects students in two ways. First, the institution attempts to legitimate its structural organization and values by formally presenting them to the student as intrinsic components of "thinking like a lawyer." Thus the law school transmits the formal structure of the institution by preparing the student for hierarchical relationships (teacher-student is equated with partner-associate, judge-counsel, and lawyer-client) as well as by telling the student that acceptance of these relationships is necessary for effective lawyering.

Second, the student is supposed to reciprocate in the process of legitimation by accepting the law school on *its* terms, including accepting as legitimate the system by which the law school evaluates and ranks its students.[172] Implicitly, then, the student recognizes that the law school has the right to rank students, that the ranking must be correct, and that the ranking represents the student's true ability to be a lawyer (at least in relation to the others in the class).[173] At the University of Pennsylvania, this process takes hold powerfully in the first year of law school.

In first-year classrooms, a gender system is established, legitimated, and subtly internalized. As one third-year student said:

> I think I am definitely more subdued. . . . I wonder how much [of]
> this is . . . getting older or maturing and how much [is] law school,
> specifically. I think law school makes you very risk-averse or at
> least that is the effect that it has on me.

Students learn their place in the gender hierarchy. All women have finally been welcomed into the law school's hierarchy, but it seems that a significant number are welcome to stay at the bottom. The combination of highly visible, competitive pedagogical strategies in large first-year classrooms, peer hazing, and an institutionalized emphasis on replacing "emotions" with "logic" and "commitments" with "neutrality" may be sufficient to socialize many students into their "place," even those who are trying to resist.[174]

B. *The Alienation and Exclusion of Women from Informal Learning Networks*

In his narrative response to the Bartow Survey, a third-year male noticed this tendency among his male colleagues:

> Whenever men at the law school open their mouths, something
> horrendous about women seems to come out. There are so many
> such incidents that to try and list them would be futile. Disparag-
> ing remarks about women's bodies, menstrual cycles, sexual orien-
> tation, etc., are the rule.

We posit that in addition to feeling alienated from the manifest structure of the educational environment, many women are, in fact, excluded from the latent learning structure. Whereas our first hypothesis is that alienation, class participation, and academic performance are interrelated variables within the *formal* learning environment, our second hypothesis looks at the way women function within the law school's *informal* learning structure.

We argue that at least some of the learning in law school takes place outside the classroom.[175] In this context, according to the Bartow Survey, women report feeling less comfortable than men students in approaching faculty outside of class, and many women report that they feel objectified by their male peers. For these reasons, many women do not enjoy equal access to important educational relationships outside of the classroom.[176]

Our data suggest that women students are less comfortable, in the aggregate, than men within the law school's informal structure. Female students are less likely than their male peers to interact with faculty outside of class.[177] Whereas male students report that they are comfortable approaching faculty of either gender, female students apparently require "friendliness cues" before they seek out faculty after class.[178] In addition, many female students believe male professors favor male students.[179] These women also complain that the hazing by their male peers both inside and outside of class forces them to retreat to all-women support groups or to form pacts with other women in order to support women participants in class.[180]

Some women law students are also less successful at negotiating barriers to informal faculty/student interactions. These barriers to informal contact, whether self-imposed or institutionally constructed, in turn adversely affect the ability of these female students to thrive in the law school's environment.[181] For example, although participation in student organizations is more important to female survey respondents than to their male counterparts, these women are less likely to perceive themselves or other women as leaders in these organizations.[182] If status positions are not achieved by women in numbers equal to men or proportionate to their presence in the student body, this then appears to reduce the respect women are granted within the law school community.[183]

Similarly, we found that the predominantly male faculty bestows a disproportionate number of graduation awards upon male students.[184] This may reflect the first-year academic performance differential that is sustained over the next two years in law school. Alternatively, or additionally, it may reflect the fact that women also suffer when subjective criteria, such as "best student in X" or "most promising student in Y," govern. Or, it may reflect the fact that male professors are more likely to mentor male students.[185]

For example, finding a mentoring relationship positively correlates with institutional success.[186] Yet relatively few female students are apparently mentored by the faculty.[187] There are several possible reasons for this. First, male students are more willing to approach male faculty than are female students because male students perceive male faculty to be generally respectful and friendly.[188] Second, mentoring relationships more often form between people who share similar values, attitudes, or backgrounds, including gender.[189] Third, many faculty do not view mentoring as part of their job.[190]

One reason that faculty give for declining to mentor students is that Socratic-style instruction in the large classroom is efficient, whereas mentoring is very time-consuming. Another justification proffered by a male colleague at the law school is that mentoring is similar to "spoon-feeding," which is antithetical to traditionally valued notions of rigorous analytic work, whose lessons are best learned in isolated or stressful circumstances. Likewise, faculty may believe that student initiative is necessary in order to justify the time commitment involved in mentoring. As a result, they mentor only selected students and primarily those who initiate the relationship.

Although the faculty may be treating both male and female students alike in this regard, the failure to initiate mentoring relationships disproportionately discourages female students. In the absence of overt friendliness cues, female students often do not seek out mentors in a male-dominated faculty.[191]

The informal barriers we describe may be so "imbedded in our ways of interacting with each other as men and women" that they are invisible to many students and faculty.[192] They may reflect the unconscious imposition of "male norms"[193] on ways of learning or mentoring that have a discrepant gender-based effect.[194] Alternatively, these women may simply be excluded from informal settings in which people who are perceived to be different are invisible or made to feel unwelcome.

In fact, others have found that homogeneity among elites promotes greater familiarity, which minimizes the need for formal rules, thus permitting communication shortcuts among socially similar peers.[195] Consequently, in informal settings students and faculty of the same sex and similar backgrounds often interact most comfortably.[196] This is consistent with the social science findings that members of minority groups experience informality as a barrier; they are more likely to feel excluded in less rule-bound, informal settings than in formal settings.[197]

In addition, informal barriers may exist in response to the proportional scarcity of women in the upper levels of the institution's hierarchy. For law students, the number of women exceeds the numerical threshold for true "tokens."[198] Nevertheless, many women function as if they were tokens, in part because they are proportionally scarce in the institution's leadership or influential roles. For example, women are proportionately underrepresented as full-time tenure-track faculty,[199] on the law journals, as leaders in student organizations, and as recipients of faculty-initiated graduation awards.[200]

We posit that women law students are at a disadvantage because their rising proportion in the student body has not been accompanied by a comparable increase in the number or proportion of female faculty. We suggest that the difficulties of being women students in an institution with a high proportion of male faculty adversely affect women's access to informal education networks. Based on findings at other institutions,[201] as well as our own data, we hypothesize that women faculty are more likely than men faculty to mentor women students, that women students are more likely to perceive women faculty as approachable, and that being able to approach faculty is as critical to students' self-perception of their role in the institution as it is to the substantive learning that takes place in various other informal settings.

Our claim is that the proportional scarcity of "elite women" sets up a dynamic of virtual tokenism, in which the more numerically significant women students are nevertheless treated as, or self-identify as, "tokens."[202] This dynamic exists in both the manifest and latent structure of the law school, as well as in both the actual treatment of female students and their perception of their treatment by male students and faculty.[203] As with true tokens, the dynamic of virtual tokenism reinforces limitations on the opportunity for success of women law students.[204] Also similar to the plight of true tokens is the fact that many female students at the law school enter the institution with identical credentials and then differentiate significantly from their male peers in terms of academic achievement, voluntary class participation, and interaction with faculty.[205] They become casualties of institutional structure, and yet they hold themselves to be personally responsible. Moreover, even if they are treated no differently than male students, many female students experience the institutional norms in a way that adversely affects their performance. Some women may simply need more encouragement to do well or to approach faculty in a male-dominated school where "merit" is arguably still measured by attributes associated with maleness or available to males.[206] Or, these women may need mentors as much as—or more than—men to counterbalance the impersonality of the large first-year Socratic classroom.[207]

We do not argue that male faculty cannot or do not ever mentor female students.[208] We do believe, however, that the mentoring dynamic adversely affects those female students who are not successful in establishing such relationships and whose need for such informal reinforcement may be even greater than that of some of their male peers.

This is not an argument for more women role models.[209] We argue that women students need faculty and student *mentors*—meaning teachers, guides, or more accomplished peers who share their knowledge or experience within the context of an interpersonal relationship. We posit, based on our data, that a disproportionately male faculty and student body—for whatever reason—fail to function effectively in informal settings to support female students to the same degree as male students are supported.

C. *Women Who Do Not Become Gentlemen Are Less Valued Members of the Law School Community*

There is also a third hypothesis that others have urged us to consider: that women are simply different. There is a tension in this "difference hypothesis." Our data lead us to conclude, on the one hand, that many women entering law school *are different* from men in various ways, including their initial interest in public interest law, their expressions of alienation from and nonparticipation in the formal educational pedagogy, and their self-reported need for more friendliness cues for informal faculty interaction. On the other hand, it is important to remember that, using standard predictors of academic success, women entering law school are fundamentally *the same* as men entering law school (as a group). We interpret this web of data to mean that *"difference" as disadvantage is created at law school over time.*

According to the difference hypothesis, women's difference makes them less equipped for law school.[210] The way things are done in law school (the Socratic method, timed issue-spotting exams, large classrooms, unpatrolled and informal networks) devalues and distorts those characteristics traditionally associated with

women, such as empathy, relational logic, and nonaggressive behavior. In this understanding, law school unintentionally uses a
male-oriented baseline to measure male/female differences, ren-
dering women as less than competent.[211]

Although aspects of this hypothesis permeate the other two, this
third explanation invariably conceals a troublesome assumption—
that it is women, not law school, that must change. Because of this
assumption, the third explanation invites another troubling response—that, despite identical entry level credentials, the *wrong*
women are being admitted to law school.[212] In other words, many
women simply should not be trained as lawyers.[213]

Our research reveals a gendered institutional experience of hierarchy and of exclusion which is masked as difference, leading us to
theorize about ways that legal education creates or enhances
"difference" and converts it into a disadvantage.[214] Even if important preinstitutional gender differences exist, the source of those
differences is not the point. Even if we assume that women who enter law school are actually less prepared to be good lawyers—a
difference hard to imagine given identical entry credentials—the
institution's pedagogy, hierarchy, and male-dominated faculty ex-
acerbate that difference.

Our study focuses on a group of women at Penn Law School who
are unable or unwilling to "become gentlemen." It is important to
recognize, however, that even within this group, "women" is not a
monolithic category. Some women who are alienated nevertheless
do well academically; these women are successful within the hierarchy and norms of the law school.

At the outset we identified two distinct "groups" of women. The
first struggles academically as well as personally; the second succeeds academically. Within this latter category, there is also a subset who do well but feel alienated. This subset of women resents the
sacrifices of self that law school requires them to make. These
women perceive that law school is a "game," and they learn the
rules in order to play, but they are acutely aware of the price they are
paying. These women are those who have been described in some of
our secondary literature as "bicultural" or "bilingual." They can
act both as "women" and as "gentlemen" and they are acutely conscious of the difference, and of the costs of each.

For this alienated subset among the "successful women," their alienation does not seem to hurt them academically. However, some of them report being punished in class, primarily by their male peers, for class participation. In particular, while a male student who is perceived as overly assertive may be called an "asshole" (especially in the game we describe in note 120), a woman who behaves the same way risks being called a "man-hating lesbian" or "feminazi dyke."[215] The former is a "neutral" slur describing behavior; the latter two impute membership in despised, and often invisible, minority groups or suggest an abhorrent belief system associated with members of such a group.

In this way, women who initially succeed may be forced into the group of weak performers because of the intensive peer policing on the part of their colleagues. Moreover, such peer policing further intimidates women who witness it.

The experiences of the two different groups of women are thus related. For example, as the first of our two main groups of women grapple with the law, legal education, and their personal and professional identities, they see those who are more successful at "the game" disparaged. In this way, the classroom environment both creates and maintains the plight of the first group of women, despite, or perhaps because of, the second group. Disparagement of some female token performers works against all women.

Among those women who succeed academically, some are "bicultural"; they learn to function as "social males" and on some level they do become "gentlemen."[216] Nevertheless, their attempted gender transformation does not make their chances of excelling within the institution's social and academic hierarchy equal to men's. The institutional treatment of their gender serves to disadvantage them, even though they resist traditional "female"-associated traits.

Moreover, implicit in this critique that women who are different should not become lawyers is an argument questioning the predictive value of the law school's admissions criteria.[217] We suggest that those who rely on a "difference" axis to justify the status quo are really defending a tautological universe.[218] The men make the rules and then develop predictors of performance under those rules. When women do not achieve predicted rates of performance, the men (and some women) question the women rather than the rules.

In our view, the important message is that some change must

come to the law school. Women who are admitted possess qualifying entry credentials. Once they are at the law school these women are the institution's "clients." Even those most comfortable with the status quo might nevertheless entertain some concern when so many of the law school's clients feel dissatisfied and ill-served.

To endorse the theory that women are not well suited to law school is to accept the premise that legal education as it currently exists is the only and best formulation of how law schools should operate. Our response is that all the quantitative and qualitative data available suggest that women import competent credentials and are quite capable of meeting standards of academic rigor. In their reactions to the law school experience, women voice important concerns and offer creative visions for what law school could be for both men and women.

Our view is that the critique many female law students present gives us an occasion to reexamine traditional assumptions about lawyering for all. This reexamination is timely in light of the changing character of the legal profession and presents an opportunity to reconsider the value of the dominant pedagogy and accompanying emphasis on adversarialism that presently permeate legal education.[219] For example, our data indicate that certain educational techniques work for some, but not all, people.

Some might use our data to question the educational methodology that attempts to determine "merit" by testing for analytical thinking exclusively in the abstract. Critics of legal education often argue that although the ability to think fast on one's feet is important, it is not the only skill necessary for practicing law successfully. Furthermore, the argument usually proceeds, abstract reasoning is not the only prototype for legal reasoning. Appellate advocates or law professors may need to develop this skill more than trial lawyers or in-house corporate counsel.[220]

Another argument for changing legal education is that it currently overemphasizes the adversarial nature of lawyering.[221] Legal education may be inadequate where it focuses on legal issues exclusively or primarily in the context of resolving disputes through litigation.[222] The law school's definition of lawyering potential—as measured by a single evaluative methodology[223] and one dominant pedagogy—may simply be outmoded in light of contemporary professional developments, which include alternative dispute resolution,[224] emphasis on negotiation rather than litigation,[225] and client counseling.[226] Moreover, few Penn Law School graduates enter the profession at a level in which highly developed abstract reasoning is the most important variable for success.[227] To lawyer effectively, a contemporary attorney may need more than the ability to spot issues or engage in quick-response legal analysis as measured by timed examinations graded on a mandatory curve.[228]

By relying on the norm of abstract, analytic and quick-witted performance to test "merit" in this manner, the institution arguably fails to consider whether those practicing law need training in multiple rather than unidimensional skills,[229] or whether on-the-job training is equally important to one's career development.[230] In either case, the school limits opportunities for women to learn their chosen profession by emphasizing the ranking of students, often to the detriment of educating them. The evaluation system ranks women and men based on a partial picture of their ability to perform as lawyers. Their ranking then defines student status within the law school and the legal community. In these ways, the institution arguably treats many of its women students unfairly and in ways that some might deem professionally irresponsible.[231]

For these reasons, we believe that Penn Law School has an obligation to minimize the gendered differences in academic performance, whatever their source—a professional and educational obligation to meet the needs of all its "clients." It cannot simply ignore the gendered academic performance differential.[232] This matters to the women themselves, who appear to internalize their academic weaknesses in the form of greater mental health distress, low self-esteem, and anger. It may also matter to members of the profession who worry that the general public views the bar with increasing skepticism.[233] Furthermore, the law school must assume some responsibility because it publishes this academic performance differential when it provides transcripts to prospective employers.[234]

From the three tentative conclusions we draw from our data, we derive two related propositions. First, the institution's examination and educational structure has a disparate psychological and academic impact on an identifiable class of its graduates; at least one identifiable group of law students suffers from being ranked, rather than well educated.[235] Second, analogous to the principles behind disparate-impact employment discrimination cases—and consistent with the school's professional and pedagogic responsibilities—

the institution should seriously reexamine its teaching and examination methodologies.[236]

In conjunction with prospective employers with whom Penn Law School shares student transcripts, the law school might discharge its professional obligations by demonstrating that its examinations, despite their disparate gendered impact, are reasonably predictive of success in the profession.[237] The school could show that its examinations are valid, reliable, and fair.[238] Without assuming that a doctrinal approach satisfactorily resolves this issue, it is worth noting that the failure of an examination to test for other relevant job-related skills is a basis in employment discrimination cases for demonstrating the invalidity of selection criteria.[239] Even in the face of a valid test, the existence of less discriminatory alternatives is relevant.[240]

We have not gathered data on the professional experience of women law school graduates, or on the skills needed to succeed as an attorney.[241] The traditional assumption is that law school examinations test students' ability to "think like" an appellate lawyer or law professor, rather than to *be* a lawyer.[242] Consequently, we can only speculate about the results of such an attempt to validate law school examinations.[243]

Whatever the outcome of a validation study, however, we believe that Penn Law School is a resilient institution, capable not only of responding to critique but also of profound change. We urge this specific institution and others like it to take seriously the transformative potential of this research. We hope our preliminary findings prompt others to investigate further the institutional, pedagogic, and evaluative problems we identify.

D. *Recommendations*

We do not underestimate the difficulty of institutional reform. As we stated earlier, the problems we identify are probably not specific to any one institution. The University of Pennsylvania Law School does not operate in a vacuum; it functions in response to a set of widely shared values that determine its comparative ranking, its ability to attract distinguished faculty and outstanding students, the marketability of its graduates, and its capacity to raise money from its alumni.

In addition, we do not purport to have definitive answers to the problem of gender and legal education. Nor would we claim unilateral wisdom or power to impose a solution. Indeed, the solution must emerge from a dialogue in which the perspectives of all those affected by legal education—including faculty, students, practitioners, and consumers of legal advice—are represented.

We offer here an opening to that conversation. We propose examples of the types of concrete changes that could eventually make the learning process more accessible to, and more respectful of, female students. Restructuring legal education to benefit these women may also improve the experience for all students. And, in the end, the process of reform, or at least reexamination, could have a beneficial effect on the practice of law itself.[244]

We have three specific recommendations for further research.

First, we suggest that the University of Pennsylvania Law School rethink the conventional assumption that the large Socratic classroom should dominate first-year instruction.[245] This should be an effort to promote a genuine diversity of constructive teaching styles, including, of course, rigorous Socratic teaching. As one second-year woman said, reflecting on her law school experience, "Being intellectually stimulated is the best thing that could happen to you in law school, as long as you are not alienated."

There have been efforts at other law schools to explore a more pluralistic approach to the format of first-year classroom instruction.[246] Even at the University of Pennsylvania Law School, one professor reports great success in randomly assigning first-year students to "working groups" in which each student must pull his or her own weight in order for the group to function.[247] By success, this professor means that "race and gender are simply not as relevant in groups of six or seven, even as they may have been in a class of thirty-six."[248] This format can be especially empowering for students who perceive their participation in a large first-year class as an unpleasant "performance" and, in particular, a performance as spokesperson for their racial or gender identity.

An intriguing method of running classroom discussions has been tried in a Japanese middle school where, to minimize the agenda control of those who raise their hands first, the teacher waits until at least 75% of the students raise their hands before she calls on anyone. By teaching the students different ways of raising their hands, the teacher also invites students to signal the nature of their comment. For example, a flat palm held away from the body would indicate a different type of response than a clenched fist would signify. This approach allows participation from the girls in the class who take time to think before they speak.[249]

These less hierarchical alternatives (and others surely exist) minimize the alienation of some students, encourage broad-based participation from those who feel disinclined to "perform" when they speak but nevertheless have something to contribute, and supplement the informal mentoring that presently aids only some students. The potential of these educational approaches is suggested by the experience of the University of Oregon Law School.[250] These alternatives also track ideas now being considered by traditional consumers and watchdogs of legal education such as the American Bar Association.[251]

Second, we suggest that the law school further investigate the limitations of the litigation-as-combat model of problem solving, at least in this model's role as the universal, exclusive norm for legal education.[252] We have documented how assumptions about the usefulness of competitive hierarchy and binary results exclude a significant proportion of the present student body.[253] We have noted that these assumptions may reinforce competitive, even harassing behavior among male students that disproportionately alienates and ridicules some women.[254] We also suggest that these assumptions may not be realistic in a contemporary legal market in which lawyers do many things other than argue in a highly stylized courtroom setting. We do not advocate abandoning an adversarial approach to problem solving. We do advocate exploring whether an adversarial, litigation-centered approach is the most, or the only, effective method for educating students about the full range of skills that contemporary lawyers need.

Indeed, cooperative approaches to negotiation not only are common in forums that emphasize mediation and alternative dispute resolution, they are also associated with traditional advocacy. For example, in a "Professional Responsibility" class simulation at the law school, those students who achieved the best results according to the professor were those who put all their cards on the table and attempted to resolve the problem cooperatively.[255] Similarly, in client-centered litigation, the ability to listen and to empathize is extremely valuable.[256]

We recognize that small class size may be a necessary precondition to learning for some law students, but changing the size of the formal classroom environment alone is not sufficient.[257] Even in a seminar-style class, a few men may dominate the discussion,[258] and a professor intent on intimidating students can still do so despite a more participatory format.[259] Nor should we overemphasize the role of the professor as the single authority figure in a class of any size. Our data suggest that peer policing of student participation acts to deter some women from engaging effectively in legal education as presently constituted. Similarly, the informal learning environment may be as significant a factor in alienating women as is the formal, Socratic classroom of a hundred or more students. A passive response by faculty to either circumstance, however, is problematic.

The University of Pennsylvania Law School, therefore, might choose to investigate further the ways in which its students learn best.[260] There are other styles of teaching that might work better for some, if not all, law students. For some, certainly, collaborative or interactive learning is necessary, not just preferred.[261] To address this problem, the law school might choose not to reconfigure its large, Socratic classroom. Instead, it might want to: (a) set aside time for formal faculty mentoring (such as Friday afternoon receptions); (b) arrange study groups in informal settings pairing first-year and third-year students or weaker and stronger students; or (c) institutionalize sessions to teach students not just how to study for exams, but also how to prepare for daily classroom exchanges and how to access faculty time and expertise. These types of intervention have had some success at other institutions.[262] In other words, we urge the law school to assume more responsibility for structuring the informal learning networks on which its students currently depend.

In addition to the possibility of rethinking the virtue of large classes in the first year, Penn Law School may want to engage faculty in discussions of democratic pedagogy so that all students feel free to participate in class and beyond, and so that all can expect an audience. This conversation could help faculty to understand their responsibility to elicit multiple voices and sustain a sense of community, which may, at times, mean interrupting and negatively sanctioning students who work to silence others.

In sum, we do not propose simply cleaning up the top of the hierarchy to make it appear more "diverse"; we believe our data offer an opportunity to consider dismantling the hierarchy itself. For us, this project provides an incentive to commit ourselves to creating an intellectual environment in which the theoretical, practical, and ethical notions of justice and injustice are discussed, critiqued, and imagined anew in ways that meet the changing needs of many women students, and men, and of contemporary society in general.

CONCLUSION

The data we have collected chronicle the insidious effects of gendered stratification in law school "socialization." We have argued that the educational strategies of the law school sustain hierarchy, legitimate inequity in the name of merit, and yield serious, adverse consequences for many women. Yet the school maintains these practices as gender-neutral.

Unlike some earlier studies of female law students that focused primarily on women's silence as a site of resistance, our research identifies women's silence in the classroom as only one aspect of a systematically alienating, three-year educational experience. From this, we question whether all women truly have access to law schools, and whether mere access, even where women students constitute a critical mass, suffices to ensure gender equality.

We believe that our research raises a "second-generation" diversity issue. If the first generation of women was challenged to demonstrate the need for access to existing previously all-male institutions, the current (second) generation is challenged to demonstrate that mere access, especially in comparatively low status positions, is inadequate. Although more women are now admitted, as now designed, law schools fail to equalize the experience and outcomes for all law students across gender. Whether because of difference or domination, legal education at Ivy League institutions in particular exacts a disproportionate toll on almost half the law student population.

Formerly all-male educational institutions cannot incorporate and take advantage of difference without changing from within.[263] Second-generation diversity requires some institutional transformation as a precondition for genuine inclusion. The major changes we observed, however, occurred within the women who attend the school, not within or by the institution.

We argue that the aims of legal education should be reconsidered critically. The problem is not simply "difference" or gendered domination—both of which play a role in the stories we have told. Nor is the problem simply that women are outsiders who opt for a powerful, stony silence. The problem lies in a system of evaluation which functions to rank students on a hierarchy that prospective employers then use to choose who *they* will actually train to be a lawyer. In addition to ensuring selectivity, the law school's pedagogy socializes students to a certain adversarial practice of law. In these complementary ways, law schools perpetuate a vision of legal practice that has contributed to a crisis in the public trust of lawyers.

The data produced by our study prompted one of the coauthors, Professor Michelle Fine, to observe:

> If law school is "boot camp" to train recruits for equally ruthless law firms, then the success of this institution is brilliant. Silence makes sense, difference has no place, and domination and alienation are the point. Alternatively, if law school is an attempt to engage and educate diverse students democratically and critically about the practices and possibilities of law for all people, then the failure of the institution is alarming. In the meantime, the price borne by women across colors is far too high and their critique far too powerful to dismiss.

The question is not about women; it is about the political project of law schools, and the price women have to pay to become gentlemen.

*   *   *

In the end, we believe that our study calls for a profound rethinking of "equal access." In these days when a facile retreat from equal access seems all too common, we seek to up the ante. Law schools such as the University of Pennsylvania Law School not only reproduce social stratification, they create and legitimate it. If we, as a community of interdisciplinary scholars, are serious about inclusion, we must work well beyond the question of "entry" toward a profound transformation of the very institutions into which historic outsiders are being invited.

Changing the number of women faculty, ensuring a critical mass of women students, or even institutionalizing gender-neutral language may help some women achieve their true potential as productive lawyers. But it is not enough just to add women and stir. These data plead instead for a reinvention of law school itself—for fundamental changes in teaching practices, institutional policies, and social organization.

APPENDIX A

The Bartow Survey questions follow:[264]

QUESTION 1:   How often do you ask questions in class?

QUESTION 2:   How often do you volunteer answers in class?

QUESTION 3:   Are you comfortable with your level of voluntary participation in class?

QUESTION 4:   Do you think that students of one sex ask more questions than students of the other sex?

QUESTION 5:   Do you think that students of one sex volunteer more answers than students of the other sex?

QUESTION 6:   Are students more tolerant of in-class comments made by students of one sex than of in-class comments made by students of the other sex?

QUESTION 7:   Do you think that students of one sex who have asked questions or volunteered answers are given more class time than students of the other sex who have asked questions or volunteered answers?

QUESTION 8:   How many times are you called on in class involuntarily (e.g., without raising your hand)?

QUESTION 9:   Are you comfortable with the number of times you are called on involuntarily (e.g., without raising your hand) in class?

QUESTION 10:   Do you think that students of one sex are called on more frequently than students of the other sex?

QUESTION 11:   Do you think that students of one sex who have been called on are given more class time than students of the other sex who have been called on?

QUESTION 12:   Do you think that students of one sex are asked questions that are more difficult than those posed to students of the other sex?

QUESTION 13:   Do you think that students of one sex receive "follow up" questions more often than students of the other sex?

QUESTION 14:   Do you think that the nature or content of classroom interactions between professors and students are affected by the sex of the student?

QUESTION 15: Do you think that the nature or content of classroom interactions between professors and students are affected by the sex of the professor?

QUESTION 16: Do you habitually use gender-neutral language outside of the law school setting?

QUESTION 17: Does your language usage change when you are in a law school setting?

QUESTION 18: How often do your professors use gender-neutral language in class?

QUESTION 19: How often do your professors use gender-neutral language outside of class?

QUESTION 20: How often do your textbooks use gender-neutral language?

QUESTION 21: How important is the use of gender-neutral language to you?

QUESTION 22: How receptive are your professors to contact with students outside of class?

QUESTION 23: How often do you approach your professors after class or in their offices?

QUESTION 24: How comfortable are you in interactions occurring outside of class with professors of the opposite sex?

QUESTION 25: Outside of class, are your professors more receptive to contact with students of a particular sex?

QUESTION 26: How comfortable are you in interactions occurring outside of class with professors of the same sex?

QUESTION 27: Do you think that your professors can determine your gender based on your handwriting?

QUESTION 28: How concerned are you that knowledge of your gender (based on your handwriting) may consciously or unconsciously influence the way that a professor grades your exam?

QUESTION 29: Have you ever felt, in any context, that a professor treated you inappropriately based on your gender?

QUESTION 30: Given your day-to-day observations of life at Penn Law School, please check all that apply:
    I think that male professors favor male students
    I think that female professors favor female students
    I think that male professors favor female students

I think that female professors favor male students

I think that male professors treat male and female students equally

I think that female professors treat male and female students equally

No opinion

QUESTION 31: What qualities do you most admire in a law school professor? (Please check all that apply)

knowledge of subject matter

knowledge of theories and policies behind law

openness to questions in class

openness to questions outside of class

enthusiasm for teaching

asks challenging questions in class

friendly with students

available to help students with personal matters

expresses ideas clearly

professional reputation

experience

good at Socratic dialogue

open to discussing exams and exam results

forces you to learn

treats students with respect

other

no opinion

QUESTION 32: Are you or have you been a member of any student organization here at Penn Law (e.g., Council of Student Representatives, Environmental Law Society, Asian and Pacific American Law Students Association, etc.)?

QUESTION 33: How important are student organizations and activities to you?

QUESTION 34: In your opinion, do students of one sex participate in the activities of student organizations in proportionally greater numbers than students of the other sex?

QUESTION 35: In your opinion, do students of one sex hold leadership positions in student organizations in proportionally greater numbers than students of the opposite sex?

QUESTION 36: Do you think that a majority of the activities of student organizations are more appealing to students of one gender?

QUESTION 37: How often do you interact socially with other law students?

QUESTION 38: How satisfied are you with this level of social interaction?

QUESTION 39: Do you spend more time with law students of one gender?

QUESTION 40: Is your group of friends here within the law school demographically different from your group of friends from elsewhere? (Please check all that apply.)

    My friends here are older

    My friends here are younger

    My friends here are the same age as my friends from elsewhere

    My friends here are more racially diverse

    My friends here are less racially diverse

    My friends here are equally as racially diverse as my friends from elsewhere

    My friends here are more sexually diverse

    My friends here are less sexually diverse

    My friends here are equally as sexually diverse as my friends from elsewhere

    No opinion

QUESTION 41: How often do you study with your peers?

QUESTION 42: How competitive are the students in this law school?

QUESTION 43: Are students of one sex more competitive than students of the other sex?

QUESTION 44: How sensitive to gender issues are most Penn Law students?

QUESTION 45: Are sexist comments and actions by students permitted under the informal "house rules" of this law school?

QUESTION 46: Have you had at least one interview for a law-related job since enrolling in law school?

QUESTION 47: During the course of a job interview, have you ever been asked questions about your marital or family status that you considered inappropriate?

QUESTION 48: Have you ever been approached socially during a job interview in a way that made you uncomfortable?

QUESTION 49: If an interviewer asked you an inappropriate gender-related question, or made an offensive gender-related comment, how likely is it that you would report the incident to the Placement Office?

QUESTION 50: What impact do you believe your gender will have on your legal career?

QUESTION 51: What were your reasons for going to law school? (Please check all that apply.)
- influence of family, teachers or friends
- intellectual stimulation and training
- like to argue and debate
- prestige of profession
- opportunity to be of service to society
- desire for varied work
- desire to go into politics
- desire to go into business
- desire to teach law
- desire to go into government service
- desire to earn a lot of money
- unable to find satisfactory job without graduate degree
- other
- no opinion

QUESTION 52: What factors are highly important to you in a law-related job? (Please check all that apply.)
- intellectual stimulation
- adversarial nature of work
- independence
- opportunity to work with a team of people
- ability to earn a high income
- wide variety of work
- ability to balance career and family
- ability to have influence in the community
- opportunity to participate in politics
- high prestige of position
- opportunity for leadership
- ability to handle important tasks
- opportunity to be of service to the society
- utilization of speaking and writing skills
- other

QUESTION 53: What kind of job do you expect to have after law school? (Please check all that apply.)
- sole practitioner
- law firm/partnership
- government

academic

legal counsel of corporation

non-legal corporate position (e.g., investment banking)

legal counsel of foundation or university

public interest/nonprofit association

other law-related job

job unrelated to law

other

QUESTION 54: What kind of law do you expect to practice? (Please check all areas you expect to spend 25% or more of your time practicing.)

administrative law

corporate law

criminal law

family law

labor law

litigation

personal injury

public interest

real estate

tax

bankruptcy

trusts and estates

other

no opinion

QUESTION 55: How long do you expect to stay at your first job after law school?

QUESTION 56: On average, how many hours do you expect to work per week after law school?

QUESTION 57: During law school, how often do you drink alcoholic beverages?

QUESTION 58: During law school, how often do you take tranquilizers, sleeping pills, or other prescription or nonprescription depressant drugs?

QUESTION 59: During law school, how often do you take amphetamines, cocaine, or other prescription or nonprescription stimulant drugs?

QUESTION 60: During law school, how often do you overeat or undereat?

QUESTION 61: During law school, how often do you fight, break things, become physically violent?

QUESTION 62: During law school, how often do you cry?

QUESTION 63: During law school, how often do you have difficulty sleeping?

QUESTION 64: During law school, how often do you experience depression or anxiety?

QUESTION 65: Have you sought counseling or psychiatric care for law school related concerns?

QUESTION 66: Did you come to law school directly after college?

QUESTION 67: What is your sex?

QUESTION 68: What is your race?

QUESTION 69: What year of law school are you in?

QUESTION 70: What is the highest educational level attained by your parents?

APPENDIX B

The Bartow Survey's open-ended question follows:

> Please use this space to describe any acts or comments made by a professor or fellow student you have witnessed or experienced at the law school that made you uncomfortable for gender-based reasons. Please be as specific as you can, but do not feel compelled to identify anyone by name. As with the rest of the survey your response will be kept confidential.

❧ III ❧

Models and Mentors

Lani Guinier

*I*N 1984 I RETURNED to Yale Law School to participate on a panel of mainly black alumni reminiscing about the thirty years since *Brown v. Board of Education.* It was a panel sponsored by the current black law students who were eager to hear the voices of those who had come before them. Each of us on the panel spoke for ten minutes in a room adorned by the traditional larger-than-life portraits of white men. It was the same classroom in which, ten years earlier, I had sat for "Business Units 1" (corporations) with a white male professor who addressed all of us, male and female, as *gentlemen.*

Every morning, at ten minutes after the hour, he would enter the classroom and greet our upturned faces: "Good morning, *gentlemen.*" He explained this ritual the first day. He had been teaching for many years; he was a creature of habit. He readily acknowledged the presence of the few "ladies" by then in attendance, but admonished those of us born into that other gender not to feel excluded by his greeting. We too, in his mind, were "gentlemen."

In his view, this was an asexual term, one reserved for those who shared a certain civilized view of the world and who exhibited a similarly civilized demeanor. While the term primarily referred to men, and in particular men of good breeding, it assumed "men" who possess neither a race nor a gender. If we were not already members of this group, law school would certainly teach us how to be like them. That lesson was at the heart of becoming a professional. By this professor's lights, the greeting was a form of honorific. It evoked the traditional values of legal education: to train detached, "neutral" problem solvers, unemotional advocates for their clients' interests. It anticipated the perception, if not the reality, of our *all* becoming gentlemen.

Now, seated at the podium back in the familiar classroom preparing to address a race- and gender-mixed audience, I felt the weight of the presence of those stern portraits. For me, this was still not a safe place.

Yet all the men on the panel reminded us how they felt to return "home," fondly revealing stories about their three years in law school. Anecdotes about their time as students, mostly funny and a touch self-congratulatory, abounded. The three black men may not have felt safe either, but they each introduced their talks with brief yet loving recollections of their law school experiences. Even the one so-called black radical among us waxed nostalgic and personal, with proud detail about his adventures as the law school troublemaker.

It was my turn. No empowering memories came to me. I had no personal anecdotes for the profound senses of alienation and isolation that caught in my throat every time I opened my mouth. Nothing resonated there for a black woman, even after my ten years as an impassioned civil rights attorney. Instead I promptly began my formal remarks, trying as hard as I could to find my voice in a room in which those portraits seemed to speak louder than I ever could. I spoke slowly, carefully, and never once admitted, except by my presence on the podium, that I had ever been at this school or in this room before. I summoned as much authority as I could in order to be heard over the sounds of silence erupting from those giant images of gentlemen hanging on the wall and from my own ever-present memory of slowly disappearing each morning and becoming one of the gentlemen of "Business Units 1."

Immediately after my presentation, the other black woman on the panel rose to speak. She did not introduce herself with personal experiences or warm reminiscences either, but, as I had tried to do, remained upright and dignified. Afterwards she and I huddled together to talk about how different the law school we had experienced was from the one recollected by our male colleagues. For both of us, the gigantic male portraits had captured and frozen in time the alienation from class, race, and gender privilege we had felt as students.

We were the minority within a minority, whose existence, even physical presence, had been swallowed up within an explicit law school tradition. Even from our places up front at the podium, those portraits were like an attic jury, reminding us that silence was the price of our presence.

Our shock seemed to need explanation. Perhaps law school was simply more homogeneous, with even more cookie-cutter institutional norms (such as value-neutral detachment) than we had either expected or experienced earlier, in college. Our sense of disassociation also appears consistent with the contemporary school experience of other black women and black girls.[1] Whatever the post-hoc explanation, in law school we had felt both closely scrutinized and invisible, watched but not quite seen.

Although admittedly neither as intense or painful, my invisibility also revived memories of my father's experience a generation ago as one of only two black students entering Harvard College in 1929. My father told me he'd been barred from the dormitories and denied financial aid, and that he'd been ignored even by students with whom he'd attended Boston English High School.

Four years later, at its first "Women of Color and the Law" conference, I again returned to Yale Law School. I was invited to speak at a panel on "Roots in our communities: What roles for lawyers and professionals?" This time I was invited by young women students of color who asked me to speak explicitly about the personal choices and conflicts I had experienced in my career as a black woman civil rights attorney. At the conference I tried to overcome my training as a surrogate gentleman who distances her personal self from her professional self. I also tried to overcome the self-protective silence that earlier had helped me survive—*as* a gentleman—in "Business Units I." This time I found my voice.

I revealed myself in context, talking about my family and my colleagues, my adversaries and my clients. In all my professional roles, I had experienced what Mari Matsuda calls multiple consciousness,[2] meaning the split in thinking that allows one to shift back and forth between one's personal consciousness and the white male perspective that dominates the legal profession. Multiple consciousness allows us to operate within mainstream discourse and "within the details of our own special knowledge," producing both madness and genius. It invokes the spirit of W. E. B. Du Bois's "double-consciousness," two dueling selves within one black body, "born with a veil," yet "gifted with second-sight."[3] Adding gender to Du Bois's "peculiar sensation" of "always looking at one's self through the eyes of others," multiple consciousness provides intellectual camouflage and emotional support for outsiders who feel the threeness of race, gender, and professional role.

I recounted to the students how shifting between identities often became a burden in my professional relationships with male lawyers and colleagues. I was never certain when to situate myself outside a white male perspective or with whom to disengage from value-neutral problem solving. Even my own mother complained that sometimes I cross-examined her.

But in my relationships with clients, multiple consciousness was liberating. As a black woman civil rights attorney with insider privileges and outsider consciousness, I moved along the spectrum of cultural norms (roots, community, race, and gender) and cultivated status (Ivy League graduate, expert, mainstream professional) as an explorer and translator of these different identities. I lost myself in my work, spending countless hours interviewing and researching, writing and thinking. I did not presume to know. Nor was I silenced by the presumed authority of others. Instead I listened, I empathized, I discerned the facts necessary to channel my clients' anger to overcome their isolation and obtain legal redress. The pain of their grievances mobilized my advocacy.

I was not unaware of the hierarchical relationships between clients and attorneys, between lawyers for the same client, between opposing counsel and my clients. Nor was I oblivious to the silencing role that either law or litigation itself may play. As a translator and facilitator for my clients, I saw it as my role to bring a previously unrepresented perspective into the courtroom, helping my clients as well as cooperating attorneys to empower themselves.

Effective representation, I discovered, requires mutual respect, honest and continuous communication, intimacy with the facts, and familiarity with the law. Furthermore, one must constantly struggle to recognize the importance of everyone's perspective in order to support serious collective action. Especially in the context of civil rights, the effective advocate hears the passion, anger, and fear expressed by clients alienated and intimidated by formal speech, and translates them into legal discourse. He or she must be anchored in the daily struggles of their poorest clients, yet encourage participation by all clients. Effective representation requires a constant process of dialogue—the "building of coalitions, the development of a voice, . . . the flexing of organizational muscle."[4] Able advocates for the disempowered are not simply ventriloquist hacks moving the lips for one abstract position in a lawsuit. Through creative collaboration with their clients, these lawyers struggle to become architects of a different kind of public space.

Skilled advocacy, for me, meant bringing a marginal perspective into the center, giving outsiders credibility in their own eyes—*un*-becoming a gentleman. In my work I found many voices.

*   *   *

Years and career options intervened. I joined the academy along with other women, including women of color. As a law professor, I now take the podium daily under the watchful eyes of those ever-dominant gentlemen whose portraits still guard the periphery. I am at the podium, but as Michelle Fine, Jane Balin, and I argue in our study of women law students, this is not always a safe place for women and people of color like myself. Our race and our gender—and the race and gender of the litigants in our casebooks—are still, for the most part, unspoken subtexts. Law school still teaches value-neutral detachment, an unfamiliar, existential luxury for those who live within "a veil." Many women and many people of color still do not feel comfortable speaking out in the large law school classrooms. No matter how self-possessed I seem on stage, I too sometimes falter when surrounded by the surreal shadow of those brooding gentlemen.

To students who feel similarly disembodied by the traditions reflected in the larger-than-life visages on the wall, my presence in legal education offers refuge. In their eyes, I am "there for them." Indeed, for some, I *am* them. I am not merely a law professor. I am a role model.

In the conventional sense of the term, I function not only as a teacher but as a symbol for certain student voices and aspirations. I bear witness as a trophy of achievement. My conspicuous presence may rebut assumptions of group inferiority that undermine student confidence and performance. My example not only legitimizes the competence of matriculating minority students; my visibility helps lure future minority and female students into the profession. Role models provide psychological uplift, affirming the status of black women as law school citizens who can participate fully in the educational process. By confirming black and female advancement, black women role models may also be seen as living symbols of the equal opportunity process.[5]

I do not object to being a role model, even if I had a choice about the matter, which I probably do not. Indeed, I do feel special responsibilities as a black woman law professor. But in my own eyes, I am a mentor more than a role model.[6] I hold my students to high expectations of *themselves*, not of me. I facilitate their learning, not my being. I view teaching as a reciprocal, interactive relationship that is primarily about *their* education.

I do not view myself in my teaching role as the purveyor of an image but as a mentor who takes from the margin to facilitate student reflection, insight, and professional responsibility. Indeed, repercussions from a recent public call for more black women role models prompt me to explore the uneasiness I have with a role model rationale as a justification of my presence in legal education.[7]

I resist the term "role model" in part because I worry about the way the role model argument is often used to diminish the actual role outsiders play, one that benefits insiders, not just other outsiders. I question the way the concept measures successful outsiders by an insider yardstick. In addition, I take issue with the idea that someone of a given person's own gender and racial or ethnic group is necessarily a model or representative for that person. Role models may grant a passport to power or status to people who then take no account of how they arrived at their destination.

The first problem with the role model argument is that it trivializes the important contribution that outsiders play in diversifying a faculty. Presenting women of color law professors primarily as role models ignores their role as scholars and intellectual leaders whose presence on a faculty might alter the institution's character, introducing a different prism and perspective. Women of color legal scholars may influence their white male colleagues to perform their own roles better.

In other words, women of color law professors symbolize more than their own singular achievement. They can be templates for how the role itself might be performed differently. For example, some black women may draw on the outsider consciousness of being a minority group advocate and member. From this vantage point, they can see that many women and students of color, already wary because of their status, respond less enthusiastically to learning by individual intimidation than to other emotional stimulants such as peer encouragement and sorority of intellectual views.

Indeed, as teachers, they may learn to use an interactive, communicative process—what Iris Marion Young calls a *communicative discourse*—to change the educational conversation.[8] A communicative, rooted discourse requires "careful listening, questioning for clarification, the willingness to express oneself many different ways, to engage in struggle and conflict without walking away."[9] Such a discourse rejects as the exclusive mode of participation a dominating, theatrical style of expression that often operates to silence and disadvantage members of some groups. Reciprocity, trust, and interest in "others" are valued instead. Giving a marginal perspective credibility in everyone's eyes does not require emotional detachment or rigid argumentation but many different forms of communication, including personal narrative.

A professor who engages students using Iris Young's communicative style of teaching refocuses attention away from the professor. She or he provides opportunity for student-initiated learning projects, encourages peer interaction where it provides intellectual stimulation, acknowledges where appropriate the relevance of race or gender, and makes explicit the value of listening carefully and of paraphrasing rather than parodying.[10] He or she reinforces skilled argument, acknowledges sophisticated perceptions, and points out constantly the nuances, the implications, the complexity of voice, of analysis, of legal rules, of policy alternatives.

Like most law teachers, I was trained that the tension of the Socratic dialogue motivates learning. But though I try hard not to silence or intimidate, I still find that many women and people of color are reluctant partners in the Socratic exchange. Performance-oriented questioning, even by a "compassionate" black woman, may diminish self-esteem, and may insult students' privacy and dignity. To reach women and people of color in particular, I encourage all students to prepare for class in teams, to talk through their ideas first in less formal settings. Students who have otherwise been silent are often more likely to share their points of view openly with their classmates in such a context. And many women and men of all colors thrive once they have a chance to hear themselves think aloud, alone with their peers.

A genuinely interactive perspective on legal education does not mean lack of rigor. The big difference, it seems, is the establishment of an atmosphere of respect in which the students can safely challenge each other. "There is a different feeling in the classroom when students go after each other than when a professor goes after them; the fear is gone and people aren't afraid to have personal viewpoints."[11] As Michelle Fine, Jane Balin, and I found in our research, many women students in particular feel more self-confident in a discourse of mutual respect.[12]

An interactive, communicative discourse may help awaken the classroom participation of some students, and subsequently enhance their learning. For others, a discourse that legitimizes alternative forms of participation, respects listening before speaking, and broadens the educational dialogue may make them better advocates by deepening their knowledge of the world around them, as well as increasing their understanding of the implications of their claims. Law students trained in a communicative discourse may become better advocates in a pluralistic society, even outside a civil rights or social change context.

Some women of color law professors also bring a sense of social responsibility to their scholarship. They can teach their colleagues how to be "organic intellectual[s] with affiliations not restricted to the walls of the academic institution."[13] They can produce law review articles and engage in educational instruction not in isolation but in solidarity with other like-minded scholars. Speaking in their own voices connects them to the richness of their own experience and empowers them to overcome silencing by even well-intentioned white male colleagues. Their stories enrich the reality of majority group members. And their efforts to connect with others are both a means of psychic self-preservation and a lessening of their own subordination.

As women of color, we may contribute to legal education not merely through our physical presence but by pulling from the richness and rootedness of our experience, by continuously reaching for the transformative possibilities of our role.[14] In this way, we are often less role models than teachers, educators who empower through feedback, guidance, and sharing rather than commanding through example, visibility, or physical stature.

Black women as role models are also defended as group spokespersons. For example, some blacks claim that as teachers they have "a clear, racial representational function," meaning that they both "comprehend" and "represent" the needs and interests of all black students.[15] Thus some argue that black women role models *represent* aspiring young black women's needs and affirm the status of black women as law school citizens who can participate in the process of making policy decisions that affect their lives in law school and beyond.

This "representational" view posits a person being accepted as an inspirational figure based disproportionately on mere physical attributes, potentially institutionalizing acceptable or assimilated "gentlemen of color" to serve as group representatives to the outside world. By their presence, such role models presumably articulate black interests and act as living symbols of the equal opportunity process. To some, the selection of black role models signals that society's institutions are "color-blind" pure meritocracies. The individual advancement of black women professors inspires black students and young people in the community to believe in the system.[16]

This representational message deemphasizes the structural aspects of exclusion while devaluing the job-related qualifications of the person who serves as the role model. The disconcerting irony of representational rhetoric is captured by Professor Adeno Addis when he observes that it makes space for women of color as it simultaneously undermines the ground on which we walk.[17] When the rhetoric of representation is used to buttress the claim that more women of color should be hired as law professors, the message to the individual selected is that she achieved the position primarily because of her symbolic value. This message, Professor Anita Allen writes, "trumpets our necessity as it whispers our inferiority."[18]

Moreover the role model as spokesperson overemphasizes the representational value of passive, individual success unconnected to a dynamic, rooted concept of socially responsible, emotionally engaged leadership. Without an introspective or reflective understanding of their own experience, and an open ear listening and responding to the voices of group and non-group members, the role model as respectable insider simply presents success as an illusion of privilege. The possibilities for social change become the possibilities for individual advancement.

The term "role model" is also used insidiously to refer only to a sort of "mascot" who counsels and keeps others in line, a pacifier of the status quo who won't bite the hand that uplifted her.[19] Using the external standard of the ingroup to measure performance by an outsider distorts the "role" being modeled. As prototypes of achievement, role models illustrate, through example, the possibility of success for their constituency. Yet these same symbols of achievement are measured by institutional reference points external to both the minority group and the individual.[20] They offer "pride" and "positive identities" rather than effective, committed teaching. They are spokesmodels—attractive group spokespersons with no accountability to group goals. Like the spokesmodels on television, they are scouted for their poise, looks, and articulation.

Without moral leadership and a critical perspective, the concept of the representational role model suggests that the problems of group disadvantage are individual ones, unconnected to a changing economy or the social and racial nature of constraints on opportunity. Showcasing the individual spokesmodel as the image of success obscures both the struggle and the discrimination involved in opening for other group members *real* opportunities, not just perceived possibilities. In fact, black role models may become powerful symbolic reference points for camouflaging the continued legacy of past discrimination. Institutionally acceptable role models may simply convey the message "we have overcome" in language calculated to exact admiration from, but not necessarily to inspire, those who still have a lot of overcoming to do in a society where equality of opportunity does not yet exist.[21]

To realize their value as catalysts for meaningful group "upward mobility" (meaning beyond their own individual advantage), role models need ties to their community. They should be more than mere "gentlemen of color"—detached, neutral, wooden images for emulation or admiration. They must lift others as they climb.[22]

As a catalyst for progressive change, genuine role models have responsibilities, not just privileges. To be a role model in this sense is a responsibility to those who come after us and to those whom we follow. Role models should be people with whom members of the outgroup identify who are then held accountable to other outsider aspirants. Especially to the extent that they are seen as representatives or agents for others, role models need to nurture their roots not just model their roles.

This rootedness needs to be incorporated more directly into the definition of the term. As a self-referential descriptor, "role model" fits me only to the extent that my own polar experiences— as a marginalized student and as an empowered and empowering civil rights attorney—root me in the sturdy soil and rocky terrain of multiple consciousness. Indeed, to the extent I am a role model, it is not because I became a gentleman with a race and a gender added.

This is why I find greater meaning in an alternative view of the role model relationship: as involving an "interdependent" or "co-productive" effort. Interdependency is a term used in the corporate context to describe efficient, effective teamwork that promotes productivity and interactive communication.[23] Coproduction also suggests a relationship that is communicative and interactive.[24]

I prefer the active voice. I prefer the term "mentor" or teacher. In the context of education, mentors are not simply cultural icons, but are continuously legitimized and reinforced by a process of dialogue that monitors student performance and holds those who follow to high expectations. Mentors see learning as a dynamic process that builds on students' emotional engagement and emphasizes the mutuality of their role in the educational conversation. In the words of poet Nikki Giovanni, "The purpose of any leadership is to build more leadership. The purpose of being a spokesperson is to speak until the people gain a voice."[25]

I find myself, therefore, experimenting with innovative teaching techniques that depart, at least occasionally, from the stereotypical Socratic method in which a single authority figure dominates a structured dialogue. As Uri Treisman observed in watching Asian-American students study calculus, those who have to speak and justify their claims to others who may be skeptical, who test their ideas on their peers before they raise them with their professors, develop self-confidence and the skills of self-criticism, both of which are essential for personal, professional, and intellectual growth.

For example, I developed a law school course called "Public Interest Lawyering" to expose students to a different and broader perspective on the practice of law and to explore the relationship of the public interest advocate to multiple clients in litigation, legislative advocacy, and administrative agency contexts. Readings include actual legal case studies, literature on the psychology of group dynamics and organizational behavior, and narratives from legal practitioners about their work. Class sessions involve simulations, advocacy role-playing, and directed conversations with practicing public interest attorneys. The students must each write a research paper with an empirical component on a contemporary problem confronting public interest attorneys. They must also either volunteer for a relevant "law reform" project or interview the project's staff and clients to assess critically the way the project responds to the important public policy problem they have identified. Students are encouraged by the course readings and class sessions to integrate their own experience into class discussions, to focus on the social and psychological skills of good advocacy, and to develop a critical perspective on the work of public interest attorneys.

My primary ambition in teaching this particular course is to help law students understand the importance of each client's perspective in shaping their advocacy, to become more responsible as legal professionals. They learn ways to interrupt the discourse of "gentlemen lawyers," to counter the power asymmetries that too often separate poor and working-class clients from the elite interests of the legal system. My secondary goal is to encourage more law students to consider public interest work as a career in which psychic satisfaction more than compensates for the salary differential in relation to more lucrative areas of private practice. My third goal is to experiment with alternative approaches to legal education. I continue to pursue an interdisciplinary approach to the task of legal education, to develop further the critique Michelle Fine, Jane Balin, and I put forth in our study of the way in which one-size-fits-all pedagogy marginalizes women and minorities.

I unpeel these preliminary, still tentative thoughts on our continuing negotiation over shared cultural space like the layers of an onion. I puzzle over demystifying the traditional image of legal educators and lawyers as detached, neutral, advocates. The nature of my own education and of the schools with which I have been associated makes it difficult either to reject the opportunities afforded me as a passive symbol of achievement or to transcend traditional, established ways of viewing the world. Yet I am certain that I do not aspire to be a cultural icon in the conventional or group representative sense. I value my role as a translator and facilitator, a beneficiary of and contributor to a transformed and transformative educational conversation with black women, people of color, and minority viewpoints of any color. But I play this role not just for black women, white women, or men and women of color. Despite special concerns and responsibilities to engage particular students, I seek to transform the educational dialogue for *all* my students. I play the role of teacher, mentor, counselor, educational facilitator for white male students too.[26]

For many of these reasons, I agree with Professor Addis when he argues that role modeling should be rearticulated as a concept "of resistance, empowerment, and transformation."[27] Black women professors need not become gentlemen in order to be heard. Instead, we can offer a counternarrative to that of the men whose portraits symbolize an authority that has too often been used to reinforce the exclusion of many marginalized groups. However, our presence alone is not enough. We must use our outsider consciousness to tell that counternarrative and help transform the educational enterprise to benefit everyone. By our actions in the classroom, we can then contribute and improve legal education for *all* students.

Thus, I collaborate with those who, like me, have sought to find their own voices and to help other people find theirs.[28] Through an interactive and communicative discourse, we can begin to tell our stories together, stories that then embolden us to explore the unclaimed territory of our experience on the margins of legal education.

Collective storytelling allows all of us many options. We can engage our personal selves with our professional role, assert the value of our lived experience, take account of the way others perceive our contributions, and attempt to empower and build community.[29]

If we find in our stories new understandings of race or gender or a wonderfully synthetic second-sighted consciousness, we can "name our reality"[30] and find our places at the center. We also may finally dislodge from our throats the alienation and isolation begotten by gentlemen's orthodoxies, including those everpresent portraits that still guard the citadel. And eventually we may help the gentlemen change the pictures.

AFTERWORD

I published an earlier version of Chapter 3 as an essay in 1991. The memory subsequently receded of the time when larger-than-life gentlemen imposed such heavy silences on women. In law school I had resisted through silence. Later I learned to question out loud how much of a gentleman I ever was, or even how much of a lady I ever could be. In the course of the Fine, Balin, and Guinier study of women at the University of Pennsylvania Law School, I saw in our research many familiar themes—the self- and structurally imposed silences, the denigration of "outsider's" points of view, the potential "smarts" of dual or multiple consciousness. Assisted by the knowledge that I was not alone, I gained the confidence to challenge those traditions that symbolically stripped me of my race, my gender, and my voice.

Indeed, at the University of Pennsylvania, with the active support of the dean, in 1990 a student group organized by women and people of color raised enough money to commission the first "official" portrait of a black woman law school graduate, Sadie T. M. Alexander. In 1991, in the course of writing this essay, I learned to my great surprise that at Yale Law School a seminar room display of graduates practicing public interest law now also includes the photograph of at least one black woman—me.

Then, in the spring of 1993, I was nominated to be Assistant Attorney General for Civil Rights, and those law student memories assumed contemporary urgency. Once again, a larger-than-life jury commanded silence.

This time I was explicitly admonished not to speak, as a courtesy to the Senate prior to confirmation hearings. I could not explain misconceptions about ideas attributed to me because I was not allowed to speak for myself or even to *be* myself. This time the jury spoke in a way more personal, more overtly hostile, and more public than any I had known before. This experience was much worse than the transformation from black woman to gentleman law student. Yet that law student experience proved an important reference point. The academy had prepared me well for the feeling of being cast outside the mainstream even as I was welcomed within it.

Unlike many male colleagues whose breeding, status, and gender assured them traditional presumptions of respectability both inside the academy and beyond, I never became my resumé. Instead, as the Assistant Attorney General for Civil Rights–designate, I was defined entirely by my opponents and those in the media who took control over my image. Like the female gentlemen of "Business Units 1," I had fallen down a rabbit hole, only this time it was in Washington, D.C.

In this Wonderland the distortions were so gross that even my own mother could not recognize me in the images the media produced. Things got curiouser and curiouser. I was like Alice, her size changing every ten minutes, facing the Caterpillar, who demanded to know just who she was:

> "I-I hardly know, sir, just at present—at least I know who I *was* when I got up this morning, but I think I must have been changed several times since then."
> "What do you mean by that?" said the Caterpillar sternly. "Explain yourself."
> "I cannot explain *myself*, I'm afraid, sir," said Alice, "because I'm not myself, you see."

Identified by my ideas—or more precisely by caricatures of them—I came to represent America's worst fears about race. Sentences, phrases, even words that were separated by whole paragraphs in my "controversial" law review articles were served up to demonstrate that I was outside the mainstream of polite society. I learned that I was still an outsider but this time differences of race and gender were targeted rather than erased.

I became a cartoon character, Bill Clinton's "Quota Queen." It didn't matter that I had never advocated quotas. It did not matter that I am a professor of law, gainfully employed, with life tenure. Like "welfare queen," "Quota Queen" was a racial and gender stereotype and a facile headline looking for a person. And, like Alice, I walked into a looking glass of manipulated images from which my real ideas were never allowed to emerge.

As a civil rights lawyer I had challenged electoral systems in which voters were alienated from actively participating in the process of self-government. As a legal scholar I promoted alternative, race-neutral remedies to empower *all* voters and to make elected officials more accountable to *all* their constituents. Through my law review articles I began to speak about the problems of a democracy in which people of color have a vote but no voice. I sought consensus, positive-sum solutions to the dilemma—identified two centuries ago by James Madison—of a self-interested majority that fails to rule on behalf of *all* the people. In those situations where 51% of the voters were excluding the other 49% on the basis of their race, their gender, or their ideas, I questioned whether 51% of the people should enjoy 100% of the power. No one, I reasoned, should have to become a *gentleman* in order to be heard.

I advocated a remedy—cumulative voting—that allocates political power in relationship to voter organization and mobilization. I had learned about cumulative voting from my gentleman professor back in "Business Units 1." He taught me that cumulative voting is a method for electing corporate boards of directors, used to protect minority stockholders.

I never got a chance to explain these ideas to the American people. Yet while I remained silent, those who opposed my nomination had a platform from which to speak, defining the parameters of conversation and debate.

> Strange name. Strange hair. Strange writings. She's history.
> If she testifies before the Senate, Real America will see her as a madwoman.
> Right now, they are Crowning "the Quota Queen." Soon she'll be the answer to a trivia question.

Even the self-described radicals among my conservative critics enjoyed the status of neutral observers.

I did not get a hearing. But this time I did not lose my voice for long. In the many intervening years since law school, I had gained the confidence to question directly speech that silences rather than enlightens. I had been forewarned by those law student memories of larger-than-life figures dominating the debate.

I began to comprehend once again what W. E. B. Du Bois eloquently described at the dawn of this century as the twoness, the double identity of being black and American. For me, there was a threeness because I also was a woman. As an outsider "within the veil," I, like Du Bois, saw myself revealed through the eyes of others.

Yes, it's true that I didn't get a hearing, but some of us (like Michelle Fine and Jane Balin) are working to ensure that ours and other voices will be heard. And by insisting on our ability to speak out about our ideas and our role, we can spark the debate that we have previously been denied. We may still have the peculiar sensation of measuring our soul by the tape of others, but, as for Alice through the looking glass, the experience eventually can become a gift, the gift of second sight.

Ours is a story about being imprismed and silenced by the status quo. Ours is the story of being admitted into Wonderland but only on condition that we for all practical purposes become something we are not. Our stories, though, are not monolithic. Nor are they monotone or monologue. Our stories help form a conversation in which we can define and redefine the world in terms that accommodate different perspectives and experiences. Through the constant process of dialogue and the struggle to communicate, we can give ourselves credibility in our own eyes. We can build coalitions, develop a voice, and begin to flex our mentoring muscle.

We have a gift, not a grievance. Legal education is strengthened by including those who were once left out. Our gift then is to help institutions turn silence into insight, to make a chorus of many voices contending. "Gifted with second-sight," we can share our stories so the rest of the world gains from our knowledge and experience. To paraphrase Nikki Giovanni, one purpose of leadership is to build more leadership. One purpose of telling our stories is to speak until those who follow gain a voice.

And if we persist, eventually we will be heard over the thunderous silence of the *gentlemen* and their larger-than-life portraits. Like *Alice in Wonderland*, our stories will become classics in their own right, because we shall speak until *all* the people gain a voice.

Lani Guinier

NOTES

CHAPTER I. WHY ISN'T *SHE* PRESIDENT?

1. Christopher Clarey, *U.S. Gymnasts Take Back Seat in All-Around*, N.Y. TIMES, July 26, 1996, at B9, B16 (explaining stumble at individual competition of Dominique Dawes, arguably the "strongest optional gymnast on the American team," quoting her coach: "She can always do it when it's for the team, but she struggles when it's for herself'"); *Strug May Skip U.C.L.A. for Fame and Fortune*, N.Y. TIMES, July 26, 1996, at B16 (describing Kerri Strug's gutsy performance despite an injured ankle, which assured women's gymnastic *team* a gold medal).

2. *See* Uri Treisman, *Studying Students Studying Calculus: A Look at the Lives of Minority Mathematics Students in College*, 23 C. MATHEMATICS J. 362, 364–65 (1992). *See also* Philip Uri Treisman, *A Study of the Mathematics Performance of Black Students at the University of California, Berkeley* 13–15, 46 (1985) (finding that the collaborative approach of Chinese-American students "provided them with valuable information that guided their day-to-day study"; these students "routinely critiqued each other's work" and thus discovered when studymates also found problems unusually difficult; as a result, students learned that their failure "was not one of simple oversight" but could be addressed by asking a teaching assistant "without fear of appearing incompetent or ill-prepared").

In 1985 Treisman also reported significant success in improving the mathematics performance of Workshop participants in the preceding two years. With only one exception, the average grade of Workshop students was at least one half grade higher than the class average of *all* students in Math 1A classes. *Id.* at 63. "The average grades received by Workshop students are consistently higher than those of their Asian and majority classmates." *Id.* at 69. Most striking, Treisman found that the average grade of black Workshop students with the lowest math SAT scores was higher than that of non-Workshop black students with the highest math SAT scores. "In every case the performance of the 'risk group' students in the Workshop has been better, often substantially better, than that of the complementary group of non-Workshop [black] students." *Id.* at 71.

3. For example, as recently as 1985, women represented only 13% of all lawyers. In 1960, women were only 3% of all lawyers. *See* Commission on Women in the Profession, "Women in the Law: A Look at the Numbers," Chicago, American Bar Association, November 1995.

4. Quoted by Harlon Dalton in *The Clouded Prism*, 22 HARV. C.R.C.L.L. REV. 435, 444 (1987).

5. *See* Susan P. Sturm, *From Gladiators to Problem-Solvers: Women, the Academy, and the Legal Profession*, DUKE JOURNAL OF GENDER, LAW, AND POLICY (January 1997).

6. DeFunis v. Odegaard, 416 U.S. 312, 328–329 (1974). Justice Douglas contin-

ued: "And no one knows how many of those who were not admitted because of their test scores would in fact have done well were they given the chance. . . . The problem is that in many cases the choice will be between 643 and 602 or 574 and 528. The numbers create an illusion of difference tending to overwhelm other facts." *Id.* at 329.

7. This is about average for law schools. *See* Michael Selmi, *Testing for Equality: Merit, Efficiency, and the Affirmative Action Debate*, 42 UCLA L. Rev. 1251, 1264 (1995) (correlation coefficients for the LSAT, which is intended to predict first-year law school grades, tend to hover around .35; correlation coefficient of .3 means that the test explains only 9% of the variation in predicted performance).

8. *See infra* Chapter 2, note 74 and accompanying text and tables. *See also supra* note 7 citing Michael Selmi. It is important to concede that the observed relationship may be misleadingly low because of "downward bias," meaning that we are only looking at the LSAT for those actually admitted to the law school. Were we to examine the LSAT for all test takers, it would probably have a higher correlation. Yet the LSAT cannot provide meaningful information about incremental differences in ranking. As Michael Selmi concludes, "This does not mean that the tests provide no useful information, only that the information will not always permit precise delineations." *See* Selmi at 1270 (challenging central assumption that test scores are closely correlated with productivity and that small test score differentials predict meaningful performance differentials).

9. The tests, however, may mask the role race and gender play. *See infra* Chapter 2, note 74. *See also Declaration of Martin M. Shapiro, Cheryl J. Hopwood et al. v. State of Texas*, Civil No. A-92-CA-563-SS (U.S.D.C. W.D. Texas, Austin Division) (finding that the correlation between first-year grade point average predicted by a combination of the LSAT and undergraduate grade point average and the actual first-year grades of African-American students at the University of Texas School of Law "is rather poor"). Professor Shapiro found that an affirmative relationship between test scores, college grades (UGPA), and first-year law school grades for African-American students was achieved only if the college grade point average of each African-American student is "multiplied by a weight equal to -3.35." In other words, only if Texas multiplied the grade point averages of black undergraduates by a negative number could the school identify any relationship predicting law school performance. Even after performing that manipulation, there was still only a small 8% predictability for African-Americans, and that small number "is achieved only if lower undergraduate grade-point averages are made to predict higher first-year averages in the Law School." *Id.* at 16.

10. *See* Peter Applebome, *For Twins, Double Jackpot on the S.A.T.*, N.Y. Times, Nov. 10, 1995, A16 (mother of fraternal twins was asked to explain their success in becoming first twins ever to earn simultaneous scores of 1600—the highest possible score—on their Scholastic Assessment Tests; Mrs. Salthouse said her children had benefited from taking the SAT repeatedly over time. Both have been taking the test since the seventh grade. Mrs. Salthouse said, "The best preparation for taking the S.A.T. is taking the S.A.T.").

11. Interestingly, one of the factors *not* identified with differential law school performance was undergraduate major. Both our study and a national study published in June 1996 and conducted by Linda Wightman for LSAC found no statistically significant differences between the undergraduate majors of men and women law students. *See* Linda F. Wightman, *Women in Legal Education: A Comparison of the Law School Performance and Law School Experiences of Women and Men*, Law School Admissions Council (LSAC) Research Report Series (1996) (herein-

after Wightman Report) at 23–26: Women tend to do less well in law school than would be predicted by their undergraduate academic records; men may tend to do better. Yet women reported higher undergraduate grades than men. Their records of undergraduate performance, however, are not a consequence of selecting less rigorous undergraduate majors.

12. Susan P. Sturm and Lani Guinier, *The Future of Affirmative Action: Reclaiming the Innovative Ideal*, 84 CAL. L. REV. 1 (July 1996). *See also* Wightman Report, *supra* note 11. The Wightman Report is based entirely on empirical quantitative data from a national longitudinal sample of 29,000 first-year students who entered law school J. D. programs at 163 different ABA-approved law schools in fall 1991. The report's findings confirm the previously reported pattern of higher LSAT scores for men than for women. The Wightman Report also found that women's academic performance in law school is slightly but persistently less outstanding than it is predicted to be by their previous academic performance, and that the gendered distribution pattern of first-year grades that Michelle Fine, Jane Balin, and I observed at a single law school is paralleled when national data are examined. *Id.* at 12. Interestingly, the Wightman Report also found that the academic underperformance by women is not independent of socioeconomic status. More than 44% of those women who performed worse than predicted were classified as low-middle in socioeconomic status, and a higher proportion of these women had fathers who were blue-collar or farm workers. By contrast, 53% of those who performed better than predicted were classified as upper or middle-upper in socio-economic status and had fathers who held professional or proprietor/managerial jobs. *Id.* at 78–79.

In an unfortunate sense, then, existing standards of supposedly objective merit may camouflage inherited privilege, including class and gender status. John Langbein has noted that with the exception of passing on the family home, the provision of a college education is the major current mechanism by which wealth is transferred between generations. John Langbein, *The Twentieth-Century Revolution in Family Wealth Transmission*, 86 U. MICH. L. REV. 722 (1988). SAT and LSAT scores are a way for middle-class parents to pass on to their children, and most especially their male children, a certain class status and the *opportunities* that presumably go along with that status. Within each racial and ethnic group, for example, Scholastic Assessment Test (formerly called the Scholastic Aptitude Test) scores increase as income rises. *See* David K. Shipler, *My Equal Opportunity, Your Free Lunch*, N.Y. TIMES, Mar. 5, 1995, at E1, E16. Money, for example, often pays for coaching or for access to preparatory schools in which students start taking the SAT as early as seventh grade. *See* Applebome, *supra* note 9 ("The best preparation for taking the S.A.T. is taking the S.A.T."). Studies by Fairtest, an organizational watchdog over standardized tests, find that coaching can increase test performance by up to 100 points.

13. Wightman Report, *supra* note 11, at 14. Our findings, based on the sample of students we studied at Penn, are supported by those of the 1996 Wightman Report, whose findings "constitute a consistent and cumulative set of data supporting the hypothesis that women tend to underperform academically in law school relative to their previous academic achievement." *Id.* at 26. Importantly, these data in no way suggest that women are *unable* to perform adequately in law school or that the performance differential between women and men is a consequence of women selecting less rigorous undergraduate majors. *Id.*

14. *Id.* at 27.

15. Hugh Price, the head of the Urban League, tells a similar story. When Price returned to Yale Law School he was hailed as one of the most distinguished mem-

bers of his class, but his law school grades would not have predicted his outstanding career.

16. Shipler, *supra* note 12, at E1.

17. *Id.* Intense extracurricular involvement in high school reflects qualities of student leadership as well as initiative, and also usually means that the student has developed a long-term relationship with an adult mentor. The mentoring relationship is critical. It usually means an adult has expressed confidence in the student's ability and provides emotional and other support even after high school graduation. *See, e.g.* Terry Williams and William Kornblum, *Growing Up Poor* (1985) at 97–109 (documenting the important role of mentoring relationships to adolescents).

18. Opportunity to succeed or fail should be inclusive, not exclusive. Certainly there are alternatives. Maybe opportunities should be allocated among people who meet a threshold set of requirements by a lottery. Maybe random selection could do the work we now assign to incremental ranking within a band of functionally equivalent applicants. Random selection, like paper-and-pencil tests, could "neutrally" allocate resources and open up opportunity. Maybe the paper-and-pencil test could establish a baseline, a floor for qualified applicants, but picking whom to hire could be done by chance.

19. Elizabeth Mertz, Wamucii Njogu, and Susan Gooding, *Race, Gender, and Status in Law School Education: A Study of Eight Contracts Classrooms* at 2–3 (unpublished manuscript, 1996) (in study of law school teaching since 1990 supported by the America Bar Foundation and the Spencer Foundation, researchers observed classroom dynamics in schools ranging across the status hierarchy: two schools were in the "elite" category, one in the "prestige" category, two in the "regional" category, two in the "local" category, and one night school class; data collection involved taping and coding the interactions during the entire first semester of "Contracts" classes). In six out of eight classrooms, male students spoke more frequently and for longer periods of time than did women. *Id.* at 45. The six included all of the classes taught by male professors and one taught by a female professor. Anecdotal observations at higher status law schools may suggest one explanation as to why the differential participation rate is particularly extreme for women students at elite institutions, for whom the presence of women professors fails to produce heightened participation by women students. *Id.* at 49. These women may be under more pressure from the men in their classes who mock or discipline the women in informal ways. *Id.* at 26. *See also* Catherine Krupnick, *Women and Men in the Classroom: Inequality and Its Remedies*, 1 ON TEACHING & LEARNING: J. OF THE HARV.-DANFORTH CENTER 18 (1985) (observation of twenty-four teachers at Harvard found that male students spoke 2.5 times longer than did women in the "predominant classroom circumstance: i.e., the situation in which the instructor is male and a majority of the students are male"; participation was "based on quick thinking instead of deep or representative thinking," and was biased toward the more verbally assertive, who tended to be white males as opposed to minorities of either gender or white females).

20. *See* Paul Farhi, *Tuning Out Testosterone: NBC Tailors Coverage To Attract Women*, WASHINGTON POST, July 23, 1996, at A1, A10.

21. *Id.*, quoting half a dozen women to explain why they prefer emotion-driven approaches to sporting events that allow them "to know who these people are" and to add an extra dimension that "makes you feel you know them better."

22. *See* Richard Sandomir, *Olympic Moments, But Hours Later on TV*, N.Y. TIMES, July 25, 1996, at A1, B14 (quoting Ed Markey, spokesman for NBC Sports: "The research leads us to the conclusion that women care more about the events than the results, and that men will sit through the events to find out the results").

23. As Elizabeth Mertz and her coauthors (*supra* note 19) discovered in observing eight "Contracts" classrooms in law schools across the country, females "respond to the emotional climate of a class more than do males, and most importantly, females' participation is related to their confidence." Mertz et al. at 12. Mertz and her coauthors concluded that "events in the classroom can affect students' self-esteem, performance, and sense of inclusion in the wider communities and professions into which they are purportedly being socialized." *Id.* at 3. Thus the process of rethinking the classroom dynamic is a continuing, urgent necessity for many women and people of color. Mertz and her coauthors are careful to notice that gender and race "are important, in some ways formative, but not completely determining aspects of classroom exchanges." *Id.* at 105. Yet those who do feel excluded "can be our best teachers about the way context and identity shape human interactions." *Id.* at 104.

24. Gary Blasi, *What Lawyers Know: Lawyering Expertise, Cognitive Science, and the Functions of Theory*, 45 J. OF LEGAL EDUC. 313, 322, 325 (September 1995) (litigation may be like tennis in which you go for the winning shot; yet even in litigation what counts is judgment and experience, and many lawyers work as members of teams representing large organizations in multiparty transactions and disputes and only rarely go to court).

25. Gerald P. Lopez, *Lay Lawyering*, 32 UCLA L. REV. 1,2 (1984).

26. It is described as including the following: identifying and diagnosing the problem, generating alternative solutions and strategies, developing a plan of action, implementing the plan, keeping the planning process open to new information and ideas. Robert MacCrate, Task Force on Law Schools and the Profession, *Narrowing the Gap: Legal Education and Professional Development—An Educational Continuum*, 1992 A.B.A. SEC. LEGAL EDUC. & ADMISSIONS B. 138 (hereinafter MacCrate Report).

27. Blasi, *supra* note 24. Lawyering is a "bundle of skills" including the lawyer's ability to "integrate factual and legal knowledge and to exercise good judgment in light of that integrated understanding." The most comprehensive effort to conceptualize the various competencies lawyers have was in the MacCrate Report. *Id.* at 326. A study of practitioners in Chicago found that the three most important qualities of lawyers were oral communication, written communication, and "instilling others' confidence in you." After these, the skills or areas of knowledge considered most important were, in order, "ability in legal analysis and legal reasoning, drafting legal documents, and *ability to diagnose and plan solutions for legal problems.*" Bryant Garth and Joanne Martin, *Law Schools and the Construction of Competence*, 43 J. LEGAL EDUC. 469, 473 (1993).

28. Carrie Menkel-Meadow, *The Legacy of Clinical Education: Theories About Lawyering*, 29 CLEV. ST. L. REV. 555, 557 (1980).

29. Deborah Zabarenko, *Women Rated Better at Key Management Tasks*, PHILADELPHIA INQUIRER, September 19, 1996, at D1, D8 (nonprofit Foundation for Future Leadership commissioned study which reviewed 6,403 questionnaires dealing with 915 corporate workers at senior levels of management, 70% of whom were men; the study did not aim to single out gender differences at the outset but clear differences emerged as the data were analyzed). While women did better than men in all but three of the areas and excelled by a wide margin in twenty-five, they were behind in a key area that was not part of the study: self-promotion. The study's author, Janet Irwin, concluded, "Women have to be more assertive in demanding recognition for their efforts." *Id.* at D8.

30. *See, e.g.*, Thomas Petzinger, Jr., *Charlene Pedrolie Rearranged Furniture and Lifted a Business*, WALL STREET JOURNAL, September 13, 1996, at B1 (a thirty-four-

year-old female, a "Yankee" outsider in the Rowe Furniture Corporation, increased plant productivity to record levels when she eliminated unnecessary layers of supervision, changed the workplace environment to make it more sunny, cross-trained workers, and most importantly, allowed workers to act on their own ideas for improving productivity).

31. *See* Clark D. Cunningham, *The Lawyer as Translator, Representation as Test: Towards an Ethnography of Legal Discourse*, 77 CORNELL L. REV. 1298, 1301 (1992) (suggesting that client satisfaction would improve if attorneys developed better listening and communication skills); Carrie Menkel-Meadow, *Portia in a Different Voice: Speculations on a Women's Lawyering Process*, 1 BERKELEY WOMEN'S L.J. 39, 57 (1985) (suggesting that a greater sense of empathy is vital to serving client needs and objectives satisfactorily); *cf.* Stacy Burling, *Study Finds Gender Gap Among Doctors*, PHILADELPHIA INQUIRER, Oct. 17, 1994, at A2 (reporting the findings that female doctors spend more time with their patients and that women doctors' communication techniques are associated with better patient compliance and understanding).

32. *See* Sturm and Guinier, *supra* note 12 (describing NYC Housing Authority informal findings and Christopher Commission Report findings in Los Angeles). The unconventional but effective technique of a gentle but firm touch from people "who have trust and credibility" also works with unsupervised teenagers in Minneapolis at the giant Mall of America, which has hired "mighty moms" as the mall's community liaisons to defuse potentially out-of-control situations when teenagers congregate on Saturday nights. *See* Kimberly Hayes Taylor, *Mighty Moms Make Mark at Megamall*, MINNEAPOLIS STAR TRIBUNE, April 27, 1996, at 1A. Most of the "mighty moms" are mothers who live in the same neighborhoods and go to the same churches as the young people whom "they have come to mentor more than monitor." They are teachers, school bus drivers, and homemakers. Eighteen of the nineteen "mighty moms" are black, and their approach is summed up by Lottie Dixon, a school bus driver with two teenage children of her own: "When you give them respect, they will respect you back." Like Dixon, Kay Smith, an education assistant at Harrison School in Minneapolis, sees her work as an investment in the future: "We are enforcers, but we do no restraining. We can make a friend. Give a hug. Share a hand. Give a smile."

33. Independent Commission of the Los Angeles Police Department, *Report of Independent Commission on the Los Angeles Riots* (Christopher Commission) (1991) at page 88: "A corollary of [traditional law enforcement] culture is an emphasis on the use of force to control a situation, and a disdain for a more patient, less aggressive approach.... [F]emale LAPD officers are involved in excessive use of force at rates substantially below those of male officers.... The statistics indicate that female officers are not reluctant to use force, but that they are not nearly as likely to be involved in the use of excessive force" due to their ability to be "more communicative, more skillful at deescalating potentially violent situations and less confrontational."

34. In law, employers often rely on measures of presumptive merit—law school grades—to determine job opportunities. But again, this is somewhat tautological since those who get the job are essentially getting the opportunity to learn how to do it. No one claims you learn all you need to be a lawyer in law school. But do those who get an opportunity based on law school grades alone turn out to be the best lawyers?

35. For example, Tsumomu Shimomura, a researcher at San Diego Supercomputer Center, used his own homebrew software program to locate a suspect who

was raiding electronic mailboxes. He pursued the "computer thief" using his own brand of kneejerk iconoclasticism—a willingness to question everything. Shimomura's success resulted from the application of an unconventional approach to a new kind of crime, computer piracy. In a profile (*see* N.Y. TIMES, Week in Review, Feb. 19, 1995), Shimomura was described as someone who has a deeply held sense of right and wrong, a member of a tight-knit community of "computer hackers"; he was committed to catching the thief because the suspect had violated Shimomura's culture of sharing—a culture that was apparently part of the original hacker ethic.

36. Some progressives also argue that such a simplistic approach limits opportunity to individuals who are identified based on group characteristics but are then permitted, even encouraged, to proceed without accountability to any other group members. This problem in essence reveals a contradiction between what is defended as a group remedy at a theoretical level and what is operationalized as an individual solution at the practical level.

37. *See* Peter Applebome, *The Last Integrationist*, N.Y. TIMES MAGAZINE, April 23, 1995 (describing the important role that a white professor played in giving John Hope Franklin, the distinguished African-American historian, $500 to attend graduate school; the professor's gift gave Franklin confidence in his own ability to succeed); Carol Hymowitz, *How a Dedicated Mentor Gave Momentum to a Woman's Career*, WALL ST. JOURNAL, April 24, 1995, at B1, B9 (quoting Professor David Thomas, of Harvard Business School, who has studied mentoring relationships; Thomas says effective mentors "create a context in which you're structured and developed, and that friendship and trust are essential ingredients of mentoring relationships).

38. Hymowitz, *supra* note 37, at B1, B9 (quoting Professor David Thomas, Harvard Business School; Thomas points out that it can be difficult for minority group members to trust a white mentor, and that most executives are white males and most choose people to mentor they can identify with: "Likes attract likes"). *See also* *supra* note 17 (noting the critical role of a mentoring relationship in ensuring college success).

39. This phenomenon tracks the way many experts "learn" their expertise—as a result of the opportunity to develop their knowledge and skills by examining actual problems, not through formal training programs. *See* Daniel A. Farber and Suzanna Sherry, *Telling Stories Out of School: An Essay on Legal Narratives*, 45 STAN. L. REV. 807, 821 and nn. 82–84 (1993) (citing studies of expert decision making to support the conclusion that expertise does not consist simply of knowing more facts or rules, but involves the skill of picking out key features in a new situation, which is learned primarily through experience with large numbers of past situations).

CHAPTER II. BECOMING GENTLEMEN

1. Our research is only about the University of Pennsylvania Law School and may not apply to other institutions of legal education which do not share Penn's history, traditions, dominant first-year pedagogy, and predominantly male faculty. *See infra* note 142 (identifying traditions and histories that may be peculiar to Ivy League institutions). On the other hand, the same phenomena we identify in legal education at this law school are, of course, in evidence in most of legal education throughout American law schools. *See* ROBERT GRANFIELD, MAKING ELITE LAW-

YERS: VISIONS OF LAW AT HARVARD AND BEYOND 106–07 (1992) (acknowledging that a significant number of women in law school feel disempowered, report low levels of class participation, do not feel competent, and find the law school experience both sexist and dehumanizing); Robert MacCrate, Task Force on Law Schools and the Profession, *Narrowing the Gap: Legal Education and Professional Development—An Educational Continuum*, 1992 A.B.A. SEC. LEGAL EDUC. & ADMISSIONS B. 22 (hereinafter MacCrate Report) (noting a gendered experience in the legal profession, both because men find the adversarial nature of their work more important with respect to job satisfaction than do women, and because persistent bias and stereotyping aid in maintaining a "glass ceiling," in both legal education and the legal profession, above which women cannot rise); *see also* Memorandum from Robert A. Gorman, Associate Dean of the Law School, University of Pennsylvania, to Lani Guinier, Professor of Law, University of Pennsylvania 3 (July 19, 1993) ("What is striking about American legal education is not the differences but the sameness"). Moreover, other studies have documented findings similar to those we present here. *See infra* notes 33–65 and accompanying text; *infra* notes 141, 142.

2. *See infra* notes 18–27 and accompanying text.

3. Our findings contradict much of the early literature on law school performance of women in the 1960s and 1970s. *See infra* notes 33–39 and accompanying text. The results of this study are also inconsistent with contemporaneous data about University of Pennsylvania undergraduates. At the college level, the grade point distribution does not appear to be gendered, according to statistics maintained by the university. Interview with Susan Shaman, Director of Institutional Research and Planning Analysis, University of Pennsylvania, in Philadelphia, Pa. (Oct. 15, 1992).

4. *See infra* part 2A of this chapter.

5. *See infra* text accompanying notes 71–73.

6. *See infra* notes 99–104 and accompanying text. This finding is based on an analysis of only one group of first-year women who responded in 1990 to a self-reporting survey. *See infra* note 19 and accompanying text. Unlike our academic performance data or our findings regarding women's alienation, this finding does not reflect a longitudinal database. Nor is it generalizable beyond the women who provided the data—those who responded to the 1990 Bartow Survey. *But cf. infra* note 100 (hypothesizing that differences between first- and third-year women are probably significant where first- and third-year men do not show comparable distinctions and where first-year women consistently distinguish their interests from first-year male counterparts in other self-reported value surveys conducted between 1988 and 1991).

7. *See infra* notes 95–98 and accompanying text.

8. *See infra* text accompanying note 99.

9. *See infra* notes 101, 102, 109 and accompanying text.

10. We refer here to the Socratic method, or case-study method, which was developed and originally implemented by Christopher Columbus Langdell at Harvard Law School in the late nineteenth century. Both Langdell and his methodology came to prominence through Harvard Law School, and for this reason, the case-study method is often called the Harvard method. In its most extreme form, the case-study method teaches law exclusively through the study of appellate decisions. Typically, the class session is devoted to the professor's questioning the student (or students) about details of the court's decision in an effort to extrapolate the legal principles embedded in the opinion. This method was intended not only to

convey legal principles, but also to aid the student in developing legal reasoning skills and becoming an independent thinker. *See* JOEL SELIGMAN, THE HIGH CITADEL: THE INFLUENCE OF HARVARD LAW SCHOOL 11–12 (1978) (relating the origins of the Socratic method); ROBERT STEVENS, LAW SCHOOL: LEGAL EDUCATION IN AMERICA FROM THE 1850S TO THE 1980S 53 (1983) (discussing the development of the Socratic method along with the case method); Edwin W. Patterson, *The Case Method in American Legal Education: Its Origins and Objectives*, 4 J. LEGAL EDUC. 1, 1–20 (1951) (describing the goals and elements of the Socratic method).

11. *See infra* notes 85–86 and accompanying text.

12. *See infra* notes 112–117 and accompanying text (describing how the Socratic method of classroom instruction does not reach a large segment of the student body at this law school). Our research suggests that women's alienation is not exclusively derivative of an intimidating classroom pedagogy, but is also related to the hostility that female students perceive the methodology generates or encourages in their male peers. *See infra* notes 120, 121, 134 and accompanying text. This conclusion is consistent with findings from a study of nine Ohio law schools. *See* COMMITTEE ON GENDER ISSUES IN THE LAW SCHOOLS, OHIO SUPREME COURT AND OHIO BAR ASS'N, THE ELEPHANT IN OHIO LAW SCHOOLS: A STUDY OF PERCEPTIONS—EXECUTIVE SUMMARY [hereinafter EXECUTIVE SUMMARY] (finding that 64% of women, compared to 51% of men, believed the Socratic method did not allow a free exchange of ideas).

13. Christine A. Littleton, *Reconstructing Sexual Equality*, 75 CAL. L. REV. 1279, 1308–09 (1987) (defining "social male" as a person assuming characteristics deemed culturally male, independent of "biological" gender); *see also infra* text preceding note 120.

14. All quotations from students are taken from the narrative portion of the Bartow Survey, the small-group interviews, or seminar discussions. *See infra* text accompanying notes 18, 19, 105–107. All speakers were guaranteed anonymity, but we have identified a speaker's year in school, gender, and race whenever important for context. In some instances, comments may reflect multiple observations from the same individual. We do not present our qualitative data to represent the opinions or views of the Penn Law School community in general. We present the actual comments to triangulate our data. *See infra* notes 22–30 and accompanying text.

15. We use the term "gentlemen" throughout this study to evoke the traditional values of legal education, including its mission to train the legal minds of detached, dispassionate advocates. For the purpose of this discussion, the term describes the lawyer's role as a neutral, unemotional, but courteous advocate for a client's interest. Although "gentlemen" primarily refers to men, and in particular men of "good breeding," it assumes men who possess neither a race nor a gender. *Cf.* Peggy McIntosh, *White Privilege and Male Privilege: A Personal Account of Coming To See Correspondences Through Work in Women's Studies* 1 (1988) (unpublished manuscript, on file with author) (arguing that white men's race and gender are an "invisible package of unearned assets").

The lawyer's role is still occasionally described in terms such as "behaving like a gentleman." *See* Lani Guinier, *Of Gentlemen and Role Models*, 6 BERKELEY WOMEN'S L.J. 93, 93 n.2 (1990–91); *see also* Rosabeth M. Kanter, *Reflections on Women and the Legal Profession: A Sociological Perspective*, 1 HARV. WOMEN'S L.J. 1, 8 (1978) (describing the law firm management as running a "gentlemen's club," an enterprise that depends on a "sharing of standards from similar cultural experiences"); *infra* note 126 (discussing the view that law schools aim to create advocates who are competitive, adversarial, and ruthless, and who favor logic over emotion, neutrality over commitment, and individual rights over community interests—all traditionally male attributes). Helene Schwartz recounts an experience in which a judge nearly addressed her as "gentleman." She did not insist that the judge acknowledge her gender. Although she was not active in the women's movement, which at the time sought to minimize formal gender distinctions, her feminist consciousness was apparently consistent with efforts to be considered "one of the boys." *See* HELENE E. SCHWARTZ, LAWYERING 139–40 (1976). Of course, an alternative explanation is that women pioneers prefer not to call undue attention to themselves. *See* Kanter, *supra*, at 12, 13 (discussing the "unobtrusiveness phenomenon").

16. *See infra* part 2A (documenting that women's academic performance lags behind that of men at Penn Law School); *infra* part 3A (positing that women experience a depressed social position at the school).

17. *See infra* notes 213–231 and accompanying text.

18. For the Bartow Survey questions, see Appendix A at the end of this chapter. For survey responses and related statistics, see Bartow Survey (1990) (on file with authors).

19. Ann Bartow, while a third-year student, brought these concerns to Professor Lani Guinier. Bartow asked that Guinier supervise an independent study to develop a film script parodying Bartow's own experiences at the University of Pennsylvania Law School. Guinier proposed the survey as a means to investigate whether the concerns of Bartow and a few other vocal female law students were widely shared. Bartow intended to develop a videotape of her law school experience along the lines of a comparable documentary produced by female medical students who reversed traditional gender roles associated with their medical school experience. The medical school videotape, entitled *Turning Around*, contains role reversal vignettes. For example, all the medical students study as typical the female body, all the professors are women, and "a female doctor leers at a male nurse, admires the fit of his uniform, pats him on the rear and calls him 'a good boy.'" Camille Peri, *Battling Stereotypes*, IMAGE, July 3, 1986, at 6.

The idea for the survey was that a videotape would be most useful if it addressed concerns shared by significant numbers of women law students about practices perceived to be sexist. Portions of the survey were adapted from a questionnaire distributed as part of a 1987 *Stanford Law Review* study. *See* Janet Taber et al., *Gender, Legal Education, and the Legal Profession: An Empirical Study of Stanford Law Students and Graduates*, 40 STAN. L. REV. 1209, 1234 (1988). Other survey questions were independently created based on concerns raised by law students in various contexts over the past few years.

20. Although we employed random sampling techniques to administer the Bartow Survey, we nevertheless ended up with a selectivity bias by gender in our final sample. A significantly larger number of women than we would have expected and a smaller number of men than expected answered the survey. $p < .001$. Because we make no generalizations and draw no conclusions about the entire cohort from which this sample was drawn and only speak about the cohort in terms of men versus women—two samples that are indeed randomly distributed—such a selectivity bias does not affect the arguments made here. In fact, although there are many possible reasons as to why a disproportionate number of women responded to the survey, we hypothesize that the gendered response bias in the final sample is related to the gender experiences described throughout this chapter.

21. Statistical analyses were conducted with a cohort sample of 981 students at Penn Law School. These students comprised the classes of 1990 through 1993.

This group of 981 included data on 676 third-year students, 700 second-year students, and 929 first-year students. We did not have complete transcripts for 101 students, who were therefore not included in the study. Some of these students may have transferred to other educational institutions; others may have dropped out or pursued joint degrees. We did not find significant differences in what we are calling the attrition rates between men and women (or between white students and students of color) in our initial cohort study of 712 students. The p value for attrition rates between men and women is $p < .30$. The p value for attrition rates between people of color and whites is $p < .50$. Fourteen percent of the men and 11% of the women during the 1987–91 period are in this category, as are 11% of the people of color and 13% of the white students. We have no reason to believe that the attrition rates in our later examination of the performance of 981 students (712 of whom were included in our initial analysis) are significantly different from those found in the original study.

22. *See, e.g.*, MARGOT ELY, DOING QUALITATIVE RESEARCH: CIRCLES WITHIN CIRCLES 2 (1991) (noting the rise in recent decades of qualitative research methods as an alternative to traditional methods of empirical research and suggesting that qualitative researchers may reduce the distortions created by their own subjectivity by consciously recognizing the perspectives and interpretations of their research subjects); Frederick Erickson, *Qualitative Methods in Research on Teaching*, in HANDBOOK OF RESEARCH ON TEACHING 119, 131–34 (Merlin C. Wittrock ed., 3d ed. 1986) (stating that qualitative research methods lead to a better understanding of effective teaching in the classroom, and of how insiders see and talk about an institution, than standard positivist research methods); Karen L. Henwood and Nick F. Pidgeon, *Qualitative Research and Psychological Theorizing*, in SOCIAL RESEARCH: PHILOSOPHY, POLITICS AND PRACTICE 14, 27–28 (Martyn Hammersley ed., 1993) (noting the current use of qualitative research methods in psychology); Elliot G. Mishler, *Meaning in Context: Is There Any Other Kind?*, 49 HARV. EDUC. REV. 1, 8–11 (1979) (arguing that the social and behavioral sciences should abandon the traditional scientific method's search for universal, context-free laws in favor of context-dependent laws, so better to explore novel hypotheses, confirm and disconfirm varied explanations, and generate new interpretations of data); *see also* SHULAMIT REINHARZ, FEMINIST METHODS IN SOCIAL RESEARCH 22 (1992) (noting that qualitative data may be presented as a corpus or offered through illustrative quotations); Rosalind Edwards, *An Education in Interviewing: Placing the Researcher and the Research*, in RESEARCHING SENSITIVE TOPICS 181, 183–85 (Claire M. Renzetti and Raymond M. Lee eds., 1993) (describing the frequent use of qualitative methods in feminist research.)

23. For the text of the open-ended question in the Bartow Survey, see *infra* note 131 and Appendix B at the end of the chapter.

24. The focus groups were held in 1992 to test and update the findings of Bartow's original survey. Students were solicited by memoranda placed in student mail folders and through recommendations from other students in order to reach editors of the *Law Review*, students in the top 10% of their class, members of several first-year legal writing sections, members of the black, Asian, and Latino law students' associations (BALSA, APALSA and LALSA, respectively), and the Women's Law Group.

We conducted seven focus groups, each of which included between three and six students. Two of the focus groups were held among white women, two were held among male and female African-American students, and the remaining three included male and female students of color and white students from diverse racial and ethnic backgrounds. Three of the focus groups included only first-year students, and the remaining four groups were composed of third-year students. The interviewers were third-year students who asked a scripted list of four questions.

At the beginning of each session, students were asked to identify themselves by race, gender, and year in law school. Each group discussion lasted forty-five minutes; discussions were tape-recorded and then transcribed. The students were asked to discuss the following four questions:

1. Are you different from the person you were when you first entered law school? In what ways? Do you consider these changes for better or worse?

2. How do you feel that other students, or the faculty and administration, perceive you?

3. What are the conditions that make a classroom situation comfortable for you?

4. Have you ever talked to professors after class or outside of class? Do you have a relationship with any professors in the school? Why or why not?

The interviews took place in April and May 1992. The participants in the focus groups were given neither information about the ongoing study nor details from the study, either prior to or during the discussion sessions.

The decision to conduct interviews was a response to suggestions made by Penn Law School faculty colleagues with whom we discussed our data. The most formal faculty meeting regarding our data took place on May 4, 1992. Seventeen faculty attended, four of whom were women. Four law students—Rebecca Bratspies, Deborah Stachel, Laura Nussbaum, and Nicole Galli—also attended and took extensive notes on the proceedings. Other, more informal discussions with faculty occurred in the fall of 1992 and the early spring of 1993.

25. These students were enrolled in a spring seminar at the law school entitled "Critical Perspectives on the Law: Issues of Race and Gender." The seminar originated in 1990 in response to the interest of students seeking to study the legal academic literature of feminist and race theorists whose perspectives they felt had been ignored by the more traditional law school curriculum. Based on continuing student demand, the seminar has become a regular course offering available to second- and third-year law students.

We presented our initial findings at two meetings of this seminar, once in 1991 and again in 1992. During our discussions with the students we observed and recorded their responses to our data. A total of forty-one students participated, including men and women of various ages from diverse racial and ethnic backgrounds. The group was self-selected based on interest in participating in a student-initiated seminar on this subject matter.

26. These students were members of the Women's Law Group of the University of Pennsylvania Law School who were interviewed as a group or individually by Professor Guinier. The Women's Law Group is a student-run organization that meets to address issues of mutual concern, including career options and networking.

27. *See supra* note 24.

28. Reliability is "[t]hat quality of measurement method that suggests that the same data would have been collected each time in repeated observations of the same phenomenon." EARL BABBIE, THE PRACTICE OF SOCIAL RESEARCH, at G7 (6th ed. 1992).

29. Validity is "a descriptive term used for a measure that accurately reflects the concept it is intended to measure." *Id.* at G8. The narrative responses to the survey,

the discussions of focus groups, and the responses to the presentation of our data are substantively valid but not necessarily generalizable. These qualitative data are not generalizable to the extent that they were collected from nonrandomly chosen samples of students active in the professional and social life of Penn Law School. We do not argue that these responses are reflective of all students' experiences at the school in 1990; nor do we generalize the attitudes and experiences expressed in our focus groups and those responding to the presentation of our data.

30. We use quotations from the transcriptions of the interviews and narrative responses to contextualize observations generated by the more reliable quantitative data to allow us to hear the "emic" perspective. *See, e.g.,* Erickson, *supra* note 22, at 150–51 (suggesting that an emic perspective is important in determining how insiders see and talk about an institution); *see also* ELY, *supra* note 22, at 58 (arguing that an interview allows a researcher to see the world from the interviewee's perspective).

31. Five empirical studies of women law students found that women engage less frequently than men in class discussion. *See* Taunya L. Banks, *Gender Bias in the Classroom,* 38 J. LEGAL EDUC. 137, 141–42 (1988) (examining five unidentified law schools); Robert Granfield, *Contextualizing the Different Voice: Women, Occupational Goals, and Legal Education,* 16 LAW & POL'Y 1, 6–12 (1994) (surveying half of the 1540 students attending Harvard Law School in 1987 regarding their orientations toward law and legal practice); Suzanne Homer and Lois Schwartz, *Admitted but Not Accepted: Outsiders Take an Inside Look at Law School,* 5 BERKELEY WOMEN'S L.J. 1, 37–38 (1989–90) (studying Boalt Hall Law School); Taber et al., *supra* note 19 at 1239 (considering Stanford Law School); Catherine Weiss and Louise Melling, *The Legal Education of Twenty Women,* 40 STAN. L. REV. 1299, 1335 (1988) (evaluating Yale Law School).

32. We try not to take a position in this paper on the nature-versus-nurture debate. *See infra* note 214 and accompanying text.

33. *See, e.g.,* Audrey J. Schwartz, *Law, Lawyers, and Law School: Perspectives from the First-Year Class,* 30 J. LEGAL EDUC. 437, 441 (1980) (examining how law students' "world views" changed during the first year of law school); Robert Stevens, *Law Schools and Law Students,* 59 VA. L. REV. 551, 556 (1973) ("A primary aim was to uncover any changes in the backgrounds, motivations, career expectations, and politics of law students during the increasing turbulence of the 1960's").

34. *See, e.g.,* David M. White and Terry E. Roth, *The Law School Admission Test and the Continuing Minority Status of Women in Law Schools,* 2 HARV. WOMEN'S L.J. 103, 103 (1979) (focusing on the effects on women resulting from law schools' increased reliance on the LSAT).

35. *See* Georgina W. LaRussa, *Portia's Decision: Women's Motives for Studying Law and Their Later Career Satisfaction as Attorneys,* 1 PSYCHOL. WOMEN Q. 350, 353–58 (1977) (examining women's motives for attending law school and how they relate to later career satisfaction); *see also* Stevens, *supra* note 33, at 611–16 (noting that men identified more with the traditional role of lawyer as adversary whereas women wanted to use the law to change society or help the underprivileged).

36. *See, e.g.,* Alice D. Jacobs, *Women in Law School: Structural Constraint and Personal Choice in the Formation of Professional Identity,* 24 J. LEGAL EDUC. 462, 467–68 (1972) (noting that women students' clannishness harmed them because it removed them from those vital parts of law school culture that serve as successful preparation for professional life); E. R. Robert and M. F. Winter, *Sex-Role and Suc-*

cess in Law School, 29 J. Legal Educ. 449, 450 (1978) (exploring how women achieve success in law school despite "the considerable disparity in sex role socialization" that seems to favor men).

37. *See, e.g.,* LaRussa, *supra* note 35 at 360–63 (examining trends in career satisfaction among women lawyers); Paul W. Mattessich and Cheryl W. Heilman, *The Career Paths of Minnesota Law School Graduates: Does Gender Make a Difference?,* 9 Law & Ineq. J. 59, 60–61 (1990) (reviewing a study commissioned by Minnesota Women Lawyers on the Status of Women in the Legal Profession); *see also* Stevens, *supra* note 33, at 611–24 (comparing several motivating factors and assessing their relative influence on the decision by women, men, and people of color to attend law school).

38. The Union College of Law (now Northwestern School of Law) was the first law school to admit women, in 1870. *See* D. Kelly Weisberg, *Barred from the Bar: Women and Legal Education in the United States 1870–1890,* 28 J. Legal Educ. 485, 494 (1977). In 1972 women gained access to all ABA-accredited law schools. *See* Donna Fossum, *Law and the Sexual Integration of Institutions: The Case of American Law Schools,* 7 Am. Legal Stud. Ass'n J. 222, 224 (1983); *see also* Cynthia F. Epstein, Women in Law 49–59 (1981) (providing a historical overview of women's admission to law schools, and noting the increase in women's admissions in the late 1960s and early 1970s).

39. Studies that attempted to answer this question focused on women in law school in the 1960s and 1970s. They found that many women performed as well as, if not better than, their male counterparts. *See, e.g.,* Stevens, *supra* note 33, at 572 n.46 ("[O]ver 53 percent of the women [in the class of 1972], compared to only 38 percent of the men, graduated in the top 10 percent of their undergraduate class. And average LSAT did not vary significantly by respondent's sex").

One can generate many hypotheses to explain the findings of these studies. Perhaps the first wave of female law school students felt they had to prove their fitness just to be in law school "taking a man's place." As early pioneers, these women may have emulated an aggressive style without the ambivalence that is often felt by their contemporary counterparts. Or, because only a small group of women were then in law school, these trailblazers may have self-selected themselves because of their "male" traits. Today, however, with a larger pool of women in law school, enrollment reflects a wider range of women with "traditionally female" values or aptitudes, whether cultural or biological. *Cf. infra* note 51 (discussing the possibility that law schools are now more hospitable to women and that women, finding themselves a larger subgroup in law schools, are more comfortable). Without actual performance data from that period, we can also speculate that the early literature, based primarily on self-reporting, may not be entirely accurate. Although the nature of this question seems to essentialize maleness, our study suggests that the failure to consider fully the gendered attributes of law school has had serious and harmful repercussions for women law students.

40. *See supra* note 31 (discussing recent empirical studies). In addition to the empirical data, there has been an ever-growing body of narrative literature about the law school experience and legal education with specific emphasis on its impact on women. *See* Catherine W. Hantzis, *Kingsfield and Kennedy: Reappraising the Male Models of Law School Teaching,* 38 J. Legal Educ. 155, 155 (1988) (analyzing two common approaches to legal instructions and arguing for a feminist approach to legal issues and teaching); Cynthia L. Hill, *Sexual Bias in the Law School Classroom: One Student's Perspective,* 38 J. Legal Educ. 603, 603 (1988) (presenting an imaginary interview concerning a woman's perceptions about the treatment of women

in law school); Faith Seidenberg, *A Neglected Minority—Women in Law School*, 10 NOVA L.J. 843, 845–49 (1986) (suggesting that legal education techniques which could better aid women in their law-related experiences be incorporated in a course structured to meet women's needs); Stephanie M. Wildman, *The Question of Silence: Techniques to Ensure Full Class Participation*, 38 J. LEGAL EDUC. 147, 152–54 (1988) (urging professors to determine why female law students tend to speak less in class than male law students and suggesting techniques to encourage greater participation in class, including support networks, role playing, and sharing of personal experiences); K. C. Worden, *Overshooting the Target: A Feminist Deconstruction of Legal Education*, 34 AM. U. L. REV. 1141, 1156 (1985) (rejecting the "[u]nquestioning acceptance of the immutability of a 'male voice' monopoly on legal thought and practice" and urging incorporation of a "female voice" in the law).

41. *See, e.g.*, Banks, *supra* note 31, at 141–45. Professor Banks focused on female law students' silence in the classroom at five unidentified law schools. Through a self-reporting survey, Banks asked questions about levels of volunteering in class, the influence of professorial attitude on class participation, how the gender of the professor affects class participation, and informants' views of gendered "humor" and comments in the classroom.

With regard to voluntary participation, Banks found that close to twice as many women as men reported never volunteering (17.6% to 9.6%, respectively), but 44.3% of men and 32.1% of women reported voluntary participation on a weekly basis. *See id.* at 141. Banks further broke down the rates of women's participation by age. Here she found significant differences: whereas 44.6% of women over age 30 volunteered weekly, only 27.7% of 25–30-year-olds and 26.5% of the 21–24 age group did the same. *See id.* at 141 n.19.

Banks found that the gender of the professor affected perceptions about whether women were called on as frequently. Almost twice as many women as men (12.9% versus 7.2%) reported that the gender of the professor affects the frequency with which they are called on in class. *See id.* at 143. Moreover, 70.8% of women respondents, as opposed to 55.4% of men, believed that women professors are more encouraging of student participation. *See id.* Nearly twice as many women as men (11.0% versus 5.8%, respectively) also reported that the gender of the professor affects their voluntary class participation. *See id.*

Banks argued that women's silence derives from their exclusion from the structure of the institution, especially the law school classroom, and from women's self-perceptions of inferiority. *See id.* at 146. The claim that women's silence was a response to alienation and exclusion helped begin to focus attention on the structural problems of the law school itself.

42. *See supra* note 19 and accompanying text; *see also* Katherine T. Bartlett, *Feminist Legal Methods*, 103 HARV. L. REV. 829, 863–67 (1990) (discussing consciousness-raising as a methodology of inductive reasoning in which individual stories become the basis for a shared consciousness about general phenomena). Another example of this is found in the Weiss and Melling study, which grew out of a women's law school discussion group. *See* Weiss and Melling, *supra* note 31, at 1299. After experiencing a classroom situation in which men participated at much greater rates than women, the authors decided to count the number of comments, both volunteered and requested, by men and women in a large number of classes. They then looked for average performance rates based upon the total number of women and men in each class. *See id.* at 1363.

43. *See generally* CAROL GILLIGAN, IN A DIFFERENT VOICE: PSYCHOLOGICAL

THEORY AND WOMEN'S DEVELOPMENT (1982). Gilligan found that women and men (and girls and boys) speak about and understand moral questions differently. Unlike many of the women she studied, men often adopted a rights-based, abstract justice approach in which they resolved moral conflict through the rigid application of general rules. The women tended to resolve conflict from a flexible standpoint of care and connectedness, in which they sought to find the compromise that would benefit the greatest number of people. *See id.* at 18, 43–44. Gilligan posits an ethic of care as a distinctly female approach to moral reasoning based on a different self-perspective. *See id.* at 19.

Gilligan's work is not without its critics. *See, e.g.,* Lucinda M. Finley, *Transcending Equality Theory: A Way out of the Maternity and the Workplace Debate,* 86 COLUM. L. REV. 1118, 1154 n.158 (1986) (noting strong feminist reaction to Gilligan's work); Ruth B. Ginsburg, *Some Thoughts on the 1980's Debate Over Special Versus Equal Treatment for Women,* 4 LAW & INEQ. J. 143, 148 (1986) (arguing that the difference debate depends on overgeneralizations without emphasizing enough the individual differences within gender). In particular, Catharine MacKinnon argues that the differences found by Gilligan reflect existing power relationships in which women's so-called different perspective is a consequence of their social, economic, and physical standing. *See* CATHARINE MACKINNON, FEMINISM UNMODIFIED 38–39 (1987); *see also* Isabel Marcus et al., *Feminist Discourse, Moral Values, and the Law—A Conversation* (Oct. 19, 1984), *in* 34 BUFF. L. REV. 11, 27 (1985) (reprinting a discussion in which Catharine MacKinnon attributes gender differences to women's status as a subordinated class).

44. *See, e.g.,* Homer and Schwartz, *supra* note 31, at 8, 18 (discussing Gilligan's theory of gender difference in moral development and reasoning); Janoff, *infra* note 52, at 201–03 (same); Taber et al., *supra* note 19, at 1212–15 (same); Weiss and Melling, *supra* note 31, at 1302–04 (same).

45. *See* MACKINNON, *supra* note 43, at 32–45; Marcus, et al., *supra* note 43, at 25–30; *see also* Taber et al., *supra* note 19, at 1217 (discussing MacKinnon's objective of destroying the hierarchy that allows men to set comparative standards); Weiss and Melling, *supra* note 31, at 1300 n.4, 1308–09 (discussing MacKinnon's goal of freeing women to control themselves and their world). MacKinnon's thesis has been supported by work in other disciplines. *See, e.g.,* Sara E. Snodgrass, *Women's Intuition: The Effect of Subordinate Role on Interpersonal Sensitivity,* 49 J. PERSONALITY & SOC. PSYCHOL. 146, 147–48 (1985) (arguing that the subordinate role of women may cause women to protect themselves by developing sensitivity to feelings of others); Wendy Wood and Stephen J. Karten, *Sex Differences in Interaction Style as a Product of Perceived Sex Differences in Competence,* 50 J. PERSONALITY & SOC. PSYCHOL. 341, 342 (1986) (maintaining that social roles involving dominance and subordination create what appear to be gender-related differences).

46. *See, e.g.,* Mari J. Matsuda, *When the First Quail Calls: Multiple Consciousness as Jurisprudential Method,* 11 WOMEN'S RTS. L. REP. 7, 8 (1989) (noting that outsiders sometimes employ a dualistic approach to the legal system, simultaneously working within the system as legal realists and attacking the injustice the system perpetuates against women and people of color). In her more recent work, Carol Gilligan also recognizes the phenomenon of "double vision" in which the adherents of one voice are also aware of the other—in fact, she contends that both men and women engage in this dynamic. *See, e.g.,* Marcus et al., *supra* note 43, at 46–49 (discussing the presence and use of both voices by both men and women).

47. *See* Homer and Schwartz, *supra* note 31, at 21–22 (discussing women as out-

siders in the law classroom setting); Weiss and Melling, *supra* note 31, at 1300–02 (referring to the status of women as outsiders); *cf.* Granfield, *supra* note 31, at 7, 10 (noting that many of the women at Harvard Law School described a sense of "marginality and otherness," and that a significantly larger proportion of women than men also claimed to have become more interested in social change while in law school).

48. *See* Taber et al., *supra* note 19, at 1212–14, 1218–22. This study was published in 1988 by the *Stanford Law Review* based on data collected from current and former Stanford Law School students. The researchers expected to find gendered responses and believed that Gilligan's theory would explain these differences. *See id.* at 1212–14. Their questionnaire included problems that were intended to serve as moral measurements. Respondents were given questions with a spectrum of responses ranging from "contextual" responses at one end to "abstract" responses at the other. Based on Gilligan's research, men were expected to choose "abstract" responses and women "contextual." *Id.* at 1236.

49. These differences were based upon the weight women and men placed on the importance of preselected factors. *See id.* at 1248–49.

50. *See id.* at 1249.

51. *Id.* at 1240. The survey editors attributed this lack of disparity to a "more responsive and hospitable" law school environment, women's "comfort in being one of a sizable subgroup within the law school population," and/or changes in women's lives that "allow women to accommodate more easily to the law school environment." *Id.* at 1242–43.

The survey did find differences among current law students for level of class participation and reasons for going to law school. *See id.* at 1238–39. On a scale of one to five, with five indicating most frequently, male students reported a higher frequency than did women of asking questions in class (2.98 versus 2.43), volunteering answers (2.96 versus 2.48), and asking professors questions outside of class (2.61 versus 2.30). *See id.* at 1239.

The survey found no gendered responses for academic performance in law school and was unable to test for differences in class rank based on gender because of the fact that Stanford does not officially rank students. Therefore, students could not self-report this information. *See id.* at 1239. The one indicator of rank the survey did use, Order of the Coif, did not reveal any gender difference from graduate reports. *See id.* at 1239–40.

52. *See, e.g.,* Sandra Janoff, *The Influence of Legal Education on Moral Reasoning,* 76 MINN. L. REV. 193, 237 (1991) ("In the study's sample, women and me revealed significantly different response patterns at the beginning of the year but showed no significant difference at the end of the year"). *But see* Weiss and Melling, *supra* note 31, at 1300 (arguing that the law school experience differs for men and women).

53. With regard to the moral reasoning section of the Stanford survey, the design of the test may have had some effect on the results. Respondents had only limited choices in response to the hypotheticals and were not given space for additional comments. *See* Taber et al., *supra* note 19, at 1234. Moreover, the legal nature of the hypotheticals may have led women to respond in a legal manner (that is, Gilligan's male, abstract voice). *See* GILLIGAN, *supra* note 43, at 32 (explaining the difference between women's contextual morality and men's abstract moral judgments). Other models that analyze moral reasoning may capture this nuance more readily. *Compare* Taber et al., *supra* note 19, at 1234 (using a rigid questionnaire) *with* Janoff, *supra* note 52, at 212–13 (using open-ended interviews to

compile responses). Indeed, if Gilligan's hypothesis is true, and women shy away from quantifiable responses to rules, an abstract survey may not "hear" women's voices.

Another problem with the Stanford study as a whole is that it was entirely self-reported. The study was therefore unable to match respondents' perceptions to actual data. *But see infra* notes 58, 64 (noting correlation between women's perception of decreased performance and actual decline in academic performance). More-over, in using Order of the Coif to measure academic performance, the study did not "consider the fact that the top ten percent of the class elected to Order of the Coif is not necessarily (or even logically) representative of the performance distribution among men and women in the other 90%." Homer and Schwartz, *supra* note 31, at 13.

54. Stanford is distinctive with regard to teaching method and style. The authors reported that most professors did not use the Socratic method. *See* Taber et al., *supra* note 19, at 1254. In addition, the dean and many members of the Stanford Law School faculty who are openly identified with critical legal studies have articulated an interest in creating a nonhierarchical classroom environment, or at least a nontraditional one. *See* Duncan Kennedy, Legal Education and the Reproduction of Hierarchy: A Polemic Against the System 78, 120–23 (1983) (criticizing the "legal hierarchy" and proposing a model solution). The authors of the Stanford study concluded that no gender gap exists because varied ways of learning and lawyering have already been incorporated into law school and the legal world. *See* Taber et al., *supra* note 19, at 1242–43.

55. *See supra* notes 31, 47 and accompanying text.

56. For example, the authors of *The Legal Education of Twenty Women* attribute power to their outsider perspective, which gave them the unique consciousness to evaluate their experience at Yale Law School and form a special bond with other outsiders. *See* Weiss and Melling, *supra* note 31, at 1300; *cf.* Matsuda, *supra* note 46, at 7–8 (noting that "outsiders" have unique perspectives relevant to legal study). The Yale women render their law school experiences a moral issue, with narratives by female law students at the heart of the piece.

Various forms of alienation were described by women during their years in law school: alienation from self, alienation from the law school, alienation from the classroom, and alienation from the content of legal education. *See* Weiss and Melling, *supra* note 31, at 1299. This was the first piece to grapple so explicitly with the qualitative aspects of women's law school experience. *See* Homer and Schwartz, *supra* note 31, at 11 (some women who read the Yale study felt that "someone [had] at last 'told it like it is'"); *cf.* Granfield, *supra* note 31, at 10 (stating that many women at Harvard Law School reported feeling isolated from the educational process and "were critical of what they perceived as the male-dominated worldview of law and legal reasoning that pervaded the law school environment"). The Granfield study found partial support for the difference theory based on 391 questionnaires representing the responses of about one-fourth of the students attending Harvard Law School in 1987, supplemented by in-depth interviews conducted from 1986 to 1988 with about a fourth of those students who returned the questionnaire. *See id.* at 6–7. Granfield concluded that women experienced legal education differently in relation to preexisting occupational goals, and not simply in relation to fundamental gender-specific personality traits. *See id.* at 15. Those women whose career goals focused on financial security, prestige, and personal advancement were more like their male counterparts than other women, including "social feminists." *See id.* at 18.

57. *See* Homer and Schwartz, *supra* note 31, at 23. The Berkeley authors had feminist goals and designed a feminist survey. The methodology combined statistical information with survey questions designed to give respondents the opportunity to speak in their own words. The survey questionnaire was divided into six parts: "(1) career plans and goals; (2) academic experience at Boalt; (3) psychological and emotional reactions to the academic experience ([entitled] 'General'); (4) academic performance; (5) demographic information . . . and (6) the section for open-ended comments." *Id.* at 24. At the end of the questionnaire the authors left respondents one and a half blank pages on which to write anything they wished. *See id.*

58. The researchers anticipated a distinction between "*what women do* in law school and *how they feel about it.*" *Id.* at 15. "Based on our hypothesis, we expected that objective indicators such as grades and academic honors would demonstrate that women had learned to play the game quite well; what we wanted to learn was how they perceived themselves for doing it." *Id.* at 25. Nevertheless, the respondents reported a decline in women's academic performance and an increase in men's performance over time. "For example, in [1988], approximately one in six men received High Honors grades in Contracts, compared to only one in sixteen women. In 1984, the proportions had been approximately one in ten for both groups." *Id.* at 30. The Berkeley study avoided the problems of self-reported grade data faced by other studies by receiving grades for two specific courses from "a source within the Boalt administration." *Id.* at 30 n.101. Entering statistics, namely college GPA and LSAT score, revealed no preexisting indicator of this performance differential. *See id.* at 39 and n.109 (showing that men and women had virtually identical entering statistics).

59. *See id.* at 24.

60. *See id.* at 43–44. The study also found that women's levels of satisfaction with academic performance were lower than men's. *See id.* at 30, 41, 51 (table 5, "Satisfaction with Academic Performance"). Over half of the women, but only 29% of the men, "felt intelligent prior to law school but not now." *Id.* at 52 (table 8A, "Self-Perception").

The study found that most women and men deemed the grading process inaccurate. Only 28% of all women thought that their grades accurately reflected their abilities as law students as compared to 39% of all men. *See id.* at 51 (table 5, "Satisfaction with Academic Performance").

61. The Berkeley study also found that race and ethnicity were "critical factor[s] in many of [its] findings." *Id.* at 27; *cf. infra* note 73 (noting that gender differences at Penn Law do not fluctuate across racial groups).

62. The Berkeley authors focus on women's silence, *see* Homer and Schwartz, *supra* note 31, at 10, with stark statistics.

TABLE N–1

NEVER ASK QUESTIONS   NEVER VOLUNTEER
(percentage of group)

	White	Of Color	White	Of Color
Women	53	61	49	65
Men	36	55	36	52

See id. at 50 (table 3, "Classroom Participation"). Nevertheless, the authors argue that being silent is a form of empowerment for those who refuse to abide by dominant rules. Rather than viewing silence as evidence of passivity within a cowed and trembling female student body, these authors theorize women's classroom silence as a powerful form of resistance, a technique for coping through an outsider perspective. *See id.* at 38 ("Silence appears to have evolved into a deliberate expression of resistance by many students to an educational system unresponsive to the free expression of nonconforming ideas"). For a general discussion of the outsider perspective and the role of resistance in that perspective, see Matsuda, *supra* note 46, at 8–9 (positing that "outsiders" can work within the system at the same time as they rebel against its injustices).

The law school experience was less gendered, but just as significant, regarding future plans. The Berkeley survey found a marked shift away from public interest work for both women and men. After being at Boalt for at least one semester, "[a]lmost half of the women who originally had public interest goals abandoned them, and over half of such men did so." Homer and Schwartz, *supra* note 31, at 42.

63. *See supra* note 24 and accompanying text.

64. This includes Granfield's 1987 study of Harvard Law School, which was not published until after we completed our own data collection. *See supra* note 31 (citing Granfield's study). No means of comparison existed in most studies between a respondent's self-reported evaluation of how she performed in law school and the actual data (either individualized or generalized for gender, race, etc.). *But see* Marilyn Tucker et al., *Whatever Happened to the Class of 1983?*, 78 Geo. L.J. 153, 156 (1989). In a preliminary study to determine the validity of self-reported data, Tucker et al. found that self-reports on rank in class had a correlation of .91 with the actual rank. Similar relationships existed for undergraduate GPAs and LSAT scores. *See id.* Therefore, while not verifiable, self-reported data from other sources may be more accurate than generally assumed.

65. *See supra* note 21 and accompanying text.

66. *See supra* note 21.

67. The Lonsdorf Index represents a formula used by the University of Pennsylvania Law School for admissions purposes during the period of time covered by our data, weighing LSAT score, median LSAT score at undergraduate institution, and undergraduate grade point average. The index is computed by a formula of $0.05399\,(\text{LSAT}) + 0.04427\,(\text{MLSAT}) + 0.0124\,(\text{RIC})$, where LSAT = applicant's LSAT score, MLSAT = mean LSAT from applicant's college, and RIC = applicant's rank in undergraduate class. Starting with the class of 1995, the law school has employed a new predictive index that reduces the weight of MLSAT.

68. GPA2 and GPA3 are cumulative statistics, incorporating the prior years' grades.

69. Because the indicators used by law schools to predict success are nearly identical for men and women, the GPA data essentially speak for themselves. We have, however, performed an ordinary least squares (OLS) regression analysis for law school GPAs, regressing for gender, LSAT, and college GPA. We do not include college rank or Lonsdorf Index in this model because college rank is too strongly correlated with college GPA and the Lonsdorf Index is only a linear combination of the LSAT and college GPA variables. Furthermore, we found no statistically significant interactions between gender and the other two independent variables in the model.

TABLE N–2

EFFECTS OF COLLEGE STATISTICS AND GENDER ON LAW SCHOOL GPAs
(figures are ordinary least squares coefficients
and their standard errors)

	Intercept	Gender	LSAT	College GPA	r^2
GPA1 =	−2.654	.161	.048	.410	.23
N = 901	(.232)	(.030)	(.003)	(.051)	
GPA2 =	−2.300	.137	.044	.386	.24
N = 685	(−.240)	(.030)	(.004)	(.051)	
GPA3 =	−2.020	.106	.039	.388	.23
N = 661	(.230)	(.029)	(.004)	(.049)	

The OLS coefficient "measures the amount of increase or decrease in [GPA] for a one-unit difference in the [indicator], controlling for the other [indicators] in the equation." GEORGE W. BOHRNSTEDT AND DAVID KNOKE, STATISTICS FOR SOCIAL DATA ANALYSIS 389 (2d ed. 1988). The intercept is the "constant value in a regression equation that shows the point at which the regression line crosses the Y axis [if all the indicators] equal zero." Id. at 494. r^2 measures the "amount of variation in the [GPA] explained or accounted for by [all the indicators in the equation]." Id. at 269. In the case of gender, r^2 is a dummy variable for which men are equal to one and women are equal to zero. Therefore, a coefficient of .16, for example, implies that men's GPAs in the first year of law school are 0.16 units higher than women's. Furthermore, all of the above coefficients are statistically significant at the .05 level.

70. All of these odds ratios are significant at the .05 level. We calculated the ratios by dividing the number of men in the top 50% of the class by the number of men in the bottom 50% and then dividing this quotient by the quotient obtained from dividing the number of women in the top 50% of the class by the number of women in the bottom 50%. In figures 2 and 3 we have illustrated the percentages of men versus women in the top 50% and top 10% of the class in years one, two, and three.

These tables can, of course, be converted back into odds ratios. For example, to determine the odds ratio between men and women for being in the top 10% of the class by year three in law school, we took the 12.6% of the men in the top 10% of the third-year class, divided this number by the percentage of men in the bottom 90% of the third-year class (87.4%), and then divided this quotient (0.144) by the quotient obtained when dividing the 6.5% of the women in the top 10% of the third-year class by the 93.5% of women in the bottom 90% of the third-year class (0.07). The calculation of these odds and odds ratios shows that men are twice as likely to be in the top 10% of the class by year three than are women. In an ideal world, regardless of the number of men and women in the class, the odds of any person being in any particular decile should be the same and should not reflect differences based on gender.

71. The actual population of men and women in the law school varies; during the period we studied, women represented between 39% and almost 47% of the student body. The percentages in figure 2, however, are not simply a rough approx-

imation of the relative numbers of men and women law students attending the school. These percentages represent the number of men in the top fiftieth percentile of the class as compared to all men in their class, and the number of women in the top fiftieth percentile of the class as compared to all women in their class. Again, ideally, we should see an equal percentage of men and women in each percentile of the class.

72. *See supra* note 67 and accompanying text.

73. This gender differential holds across racial groups but is statistically significant at the $p < .05$ level only for white students.

In terms of our race data, we find that people of color experience trends in academic performance similar to those experienced by women. Even when we hold constant LSAT and college GPA, race alone continues to be a highly significant predictor of law school performance across the first, second, and third years:

TABLE N–3

EFFECTS OF COLLEGE STATISTICS AND RACE ON LAW SCHOOL GPAS
(figures are ordinary least squares coefficients
and their standard errors)

	Intercept	Race	LSAT	College GPA	r^2
GPA1 =	−1.362	−.307	.034	.258	.24
N = 901	(.302)	(.051)	(.004)	(.056)	
GPA2 =	−0.929	−.348	.027	.235	.26
N = 685	(.309)	(.054)	(.005)	(.056)	
GPA3 =	−0.816	−.310	.023	.258	.25
N = 661	(.298)	(.053)	(.005)	(.053)	

Despite the fact that people of color are entering law school with significantly different background statistics, our regression equations indicate that race continues to play a strong independent role in predicting law school performance. In the above model, race is also a dummy variable for which people of color equal one and caucasians equal zero. All of the coefficients in this model are statistically significant at the .05 level.

74. LSAT explains only 21% ($r^2 = .21$ $p-.0001$) of the variance in student performance by year three, and even less in years one and two—14% ($r^2 = .14$ $p-.0001$) and 15% ($r^2 = .15$ $p-.0001$) respectively. In other words, when LSAT is the only variable in a bivariate regression equation, it explains 14% of the variance in first-year law school GPA. The regression coefficient is .05, meaning that with a one-unit increase in LSAT, first-year law school GPA will increase .05 units. Yet when gender and race are added to the regression equation the impact of LSAT decreases (from .05 to .03) and the explanatory power (denoted by the r^2) increases from .14 to .26 for the entire equation. The significance of gender and race in this multivariate equation and the increasing explanatory power of the model underscores the hidden impact of these two variables on law school GPA and the limited explanatory power of LSAT alone. Thus it is not LSAT that explains the law school performance of men and women.

Some may challenge this conclusion on the basis that Penn Law School students are drawn from the high end of a remarkably narrow band on the LSAT. These critics would argue that the LSAT in fact does predict performance when those who meet Penn's admission criteria are compared to those at the bottom of the LSAT pool. There is in fact evidence of a performance differential for those who are admitted from the very, very bottom of the LSAT pool. For this reason, using the LSAT as an entry level floor (basically a pass/fail bar) may make sense. The problem is that the law school does not simply use the LSAT as if it were a blunt instrument separating the wheat from the chaff. It uses the LSAT as if incremental differences within a relatively wide band above the floor are meaningful, despite the fact that those incremental differences do not predict law school performance for most male or female Penn students.

Below are our results when we did regression equations in three steps. Notice the decreasing value of the regression coefficients for LSAT as we add race and gender to our equations (which in steps 2 and 3 also include college GPA and college rank) and the increasing value of the r^2 (the statistic which gives us a sense of the significance of the equation as a whole, and the percentage of variance in the dependent variable explained by the equation):

TABLE N–4

STEPWISE REGRESSIONS

GPA1

Step One	GPA1 = LSAT					$r^2 = .14$
	.05					
	$p = .000$	$p = .000$				

Step Two	GPA1 = LSAT	CGPA	RANK			$r^2 = .20$
	.05	.43	(NS)			
	$p = .000$	$p = .000$				$p = .0000$

Step Three	GPA1 = LSAT	CGPA	RANK	GENDER	RACE	$r^2 = .26$
	.03	.36	(NS)	.18	.31	
	$p = .000$	$p = .000$		$p = .000$	$p = .000$	$p = .000$

GPA2

Step One	GPA2 = LSAT					$r^2 = .15$
	.04					
	$p = .000$	$p = .000$				

Step Two	GPA2 = LSAT	CGPA	RANK			$r^2 = .23$
	.04	.24	(NS)			
	$p = .000$	$p = .012$				$p = .0000$

Step Three	GPA2 = LSAT	CGPA	RANK	GENDER	RACE	$r^2 = .28$
	.03	.21	(NS)	$-.22$	.33	
	$p = .000$	$p = .000$		$p = .000$	$p = .000$	$p = .000$

GPA3

Step One   GPA3 = LSAT $r^2 = .21$
            .05
            $p = .000$ $p = .000$

Step Two   GPA3 = LSAT   CGPA   RANK $r^2 = .23$
            .04   .23   (NS)
            $p = .000$ $p = .014$ $p = .0000$

Step Three   GPA3 = LSAT   CGPA   RANK   GENDER   RACE $r^2 = .26$
              .02   .19   (NS)   −.10   .30
              $p = .000$ $p = .000$ $p = .000$ $p = .000$ $p = .000$

75. The figures in table 3 represent the number of men selected for various honors and the number of women selected for these same honors.

76. These figures represent the number of individual male and female students selected, based on faculty recommendation rather than the student's grades, to receive awards for their law school achievements. These figures may understate the gender differential for all graduation awards (including those based on grades) because eighteen people received multiple awards during the three-year period. For example, in 1992 there were a total of thirty-six awards given to twenty-eight persons. All of those receiving multiple awards in 1992 were men.

77. This pattern apparently continues. Although not part of the original study, in the class of 1994, five out of the twenty-three students elected to the Order of the Coif were women. *See* UNIVERSITY OF PA. LAW SCH., COMMENCEMENT PROGRAM: CLASS OF 1994, at 4 (1994).

78. Any first-year student who wishes to join the *University of Pennsylvania Law Review*, the most competitive and prestigious of the three journals at the school, must complete a writing competition in the week following spring semester exams. Students must pick up the competition materials immediately following their last exam and turn them in eleven days later. Based on a combination of competition score (graded anonymously) and first-year grades, the *Law Review* selects approximately forty-five people to serve as associate editors in their second year of law school.

For the years under study, the "pick-up" and "return" rates for men and women were virtually identical to their representation in the class. Under these circumstances, one would expect that the students selected would also represent the gender ratios of the class. This did not prove to be the case.

With respect to the class of 1994, sixteen women were selected for *Law Review*, breaking a historical ceiling (fourteen) for the number of women selected in any previous year. Even so, the number of women was still not proportionate to the number of women in the class or the participation rate of women in the competition. This increase merits further study. Although it is beyond the scope of this study, an initial assessment would suggest that a choice by the *Law Review* in 1992 to reduce the weight of grades in calculating the competition score may have been partially responsible for the breakthrough increase in the representation of women.

For several reasons, the figures representing the number of male and female students selected for *Law Review* differ from the figures in table 3 that illustrate male and female *Law Review* members. *Cf.* table 3. First, the former category does not include third-year students who "write on" to *Law Review* by submitting a publishable comment; the table 3 figures do include these students. Likewise, "Number Selected" does not encompass the selection of transfer students, who participate in a separate competition in the beginning of their second year; the "*Law Review* Member" category does reflect the presence of transfer students who become members. Also, some students selected for the *Law Review* do not accept the offer of membership; these students are included in "Number Selected" but are excluded from the table 3 figure. Finally, the "*Law Review* Member" category also excludes those students encompassed within the "*Law Review* Board" category; all of these students are included in "Number Selected," however.

TABLE N–5

LAW REVIEW COMPETITION STATISTICS

	Class of 1990		Class of 1991		Class of 1992		Class of 1993	
	Men	Women	Men	Women	Men	Women	Men	Women
Number in class	129	94	130	105	169	110	118	104
% of class	58	42	55	45	61	39	53	47
% turned in as part of total turned in	64	36	56	44	60	40	54	46
% selected as part of total selected	85	15	68	32	68	32	68	32
Number selected	34	6	30	14	29	15	30	14

79. *See supra* table 3; *see also supra* figure 3 (illustrating the percentage of male and female students in the top 10% of their class).

80. Some examples of faculty- or student-initiated graduation awards at the University of Pennsylvania Law School include the Dean Jefferson B. Fordham Human Rights Award ("to the student in the Law School who during the year has made the most outstanding contribution to the advancement of individual freedom and human dignity"), the Edwin R. Keedy Law Review Award ("to the editor of the *Law Review* who, during his or her third year, makes, in the opinion of the dean, the most scholarly or otherwise most significant contribution to the *Law Review*"), the Fred G. Leebron Memorial Prize ("to the graduating student who has written the best paper in the field of constitutional law"), the Samuel F. Pryor, III, Esq. Prize ("for the student comment that, in the opinion of the Board of Editors of the *Journal of International Business Law*, best exemplifies the *Journal*'s commitment to the exchange of ideas and information about the legal environment of business throughout the world"), and the Wapner, Newman and Wigrizer Award ("to the graduating student demonstrating special promise in the area of civil trial advocacy"). UNIVERSITY OF PA. LAW SCH., COMMENCEMENT PROGRAM: CLASS OF 1994, at 5–6 (1994).

For an additional perspective on subjective judgments, compare Kanter, *supra* note 15, at 7 ("[W]henever standards for performance are vague, people tend to fall back on social standards and social characteristics in making their judgments").

81. It should be noted that for the first time in five years, the *Law Review* selected a woman student to be editor-in-chief for the 1993–1994 academic year.

82. For the class of 1990, thirteen out of fifteen of the board members were male; twelve out of fifteen were male for the class of 1991; eleven out of fifteen were male for the class of 1992. For the classes of 1993 and 1994, five of the fifteen editorial positions were held by women. After completing the second year as an associate editor, each *Law Review* member may elect to run for the editorial board, become a third-year editor, or decline to participate on the *Law Review*. Any *Law Review* member may run for a position on the board, as long as she has fulfilled the writing requirement by submitting a completed comment. The current board selects the new board by evaluating each candidate's performance as an associate editor. Objective criteria and formal scoring mechanisms are not utilized. Grades are not factored into this process either, because board members are not given access to them. Informal knowledge of grades, however, may taint the *Law Review* board's evaluation of each candidate. Additionally, grades may affect which associate editors choose to apply for board positions.

Because the proportion of men and women who applied for the *Law Review* board is unknown, it is impossible to say whether women were in fact underrepresented in comparison to the number who ran. Whatever the reason, be it the selection criteria or the participation rates, the end result is a consistent underrepresentation of women in prestigious positions on the *Law Review*.

83. The moot court competition is held during the second semester of the students' second year. Students enroll in the competition—run by the third-year students on the moot court board—which requires them to write an appellate brief and deliver a series of oral arguments with randomly selected partners. The arguments and briefs are based on a case pending before the United States Supreme Court.

The briefs and oral arguments are graded by the third-year students on a point system based on objective criteria. The briefs are graded anonymously. Oral arguments are graded based on performance before local, mostly male practitioners. With slight variations each year, the seven students with the highest number of points become the competitors in the two moot court tournaments sponsored by the school. The five next-highest point receivers become members of the moot court board. The eleven other board members are appointed by the law school, which chooses those students with high grades who are not on the editorial board of one of the school's law journals.

For the class of 1990, only four out of sixteen moot court board members were female, and every single moot court competition finalist (seven out of seven in 1990) was male. For the class of 1992, there were two women on the board and one woman among the eight competition finalists (with one woman overlapping). For the classes of 1991 and 1993, only one moot court board member was a woman, and in 1991 this individual was one of the two women among the six competition finalists.

Again, the reason for women's underrepresentation compared to their population in the class cannot be immediately assessed. Participation rates, unavailable at the present time, may play a role. We can only speculate that the inherently subjective nature of grading oral or written presentations may have a greater impact be-

NOTES TO PAGES 42–43

cause most of the graders and questioners are male. The formal and informal use of grades may also be involved. Regardless of the precise cause, women's continued relative absence is a matter of concern.

84. With few exceptions, professors at the University of Pennsylvania award grades of Excellent (E), Good (G), and Qualified (Q). In the first year, Penn Law School, as a matter of policy, institutes a mandatory grading curve whereby approximately 20% of the students in each course receive Excellents, 40% receive Goods, and 40% receive Qualifieds. In the second and third years, the mandatory curve is officially eliminated, and the general distribution of grades shifts upward. Occasionally, professors award a superlative grade of Distinguished (DD), or they may give a failing grade of Unsatisfactory (U). (Since 1995, Penn Law School has used the more conventional ABC letter designations for grades, but the mandatory first-year grading curve itself remains unchanged.)

85. The significance of the difference between the number of men versus women responding to the question in this way was examined through one-way analysis of variance (ANOVA) tests. One-way ANOVA tests are one type of hypothesis test based on inferential statistics. Grimm and Wozniak explain that the use of inferential statistical techniques

permits a decision to be made, with a known probability of error, about whether a sample characteristic is different from a population characteristic (the single sample cases), or whether differences between samples are large enough to allow the conclusion that the populations represented by the samples are different on a certain characteristic (the cases with two or more samples).

JAMES W. GRIMM AND PAUL R. WOZNIAK, BASIC SOCIAL STATISTICS AND QUANTITATIVE RESEARCH METHODS 301 (1990).

When employing hypothesis testing, social scientists state a null hypothesis and an alternate hypothesis. Grimm and Wozniak explain:

The null hypothesis (H_0) states that there is no difference, or that means, variances, or proportions are equal. The alternative hypothesis (H_1) states that there is a difference and may specify the direction of the difference. . . .

In all of science and in all tests of hypotheses in social research, it is always and only the null hypothesis that is tested. Tests of hypotheses provide information on the probability of rejecting a true null hypothesis. The error of rejecting a true null hypothesis is called an alpha (α) or Type I error. . . .

The error of failing to reject a false null hypothesis is called a beta (β), or Type II, error. As the likelihood of committing an alpha error is reduced, the probability of committing a beta error increases. However, the magnitude of the beta error depends on what exact value of the alternative hypothesis is specified. . . .

The decision to reject a null hypothesis occurs only if the probability of committing an alpha error is at an acceptably low level, customarily $\alpha = .05$ or $\alpha = .01$.

. . . Most researchers feel confident in rejecting a null hypothesis as long as there is a less than 5 in 100 ($\alpha = .05$) or a less than 1 in 100 ($\alpha = .01$) chance of being wrong.

Id. at 302–03.

Throughout this study, the null hypothesis is that no differences exist between the male and female populations. We report the probability of committing a Type I, or alpha, error as "$p < .xxx$" after each related observation. Analysis of variance one-way tests are administered when testing the hypothesis that several means or proportions are equal or that they all come from the same population. *See id.* at 316. Finally, for all the items in this paragraph, the differences between men's and women's response rates were statistically significant at $p < .0001$.

86. Women ask and volunteer very little in class. In fact, men report a participation rate that is almost twice as frequent as that reported by women.

TABLE N–6

NEVER ASK QUESTIONS   NEVER VOLUNTEER
(percentage in gender group)

	First Year	Third Year	First Year	Third Year
Women	67	72	55	68
Men	44	62	35	57

When the three years are aggregated, twice as many men as women ask questions at least once a week and more than half of the women never or only occasionally ask questions or volunteer answers. Men ask and volunteer less over time—they become more like the women in this respect—and all grow satisfied with their relative silence as students.

Note, however, that similar issues emerge somewhat differently in studies of the performance of working-class and poor women in law school. Telephone interview with Catherine G. Krupnick, Professor of Education, Harvard University (July 11, 1994) (describing a presentation at New England Law School (in Boston) on women in legal education). Professor Krupnick asked these women, who were vocal, active class participants, why they thought their performance did not follow the trend of women at more elite schools, who were silent during classes. *See id.* In response the women explained: "If we came from Ivy League schools we'd be concerned with doing things right." *Id.* These working-class women had grown accustomed to challenging societally prescribed roles during their struggle to gain admission to law school. Once they were in law school, they were not about to give up. In other words, these women had socialized themselves to be successful, active participants who took charge of their education as they had taken charge of the course of their lives and careers. *See also* GLORIA STEINEM, REVOLUTION FROM WITHIN 111–17 (1992) (discussing the relative strength of working-class women compared to college-educated women).

87. Table N–7 summarizes our findings regarding the faculty. For a discussion of peer hazing, *see infra*, section C, especially notes 108–14, 120–22, and accompanying text.

TABLE N–7

PERCEPTIONS OF FACULTY FAVORITISM BASED ON GENDER
(percentage of group)
(columns may exceed 100% because multiple selections permitted)

	First-Year		Third-Year	
	Women	Men	Women	Men
Male faculty favor men	33	8	26	5
Male faculty favor women	3	4	0	7
Female faculty favor men	14	3	4	0
Female faculty favor women	0	13	12	21
Male faculty treat equally	16	25	8	7
Female faculty treat equally	14	6	16	5
Male and female faculty treat equally	32	48	48	53

88. By contrast, 79% of men valued a professor who treats students with respect.

89. $p < .05$. By contrast, 88% of women valued a professor who expresses ideas clearly. When students in a 1991 seminar were asked why men and women might choose different qualities as important, they responded that men are already treated with respect and therefore do not value that quality as much. An alternative explanation offered by a female colleague is that respect is related to Gilligan's ethic of care. *See supra* note 43.

90. $p < .05$ for both items. On one quality, however, both men and women agreed: both valued "good at Socratic dialogue" to the same degree and almost twice as often in the first year as in the third year. Forty-two percent of first-year students valued "good at Socratic dialogue" compared to 21% of third-year students. Year-based responses to this quality were significantly different at $p < .05$.

91. In interactions outside of class, 58% of the men were very comfortable speaking with male professors; 62% of the men were very comfortable speaking with female professors. Only 40% of the women were very comfortable speaking with professors outside of class, with virtually no difference based on the gender of the professor.

92. $p < .001$.

93. $p < .001$.

94. $p < .05$. Some of the difference in comfort level may reflect the fact that during their second and third years at Penn students have more flexibility in course selection, with the option of choosing courses based on class size and teaching methodology. On the other hand, the level of self-reported participation for second- and third-year women did not change significantly from first year.

Moreover, we are not asserting that these women are completely satisfied that they are being treated fairly. Women are more likely to agree that the "nature and content of classroom interactions between professor and students are affected by the sex of the student" and that the use of gender-neutral language is "very important" ($p < .0001$ for all items).

Women were, across the board, more likely to use gender-neutral language and *not* change to gender-specific language when outside the law school. On the other hand, men appeared,over time in the law school, to grow somewhat more adept at using gender-neutral language (from 32% to 41%), and to become less likely to revert to gender-specific language away from the school (from 33% to 28%). Over the three years of law school, however, men remained more likely than women to change to gender-specific language when they left the law school building.

TABLE N–8

STUDENT USE OF GENDER-NEUTRAL LANGUAGE
(percentage of group)

	First-Year		Third-Year	
	Women	Men	Women	Men
Use gender-neutral language	54	32	50	41
Change to gender-specific language outside the law school	19	33	16	28

In addition, women were significantly more "concerned that knowledge of . . . gender (based on handwriting) may consciously or unconsciously influence the way that a professor grades your exam" ($p < .001$). Women rated their peers as more competitive than men did, and women saw male students particularly as more competitive than female students ($p < .001$). Women were significantly more likely to agree that "sexist comments and actions by students are permitted under the informal 'house rules' of this law school" ($p < .001$), and a majority of women and a plurality of men reported that sexist comments were permitted under the informal house rules ($p = .001$). *Cf. infra* notes 135–138.

95. In the Bartow Survey, 41.2% of first-year women reported that men were called on more frequently in class than women, compared to 32.8% of second-year women, 14.0% of third-year women, 11.3% of first-year men, 7.9% of second-year men, and 8.6% of third-year men.

96. Our findings show that 34.9% of first-year women thought men who had been called on received more class time than women who had been called on, compared to 34.5% of second-year women, 12.0% of third-year women, 1.4% of first-year men, 3.2% of second-year men, and 5.1% of third-year men. Additionally, 39.7% of first-year women believed that men received more follow-up questions in class than women, compared to 36.1% of second-year women, 12.0% of third-year women, 7.0% of first-year men, 7.9% of second-year men, and 8.6% of third-year men.

97. The Bartow Survey data illustrates that 88.9% of first-year women reported that the sex of students has some effect on class experience, compared to 88.6% of second-year women, 72% of third-year women, 63.3% of first-year men, 65% of second-year men, and 62% of third-year men.

98. Another finding of the Bartow Survey was that 84.1% of first-year women reported that sexist comments are permitted, compared to 68.8% of second-year women, 64.0% of third-year women, 46.4% of first-year men, 58.7% of second-year men, and 48.3% of third-year men.

99. *See infra* notes 135–140 and accompanying text. By contrast, mental health problems are reported more frequently in women than men and persist consistently across law school years. *See infra* text preceding note 109. Of course, we acknowledge that our data on frequency of crying and other indicia of mental distress may reflect preexisting problems or gendered socialization regarding acceptable ways to express those problems. *But cf. infra* note 117.

100. Of course, the self-reported survey data on which we rely is merely a snapshot of Penn Law School at one point in time. We do not have statistically significant longitudinal data about the process of women's assimilation. Some may argue, therefore, that the survey reflects a picture of a unique group of first-year students. We have considered this argument but are persuaded that the implications of our data deserve attention for several reasons. First, the incoming credentials of the women in the class of 1992 are comparable to those in the other classes studied. Their responses to the Center on Professionalism Values Survey are also comparable to responses from the women in the classes of 1991 and 1993. Across all three years, the responses of first-year women showed a similar demographic breakdown with respect to age (around 80% of respondents under age twenty-five, and over 90% of respondents under age thirty); indicated that the most common undergraduate major of women respondents in all three years was political science/government; and consistently illustrated a greater interest in the field of public interest law among first-year women than among first-year men (7% of the women in the class of 1991, compared to none of the men; 11% of the women versus 2% of the men in the class of 1992; and 22% of the women to 13% of the men in the class of 1993). See CENTER ON PROFESSIONALISM, UNIVERSITY OF PA. LAW SCH., SURVEY OF ATTITUDES AND VALUES: FIRST YEAR LAW STUDENTS, SEPTEMBER, 1988, CLASS OF 1991, at 6–9 (1988); CENTER ON PROFESSIONALISM, UNIVERSITY OF PA. LAW SCH., SURVEY OF ATTITUDES AND VALUES: FIRST YEAR LAW STUDENTS, AUGUST, 1989, CLASS OF 1992, at 5–9 (1989); CENTER ON PROFESSIONALISM, UNIVERSITY OF PA. LAW SCH., SURVEY OF ATTITUDES AND VALUES: FIRST YEAR LAW STUDENTS, AUGUST, 1990, CLASS OF 1993, at 6–9 (1990). Second, our archival cohort analysis and group interview data confirm our interpretation that the first-year women who responded to the survey in April 1990 are more typical than unique. Third, the first-year men who responded to the survey look very much like their third-year counterparts. Finally, since the Penn Law School admissions office did not use any special process for admitting women to the class of 1992, we have no reason to believe that the women are any less representative than the men in that class.

Some may conclude that our data instead show that sexist incidents decrease by the third year. See infra note 139. This is possible, especially because the large first-year Socratic classroom with its mandatory grading curve is not as pervasive in upper-level courses. See infra note 112.

101. $p < .001$. Students were asked, "What kind of job do you expect to have after law school?" Choices included: sole practitioner, law firm, government, academic, corporate general counsel, nonlegal corporate, foundation/university counsel, and public interest. For the most popular jobs, we found the following distribution:

TABLE N–9

EXPECTED JOB—MOST POPULAR SELECTIONS
(percentage of group)
(columns may exceed 100% because multiple selections permitted)

	First-Year Women	Third-Year Women	First-Year Men	Third-Year Men
Law Firm	57	84	88	79
Government	22	12	12	18
Public Interest	25	8	7	7

102. $p<.001$. These ranges reflect the responses in tables N–9 and 4. One explanation for this shift in career emphasis is that women are simply responding to market forces. The pre–law school perception that the public interest and public service areas were among those most open to women, *see* Kanter, *supra* note 15, at 9, is also consistent with this explanation. This assumption may have triggered women's initial decisions to attend law school, and once the assumption was revised in response to information about actual job opportunities, women may have reoriented their career goals.

Market forces, however, do not explain the remarkably gendered difference within the first-year class itself regarding aspirations for a public interest career. First-year women may be responding less to financial incentives and more to gendered perceptions of their "role" as lawyer. *See, e.g., id.* at 5 (noting that women are more likely to become engaged with cases in which the client is either "diffuse and abstract (such as the public) or is not directly choosing or paying the lawyer. The office provides the identity, and the woman does not have to worry about establishing her individual reputation. Women are ... drawn to legal services as a protected setting with a social welfare orientation"); *id.* at 9 (reporting that traditionally women treated law as a " 'helping profession,' " which they entered to do " 'do good' " (quoting Cynthia Epstein, Discussion at Harvard Law School Conference on Legal Profession (June 2, 1977))); *see also* Jacquelynne S. Eccles, *Gender Roles and Women's Achievement-Related Decisions*, 11 Psychol. Women Q. 135, 151 (1987) (finding that women's career choices reflect greater interest in family and relationships). These forces also do not justify the gendered treatment some women report in law firm interviews. For example, females more than males have, "during the course of a job interview, been asked questions about marital or family status that [were] ... considered inappropriate" ($p<.001$). Also relevant is the finding that women are more likely to anticipate that "gender will be [a] hindrance" to their legal careers ($p<.001$).

103. *See supra* text accompanying notes 13–14. Although their career aspirations merge after three years in law school, sex-based differences remain an explanation of their choices. When asked, "What factors are highly important to you in a law-related job?" 68% of the third-year women and 52% of the third-year men valued "independence" ($p<.1$); 42% of the third-year women and 62% of the third-year men valued the "ability to earn a high income" ($p<.05$).

104. The attitudinal transformation compares first-year and third-year responses. The academic changes measure differences among entry-level credentials, first-year performance, and third-year graduating statistics.

105. *See supra* note 25.

106. *See supra* note 26.

107. *See supra* note 24.

108. *See infra* note 120 and accompanying text.

109. $p<.001$ for all items.

110. The pacts were described in two different focus groups in 1992; one consisted exclusively of first-year students and the other of third-year students. The first-year focus group was surprised to learn that their third-year peers had made the same pact.

A similar experience occurred at the University of Michigan Law School, where a group of first-year women organized Take Back the Class, an effort to encourage women to speak up because "the women in our classes have not been very vocal this semester." Memorandum from Take Back the Class, University of Michigan Law School 1 (1992) (on file with authors). The group met twenty minutes before two of their classes to exchange ideas and give encouragement to each other to participate. In class, the women prefaced their statements with "As *X* stated, ..." as a means of reinforcing a female speaker and validating her remarks. *See also* Weiss and Melling, *supra* note 31, at 1311, 1335, 1343 (describing a similar pact at Yale Law School).

111. *See, e.g.*, Jacobs, *supra* note 36, at 468 (noting that women's patterns of association, though beneficial in terms of providing comfort and encouragement, remove women from vital parts of law school culture); *cf.* EXECUTIVE SUMMARY, *supra* note 12, at 5–6 (finding that a higher percentage of female students than male students report a loss of self-confidence since entering law school and attributing this decline in self-esteem to "something in the law school experience," which values "male" characteristics); Robert A. Josephs et al., *Gender and Self-Esteem*, 63 J. PERSONALITY & SOC. PSYCHOL. 391, 391 (1992) (discussing self-esteem difference between men and women and noting that men's self-esteem "can be linked to a[n] individuation process in which one's personal distinguishing achievements are emphasized" while women's self-esteem "can be linked to a process in which connections and attachments to important others are emphasized").

112. To say that the Socratic method is used universally is not to suggest that it is used uniformly. There are certainly as many different approaches to the use of the Socratic method as there are law teachers. At Penn, however, all of the first-year courses (Contracts, Property, Torts, Criminal Law, Civil Procedure, Constitutional Law, and Labor Law), with the exception of the spring elective, are taught in the large classroom, Socratic style. After the first year of coursework professors at Penn employ the Socratic method much less frequently, or use Socratic questioning to initiate a dialogue rather than to dominate or intimidate.

113. This model lawyer displays all of the characteristics Gilligan and others attributed to male patterns of reasoning. *See* GILLIGAN, *supra* note 43, at 31–38. He is a lawyer who uses rights-based reasoning to analyze legal problems in terms of competing, mutually exclusive claims. He can argue all sides of any issue, because he has no personal stake in any of his arguments. In form, the model lawyer also demonstrates characteristics traditionally associated with maleness: aggression, willingness to fight, emotional detachment, and exaggerated bravado. Women who learn that lawyering equals maleness may be stifled in their ability to form a whole, integrated professional identity. *See* PETER WOODS, SOCIOLOGY AND THE SCHOOL: AN INTERACTIONIST VIEWPOINT 2 (1983) ("Individuals can only develop complete selves to the degree that they are able to assume the attitude of the social group, of which they are members, toward the group's activities"). Although female students can mimic maleness, they can never attain it. For all practical purposes, many women students are faced with the choice of trading their identities as women for identities as lawyers. *See* Guinier, *supra* note 15, at 93–94 (discussing how the author's law school professor continually referred to the class as "gentlemen," which "symbolically stripp[ed] the author] of [her] race, . . . gender, and . . . voice").

114. *See infra* note 162 (discussing the feelings of students of color when asked to "testify" with respect to issues of race). Some students noted that when a professor used the word "nigger" in a hypo during a first-year class, none of the African-American students spoke up. These African-American students were silent even as white students copied the professor's language in responses modifying the hypo. Several African-American and Asian-American students reported getting physically "hot" but remained quiet because of the burden of being a group spokesperson. *Cf.* Kimberlé W. Crenshaw, *Foreward: Toward a Race-Conscious Pedagogy in Le-*

gal Education, 11 NAT'L BLACK L.J. 1, 6–9 (1989) (describing the silencing effect of testifying as a racial partisan).

115. *See supra* exchange preceding note 109; *cf. infra* text preceding note 119 (describing law school survival as learning to "play the game"). This seems to reflect findings that women, more than men, tend to internalize defeat or interpret it as personal failure. *See supra* text accompanying notes 108, 109.

116. *See infra* notes 127–133 and accompanying text (finding that the mandatory grading curve and other pedagogical "features" of the first year translate "demographic" credentials into deeply raced and gendered definitions of merit); *see also* Josephs et al., *supra* note 111, at 391 (finding that women are more likely to have a "*collectivist, ensembled*, or *connected* schema for the self" whereas men are more likely to have "an *individualist, independent,* or *autonomous* schema"). For some women, then, other people are part of the self; for many men, other people are distinct. If self-esteem "derives from succeeding at what is valued in a given sociocultural niche," then positive self-evaluations for many men involve a sense of "being independent, autonomous, separate, and better than others." *Id.* at 392. For many women, "feeling good about one's self . . . [derives from] being sensitive to, attuned to, connected to, and generally interdependent with others." *Id.*

117. Although higher levels of psychological distress in women law students compared to men law students may simply reflect general population differences by gender, studies of medical students do not find comparable gender-based levels of distress. *See, e.g.,* Stephen B. Shanfield and G. Andrew H. Benjamin, *Psychiatric Distress in Law Students*, 35 J. LEGAL EDUC. 65, 71–72 (1985) (citing epidemiological findings). Shanfield, a professor of psychiatry, and Benjamin, a clinical psychologist, conclude from a comparison between their own survey of medical students and their investigation of law student distress at the University of Arizona that the high levels of distress they observed in women law students "are not an inevitable part of professional training." *Id.* at 72.

118. Indeed, some argue that women in law school learn to be actively *bicultural*, displaying attitudes, preferences, and behaviors that typify men, but retaining attitudes, preferences, and behaviors of feminist resistance. *See* Matsuda, *supra* note 46, at 8 (referring to a woman of color's "bifurcated thinking"); *see also* Shauna Van Praagh, *Stories in Law School: An Essay on Language, Participation, and the Power of Legal Education*, 2 COLUM. J. GENDER & L. 111, 141 (1992) (describing the same phenomenon as "bilingualism"). At worst, those who float between two intellectual/political cultures—progressive feminism and corporate maleness—with little institutional support for the former and much for the latter, become confused and disappointed. *See* EXECUTIVE SUMMARY, *supra* note 12, at 5 (in a study of nine Ohio law schools, only 16.6% of males, but 41% of females agreed with the statement, "Before law school I thought of myself as intelligent and articulate but I don't feel that way about myself now"); *see also* Howard Lesnick, *The Wellsprings of Legal Responses to Inequality: A Perspective on Perspectives*, 1991 DUKE L.J. 413, 420–26 (arguing that conservativism emphasizes individualism as opposed to community).

119. *Second-year woman:* "Although I think that I've become much more objective, and I'm not, I guess I'm less likely to let my emotions dictate especially just, I guess in all situations how, um, how, how I think, what the end result of something should be. Whether that's good or not, I don't know. I'm definitely a different person from when I entered law school. I find that, um, um, I'm worried more with trying to be tough. Like, to be, I'm more willing to be rude, to cut people off in conversations."

Third-year woman: "Um, I guess the other thing was before I came to law school I think I was more concerned about, um, other people's opinions, not only about me, but also about understanding the positions of other people, and you know, really trying to put myself in other people['s] shoes. But as I've been here I, I found that nobody else really is willing to do that and I think that I tend to dismiss other people's opinions now more than I would in the past because I just think that sometimes your opinions are just irreconcilable, and that, there are just so many people that I've met here who I don't even want to bother to think the way that they think."

Cf. C. Garrison Lepow, *Deconstructing Los Angeles or a Secret Fax from Magritte Regarding Postliterate Legal Reasoning: A Critique of Legal Education,* 26 MICH. J.L. REFORM 69, 77 (1992) (describing legal education as training students to ask rude questions, and noting that although most people ask questions to get information, lawyers are trained not to ask questions unless they already know the answers).

120. One woman student reported hearing negative comments about her frequent class participation while in a stall in the women's bathroom. Although married, she was decried as a "man-hating lesbian." She reports that she almost dropped out of law school that day. Another woman reported that she was called a "feminazi dyke" for her frequent comments in first-year classes. This student, who is Jewish, immediately stopped speaking in all her first-year classes. Still another woman said she felt "like wherever I went [the hissing] would follow me. It really shut me up."

These comments may simply reflect a general hostility towards those who speak regularly in class. In private conversations with Professor Guinier, students described a game of "asshole bingo" in which the object is to identify those "assholes" who dominate class discussion. Students playing the game agree in advance of class upon a code word, a word that they can incorporate into an oral question or answer to a professor's inquiry that indicates to fellow students when they "score." Scoring requires predicting a pattern, like a tic-tac-toe board, of who will speak in class. Female and male students who dominate the particular class become the "assholes" on the "bingo board."

The students report that male "assholes," however, are referred to as "nerds"; women "assholes" are referred to as "man-hating lesbians." The difference suggests a gendered nature to the opprobrium. By participating in class, these women become legitimate targets for their colleagues' resentment and fear. *Cf.* SCHWARTZ, *supra* note 15, at 89 (describing a situation in which a female Wall Street lawyer's success was attributed to her use of sexuality to gain an unfair advantage, leading her father to explain, "They're afraid of you. In business, if a man beats you in your own field, he's an SOB. If a woman does it, she's a whore").

Admittedly, "asshole bingo" may manifest more anti-intellectual camaraderie than antiwoman bias. Our claim is simply that women "assholes" are disparaged on the basis of sexuality, negative views toward certain sexual orientations, and assumptions about assertive women's attitudes toward men. This same phenomenon occurs when students speculate about how some female professors obtained their jobs. Successful women are apparently more threatening than successful men, at least to the two first-year men in our focus groups who mentioned their suspicions regarding female professors' qualifications. *Cf.* JEAN O. HUGHES AND BERNICE R. SANDLER, ASSOCIATION OF AMERICAN COLLEGES' PROJECT ON THE STATUS AND EDUCATION OF WOMEN PEER HARASSMENT: HASSLES FOR WOMEN ON CAMPUS 6 (1988) (finding that male students often call women lesbians as a way of intimidating or silencing them); *see also infra* text following note 215 (observing that "asshole" is a neutral slur and "man-hating lesbian" a personal identity slur; the former targets behavior whereas the latter imputes membership in a despised, invisible minority group). Calling a woman a "feminazi dyke" or "man-hating lesbian" tars the individual personally, and permanently, as holding unpopular beliefs or exhibiting personal qualities, either of which marginalizes the individual in the particular culture of the law school.

121. "My experience has been different.... I came from graduate school, and I have done well here. But in my section [because I spoke out in class] I was the man-hating lesbian." *See also supra* note 120 (describing experience of several other women labeled as lesbians for speaking out in class).

122. $p < .001$ for all items. In the 1990 Bartow Survey, respondents were asked: "In your opinion, do students of one sex hold leadership positions in student organizations in proportionally greater numbers than students of the other sex?"

TABLE N–10

PERCEPTION OF GENDER DOMINATION
OF STUDENT LEADERSHIP POSITIONS
(percentage of group)

	First-Year		Third-Year	
	Women	*Men*	*Women*	*Men*
More male leaders	33	24	38	15
Equal male and female	33	31	40	45
More female leaders	0	4	4	7

Examples of "student organizations" provided in the survey were "Council of Student Representatives, Environmental Law Society, Asian and Pacific American Law Students Association, etc." Thus, these results do not reflect the male dominance only of the law journals and moot court. *See supra* table 3; *supra* notes 78, 81–83 and accompanying text. Although the 1994–1995 academic year falls outside the scope of our research, we note that all three student-of-color organizations are headed by women this year.

123. This phenomenon was particularly acute among male faculty members. When Professor Guinier presented this information to an ad hoc faculty session attended by about 50% of the full-time faculty, including four women professors, with a few exceptions the male faculty attempted to attribute the data to experiences before law school (for example, men may participate in varsity sports in college which divert their attention, but when they get to law school they then channel *all* their energies into their studies), to the failure of women to behave like "good lawyers" (for example, defining a good lawyer as a change agent and then blaming the female law students who fail to change their sexist male peers), or to speculations about the anticipated effect of post-law-school experience either in law firm jobs or in the way that women learn the "market forces" that change their career expectations when they discover the dearth of public interest jobs. There is some support in the literature for this last hypothesis. *See supra* note 102.

124.   TABLE N–11

UNDERGRADUATE MAJORS OF INCOMING LAW STUDENTS
CLASSES OF 1990, 1991, AND 1992
(percentage of group)

	Natural Sci.	Econ.	Eng'g	Social Sci.	Arts & Hum.	Fin./ Acct.	Other
Men	3	15	3	41	18	10	10
Women	5	10	2	43	24	10	6

125. We did not explore the gender differential for undergraduate participation in varsity sports; we do note evidence of similar concerns that gendered rates of participation in varsity sports might inhibit women from breaking the glass ceiling in academia. *See* Molly O'Neill, *In an Ivy League of Her Own*, N.Y. TIMES, Oct. 20, 1994, at C1, C4 (quoting Donna Shalala, Secretary of Health and Human Services, arguing that the reason only four of forty-five top universities have female presidents boils down to intercollegiate athletics and "'the lingering question: Can she manage the football coach?'").

126. We found this response consistent with other studies on the causes of performance gaps between white students and minorities. For example, in Uri Treisman's work on the performance of African-American and Latino students in calculus classes at the University of California at Berkeley, he and his colleagues assumed that a variety of factors not related to the school itself created the problem. *See* Uri Treisman, *Studying Students Studying Calculus: A Look at the Lives of Minority Mathematics Students in College*, 23 C. MATHEMATICS J. 362, 364–65 (1992). He conducted a survey of his fellow mathematics professors across the country and found that they shared his assumptions about these students' poor performance, namely: low income, low motivation, poor academic preparation, and lack of family support. *See id.* at 365. When Treisman began researching the study habits and backgrounds of his students in an attempt to design an appropriate tutoring program, he found all four of those assumptions to be incorrect. *See id.* Thus Treisman discovered that the faculty most concerned with minority student performance had very little understanding of why these students did not do well, and their incorrect assumptions tended to place the causes of failure outside of the institution. *See id.* at 364–65.

Some Penn Law School faculty were ultimately willing to concede that there is a gendered story to tell. But then some of them were not so alarmed. The point of law school, they would contend, is to produce, shape, and promote a particular type of legal thinker who is competitive, adversarial, and ruthless—one who privileges logic over emotion and neutrality over commitments, and supports individual rights over community interests.

To these faculty members who are not troubled by our data, this study confirmed *who* is likely to be the best and the brightest, who is the most able "product" for law firms—which are considered the law school's "client."

127. The results of our age and experience comparison show that there was no significant gender difference for ages or years between undergraduate and law school. *But cf.* Banks, *supra* note 31, at 141 (finding class participation differences among women of different ages).

128. Several male colleagues, upon hearing of these gender differences, also sought to explain them in "power neutral" terms, such as differences in undergraduate majors. One male colleague suggested that the equivalence of undergraduate GPAs "might be deceptive." We explored this hypothesis and found no statistically significant gender differences in undergraduate majors, at least when using blunt measures such as social or natural sciences to aggregate more specialized areas of study. *See supra* note 124.

129. *See supra* text accompanying note 124. In addition, the women's slightly higher undergraduate GPA suggests that the Penn Law School gendered academic performance differential is not merely derivative of a previously documented differential. *See supra* note 3. Indeed, studies of college women find that they exceed their male counterparts in terms of grades. *See, e.g.,* Helen M. Berg and Marianne A. Ferber, *Men and Women Graduate Students: Who Succeeds and Why?*, 54 J. Higher Educ. 629, 632 (1983) ("[T]hese factors may be expected to influence the careers of these able women who, in terms of grades, had been better students than their male colleagues up to the time they began graduate work").

130. This is not surprising if these men construe gender variables as a source of individualizing "blame" for the performance differentials we found. Our hypothesis, however, is that the problem is not individual men or women but a hierarchical, ruthlessly competitive, and aloof institutional design. *Cf.* Granfield, *supra* note 31, at 20 ("[M]any women *support* the dominant discourse within law schools"); *infra* note 140 and accompanying text.

131. A thematic analysis of the narratives enabled us to code the responses to the following open-ended narrative question:

Please use this space to describe any acts or comments make by a professor or fellow student you have witnessed or experienced at the law school that made you uncomfortable for gender-based reasons. Please be as specific as you can, but do not feel compelled to identify anyone by name. As with the rest of the survey your response will be kept confidential.

Seven codes were generated to label and categorize each response. The codes included:

- Survey was biased so as to uncover gender tensions
- Gender tensions exist at the Law School among/between students and faculty
- I haven't noticed any bias
- No answer/not applicable
- Women students are too sensitive/paranoid
- There is evidence of reverse discrimination against men/white men
- Professors and peers are sensitive to gender issues

132. An illustrative response given by a few men, but no women, was: "I think this survey is the most gender-biased thing I have seen here at law school."

133. *First-year male student:* I feel that some female students at this law school have a specific agenda with regard to feminist issues. As a result, every action by a professor seems to be closely scrutinized and skewed to relate to this agenda. Any classroom conversation even remotely related to a gender issue becomes a debate point, and the entire subject being discussed is interrupted so as to raise this agenda, which is only important to a small percentage of the class.

One-third of first-year men responding to the open-ended survey question gave responses similar to this one.

134. Almost half of the third-year men who responded, but only one of the third-year women, used the open-ended narrative space to voice a concern similar to this one:

One female professor seemed to favor women and seemed to have specific bias against men in the class. This was not only a suspicion, but was obvious to both me and women in the class.

Three separate women faculty were identified by name as practicing "reverse discrimination" and were held responsible for the "intimidating environment" created by women who are concerned with feminist issues.

We do not mean to discount these observations of the students. Their perceptions are an important ingredient in the school's environment. Their claims, however, whatever their basis, apparently do not affect their academic performance levels or alienation in the aggregate. Even if women faculty practice "reverse discrimination," neither women's nor men's academic performance apparently suffers.

In addition, the research of scholars like Catherine Krupnick offers an alternative explanation to the "reverse discrimination" that men perceive. Her studies indicate that when women participate in proportion to their numbers in a class, both women and men perceive them to be "over-participating." Telephone interview with Catherine G. Krupnick, *supra* note 86. *But see also infra* note 152 (discussing Krupnick's findings regarding undergraduates at Harvard College). Thus, because they are expected to participate less, women may appear to be dominating a classroom when they are merely participating as much as their male peers. On the other hand, some female students do criticize female faculty. One first-year woman perceived bias toward men among female faculty, one of whom was "flirting with male law students in the first row by making physical contact." A second-year woman found a female professor annoying both men and women "with her feministic pronouns."

135. Many agreed that "mostly fellow students are the problem." One second-year woman quoted a first-year man who admitted he tunes out "whenever a female speaks in class because she probably won't have anything worthwhile to say, especially if she's good looking."

136. The first-year man stated in his narrative response to the Bartow Survey:

I was shocked and amazed at the level of discussion concerning rape in our criminal law class. . . . To be one of the few individuals who felt the issue was being trivialized was surprising.

This concern was echoed in group interviews. One-third of the women in our focus groups reported comments such as the following: "In our first-year crim course everything was a rape hypo." "Discussions about rape are offensive." No men in the focus groups initiated discussion of similar concerns. Several women remarked that the treatment of rape in the first-year criminal law class focused solely on the perspective of the rapist rather than that of the victim. Others were concerned that professors did not seem to acknowledge, in their treatment of the subject, the possibility that some students in the class had been raped or sexually assaulted. None of the three professors who taught first-year criminal law at Penn between 1990 and 1992 was a woman.

137. "[One professor] has a 'me against the class' game going on over gender issues. He defends sexist statutes and then belittles the class for disagreeing with him."

138. "A male student slapped a female student on the ass in greeting her." Sev-

eral men did acknowledge harassment of women by male students. *See supra* notes 121, 136. Even more frequently, men reported sexism or "reverse discrimination" from female faculty and students.

139. "The men and a lot of women in my section generally have no idea that women are discriminated against, especially in white-collar settings. This isn't specific, I know, but it's uncomfortable."

140. We acknowledge that these same data could suggest that male law students become more sensitive to gender-related issues over the course of their three years in law school. There is some support for this view. *See supra* table N–8 (suggesting that men increasingly use gender-neutral language).

141. GRANFIELD, *supra* note 1, at 108. Granfield's analysis draws from much of the literature about other law schools, although his study is based on his doctoral dissertation about Harvard Law School. Although Granfield acknowledges that "gender may serve as a basis for resistance," he emphasizes the voices of other women who, because of the expansion of opportunities (real or perceived), support the dominant value system of legal education. Granfield distinguishes between "social feminists" and other women. *See id.* at 107–08. We also identify different groups of women at Penn Law. *See supra* note 130 and accompanying text; *infra* notes 215, 216 and accompanying text.

142. *See supra* note 1. The fact that this research has been conducted about (and at) an Ivy League law school may be quite relevant. The coupling of patriarchy and elitism at Ivy League institutions may be quite distinct from the situation at other schools with different histories and traditions. Ivy League traditions may themselves have fostered a particular culture of legal education. *See* Anthony DePalma, *Rare in Ivy League: Women Who Work as Full Professors*, N.Y. TIMES, Jan. 24, 1993, at A1, A23 (explaining that Ivy League schools have changed slowly, refusing to accept female students or show concern for hiring female professors until the late 1960s and early 1970s; and suggesting that women faculty are often driven from Ivy League campuses to more congenial settings, exacerbating the paucity of female faculty, because the stakes are so high and the pressures to perform, publish, and win research grants are so great at Ivy League schools).

143. For example, Professor Lewis A. Kornhauser of the New York University School of Law conducted his own analysis of N.Y.U.'s selection for the Order of the Coif from 1980 to 1993 and found that women made up on average 45.53% of the classes, yet they only received 35.65% of the awards. In the thirteen years that he studied, there were only three years in which the percentage of women receiving awards came close to their percentages in the class. In most years, women lagged by 5%, and in some by as much as 30%. *See* Letter from Lewis A. Kornhauser, Professor of Law, New York University, to Lani Guinier, Professor of Law, University of Pennsylvania 1, 3 (July 14, 1994) (on file with author). Kornhauser interprets these statistics to mean that the grade distribution for men and women "do[es] not reject the hypotheses of identity of the means or of equality of the distributions. Indeed the percentage of women in the top 10% of the class in each of these years is roughly equal to the percentage of women in the class." *Id.* at 1–2.

144. *See, e.g.*, Memorandum from Colin S. Diver, Dean of the Law School, University of Pennsylvania, to Robert A. Gorman, Associate Dean of the Law School, University of Pennsylvania 1 (Jan. 18, 1993) (on file with author) (describing a "very powerful and uniform allegiance" among American law schools to the prevailing pedagogy and approach to curricular design; recognizing, in view of "the strength and pervasiveness" of prevailing ethos, that change "would take a huge

effort for any one law school," especially if it intended to "sustain such an approach over the long haul").

Accordingly, we believe it likely that we have identified problems associated with the structure of legal education, at least as it functions in elite, hierarchical, male-dominated institutions. In fact, other studies document similar or related phenomena at other elite schools. *See* GRANFIELD, *supra* note 1, at 107 (describing the experience of a significant group of women at Harvard Law School); *see also* John J. Costonis, *The MacCrate Report: Of Loaves, Fishes, and the Future of American Legal Education*, 43 J. LEGAL EDUC. 157, 157 (1993) (discussing the MacCrate Report's embrace of a practitioner-oriented concept of legal education); *supra* part 1B (describing research at Harvard, Boalt Hall, Stanford, and Yale Law Schools).

145. *See supra* note 10 (describing the Socratic method).

146. *See, e.g.*, Alice K. Dueker, *Diversity and Learning: Imagining a Pedagogy of Difference*, 19 N.Y.U. REV. L. & SOC. CHANGE 101, 105 (1991–92) (stating that psychological preparation is a necessary part of academic success).

147. We base this linkage theory on the psychosociological literature that finds that students do best if they have high self-esteem. In other words, where the formal teaching methodology leads to alienation and self-doubt, those self-doubts adversely affect student performance. *See* Berg and Ferber, *supra* note 129, at 631, 638 (noting a difference in academic self-confidence of men and women); Kanter, *supra* note 15, at 9 (asserting that self-confidence plays a large part in success in the legal profession, and that limited opportunity tends to depress aspirations and self-esteem); *see also* EXECUTIVE SUMMARY, *supra* note 12, at 5 (finding that 11% fewer women than men feel as competent as other law students); Terence J. Tracey and William E. Sedlacek, *A Comparison of White and Black Student Academic Success Using Noncognitive Variables*, 27 RES. HIGHER EDUC. 333, 344–45 (1987) (claiming that white students' success in college is partially linked to academic ability, whereas black students' collegiate success is linked to positive self-concept, a realistic self-appraisal, a preference for long-range goals, and leadership experience). For our purposes, this study is useful because it indicates that other nonacademic factors may affect the ways in which certain groups of students perform.

148. In this sense, gendered participation rates in undergraduate varsity sports may be relevant:

[Studies suggest that] women and men think differently about aggression and . . . that these differing beliefs are important mediators of sex differences in aggressive behavior. Women reported more guilt and anxiety as a consequence of aggression, more vigilance about the harm that aggression causes its victims, and more concern about the danger that their aggression might bring to themselves.

ALICE H. EAGLY, SEX DIFFERENCES IN SOCIAL BEHAVIOR: A SOCIAL-ROLE INTERPRETATION 94 (1987). Deborah Tannen has observed that boys, but not girls, may engage in mock fights or arguments to ascertain whether or not other boys want to initiate friendships. This implies that combative styles are more familiar to boys than to girls, and that therefore men might find the aggressive atmosphere of the Socratic classroom more comfortable than women do. *See* DEBORAH TANNEN, GENDER AND DISCOURSE 42–44 (1994).

Some argue that this gendered difference makes women less effective lawyers. *See infra* notes 212–214 and accompanying text; *see also* Nancy E. Betz, *Implications of the Null Environment Hypothesis for Women's Career Development and for Counseling Psychology*, 17 COUNSELING PSYCHOLOGIST 136, 137, 141–42 (1989) (arguing that women who enter male-dominated professions require greater encouragement, and if neither male nor female students are encouraged, the effect actually discriminates against the women).

149. *See* Anthony D'Amato, *The Decline and Fall of Law Teaching in the Age of Student Consumerism*, 37 J. LEGAL EDUC. 461, 473 (1987); *see also* H. Russell Cort and Jack L. Sammons, *The Search for "Good Lawyering": A Concept and Model of Lawyering Competencies*, 29 CLEV. ST. L. REV. 397, 415–18 (1980)(stating that law students' legal analysis skills are evaluated based on "unarticulated" and "idiosyncratic" models created by individual professors).

150. Our research confirms that some women do not learn when intimidated. *See supra* notes 113–117 and accompanying text. As a result, they may fail to master the equally important skills of "organization, analysis, writing style, persuasion and synthesis." Janet Motley, *A Foolish Consistency: The Law School Exam*, 10 NOVA L.J. 723, 725 (1986).

151. Alex M. Johnson, Jr., *Think Like a Lawyer, Work Like a Machine: The Dissonance Between Law School and Law Practice*, 64 S. CAL. L. REV. 1231, 1252 (1991) (arguing that "[e]lite law school education contrasts starkly with the reality of practice, and students suffer as a result"). It may be that the theory of legal education, which assumes that stress is necessary to motivate self-learning, is based on empirical studies done with primarily male subjects. Or, alternatively, the level of stress in a large Socratic classroom may be calibrated correctly for students whose goal it is to be litigators or law professors, but not for law students in the aggregate. For many in the latter group, a disproportionate number of whom are women, the level of stress may be so high as to create a dysfunctional learning environment.

152. *See supra* notes 110–114 and accompanying text. Other studies have also documented this phenomenon. *See* Catherine G. Krupnick, *Women and Men in the Classroom: Inequality and Its Remedies*, ON TEACHING & LEARNING: J. HARV.-DANFORTH CENTER, May 1985, at 18, 18–19, 22 (finding that males dominate classroom discussion at Harvard College); Sarah H. Sternglanz and Shirley Lyberger-Ficek, *Sex Differences in Student-Teacher Interactions in the College Classroom*, 3 SEX ROLES 345, 349 (1977) (observing that college male students dominate classroom interactions whether they are in the minority or majority); Weiss and Melling, *supra* note 31, at 1364–69 (presenting tables of male/female participation ratios in law school classes); Elizabeth Mertz, Research Fellow, American bar Foundation, in Philadelphia, Pa. (May 30, 1992) (describing research by anthropological linguists who measured the number of times and the length of time students spoke in law school contracts classes, and noting that preliminary findings suggest men speak not only more often, but also for longer periods). Other studies document this same phenomenon of differential participation and feedback for girls and boys beginning in elementary school and continuing through secondary school. *See, e.g.,* MYRA AND DAVID SADKER, FAILING AT FAIRNESS: HOW AMERICA'S SCHOOLS CHEAT GIRLS 1, 42–44, 269 (1994) (cataloguing subtle ways that girls, who outperform boys based on grades in elementary and secondary school, are silenced in the classroom). In the Sadkers' study, trained raters observed more than one hundred classrooms of fourth, sixth, and eighth graders in four Eastern states and the District of Columbia and also collected additional data at the college level. *See id.* at x. Their observations and data reveal that teachers respond to boys more than girls and that white males receive the most teacher attention. *See id.* at 50.

153. *See* Bernice R. Sandler, *The Classroom Climate: Still a Chilly One for Women, in* EDUCATING MEN AND WOMEN TOGETHER: COEDUCATION IN A CHANGING

WORLD 113 (Carol Lasser ed., 1987) (concluding that the devaluation of "female" characteristics and values results in subtle and sometimes inadvertent differential behavior by professors that "chills" women's participation, interferes with their education, and lowers their self-esteem more than men); *supra* note 111 (discussing female law students' reports of the loss of their self-esteem). Others suggest it is women's internal assessment of their own abilities that serves to erode their self-esteem. Therefore, even those women with stellar credentials may have low self-esteem if their inner conception of self does not match their actual performance. *See* MAGGIE MULQUEEN, ON OUR OWN TERMS: REDEFINING COMPETENCE AND FEMININITY 6–7 (1992) (stating that a sense of competence and actual competence are not always identical, and that women often receive mixed signals about their competence); *see also* Grace K. Baruch, *The Traditional Feminine Role: Some Negative Effects*, 21 SCH. COUNS. 285, 286 (1974) ("Competence is apparently viewed as a masculine trait, but our society values achievement and competence highly. Thus, women are caught in a double bind: If they develop their competence, they are 'masculine'; if they do not, they are not socially valued and learn to devalue themselves"); Kimberly A. Daubman et al., *Gender and the Self-Presentation of Academic Achievement*, 27 SEX ROLES 187, 197–98 (1992) (finding that women in public settings tend to provide lower estimates of their performance or ability than do men, who tend towards boastfulness and exaggeration); *infra* note 231 and preceding text.

154. This is the conclusion of the Berkeley study, which posits that silence represents resistance or a pragmatic coping mechanism. *See* Homer and Schwartz, *supra* note 31, at 37–38. Yet, "opting out" of the educational process does not enhance students' learning experiences. In other words, silence, even when powerful and political, is not without costs in terms of self-esteem, alienation, and professional achievement.

An alternative explanation is that women wait to participate until they are certain they have something to say, whereas men dominate the class because they are quicker to raise their hands. *See* telephone interview with Catherine Krupnick, *supra* note 86, explaining further that once called on, boys take longer to speak because they think through their comments as they are talking; girls, on the other hand, tend to edit their remarks in their minds before raising their hands. *See also*, *infra* notes 257, 258 (describing male domination of large and small classes).

155. *See supra* notes 113–116 and accompanying text.

156. *See supra* notes 120–121 and accompanying text.

157. A study that examined predictors of feminist self-labeling confirmed previous studies suggesting that many women, although attitudinally feminist, are unwilling to define themselves as such because of negative perceptions of feminists or feminism. *See* Gloria Cowan et al., *Predictors of Feminist Self-Labeling*, 27 SEX ROLES 321, 321–22 (1992).

158. *See supra* notes 120–121 and accompanying text.

159. *See supra* notes 120–121 and accompanying text; *see also* HUGHES AND SANDLER, *supra* note 120, at 5 (discussing the "academic harassment" of female students by their male peers and noting that the failure of faculty to intervene reinforces the idea that such harassment is acceptable); *cf.* Philip Brickman and Ronnie J. Bulman, *Pleasure and Pain in Social Comparison, in* SOCIAL COMPARISON PROCESSES: THEORETICAL AND EMPIRICAL PERSPECTIVES 149, 158, 166–67 (Jerry M. Suls and Richard L. Miller eds., 1977) (citing studies supporting proposition that those with higher status tend to disparage those with lower status).

160. *See supra* note 147; *see also* Phyllis W. Beck and David Burns, *Anxiety and*

Depression in Law Students: Cognitive Intervention, 30 J. LEGAL EDUC. 270, 287 (1979) (noting that many law students' success in prior academic settings leads them to develop "a belief system which equates self-worth with achievement" and that the "law school experience [of heavy work loads and confrontational instruction techniques such as the Socratic method] may be damaging to an individual whose self-esteem depends on continual demonstrations of success"); Roger C. Cramton, *The Current State of the Law Curriculum*, 32 J. LEGAL EDUC. 321, 329 (1982) (remarking that first-year grades control the "distribution of goodies" such as "honors, law review, job placement, and, because of the importance placed on these matters by the law school culture, even the student's sense of personal worth").

161. *See supra* text accompanying note 84.

162. This parallels the experience reported by students of color when issues of race permeate class discussions and they are called upon to "testify" as experts. *See supra* text accompanying note 114; *see also* Crenshaw, *supra* note 114, at 6–7 (describing the pressure and stigmatization experienced by black students "put on the spot" to "testify" about their personal experience and to incorporate their racial identity into their answers, and noting that such remarks are considered "special testimony" and disregarded as "biased, self-interested or subjective"). Consider as well the comments of the following students:

Third-year white woman: The white majority is kind of [an] arbiter and the minorities are supposed to report [minority] views and convince the white majority of the legitimacy of them or of a particular view.

First-year Latino student: It's one of the . . . the pressures, the initial pressures, of being in the very social environment like law school . . . feeling that what you contribute is not being weighed as much as everyone else's contribution because someone is attaching something to what you're saying. That's very disconcerting for me and it makes me kind of zone out from the whole process and see it as a spectator which I think really harms me in the final analysis. . . . Like right now I feel I have to break the barriers first and then see people as individuals second which is something that I don't feel whites have to do among each other. They already understand each other and they don't have those pre-conceived notions and I think that affects me and I'm sure it affects a lot of other people.

First-year black male: Whenever a minority issue comes up one is expected to say something and if you don't say something it's almost as if you're shunning your race. So you're battling with both sides of the coin. . . . When you do come forth, . . . feeling like this was your day to say some statement, you get a response like, "Wow, you know I am really impressed that you made that statement. That was really an intelligent comment." As if that was the first time that person saw you in class and had no idea that you ever acquired an education before law school. I find that very disturbing at times and you learn to deal with it and go along with the rest of the law school. . . . I think that is just part of the, once again, the situation we are in.

163. *See supra* note 15 (describing the role of the "gentleman" in the law). While it is entirely appropriate for the law school to enable students to adopt a professional demeanor, the "gentleman" model presented by the school is presumptively that of a white male. The law school's ideal lawyer is based on the role and techniques of lawyering developed at a time when no women or people of color were part of the profession.

Recent work suggests that the presentation of the model lawyer as an idealized man has its roots in the broader culture in which competence (professional and otherwise) is associated with masculinity. For women, the conflict between the desire to be competent and the desire to be feminine may lead to a negative assessment of their own competence which in turn leads to a lowered sense of self-esteem. *See* MULQUEEN, *supra* note 153, at 1 (stating that "[w]omen face the 'choice' of being perceived as either competent or feminine").

164. A significant aspect of the Socratic classroom is the way it seems to promote competition among some students. This competitive environment unnerves some law students who are accustomed to doing well in school and receiving accolades from professors. Indeed, in light of Penn's entry-level standards, being an academic high-achiever is probably a part of most students' identities. In addition, it is quite likely that individuals who have such a personal stake in academic achievement are somewhat competitive about their achievements in this area. *Cf.* Michael E. Carney, *Narcissistic Concerns in the Educational Experience of Law Students*, 18 J. PSYCHIATRY & L. 9, 16 (1990) (positing that students who are "accustomed to academic successes" see it "as an affront when they do not reach the top stratum of their law school").

165. We posit several tentative explanations for the powerful effect of the first-year pedagogy. First, the exposure to the Socratic method during the first year is magnified due to the fact that the heavy workload of the first year leaves students little time to pursue extracurricular activities or reflect upon their classroom experiences. Therefore, first-year students' predominant connection to the institution is through their professors and classroom experiences. Examining the first-year experience at Penn has particular salience due to the forced grading curve that professors must follow.

Second, the Socratic method is distinctly identified with law school and law teaching. It is a pedagogic method that was created with the specific intent of teaching and conveying a particular approach to law.

Finally, the law school presents the Socratic method to students as the unique format of legal education. At Penn, for example, first-year students are introduced to the Socratic classroom during a mock session prior to the start of classes. From this special preparation, the law school sends the message to incoming students that the particular style of cold calling on students is a specialized technique that must be mastered if one is to have a successful law school and legal career. At least one third-year student describes her memory of this session—the mixed fear and excitement of being called on—as the most vivid memory of her entire first year.

166. *See, e.g.*, Jerry M. Suls, *Social Comparison Theory and Research: An Overview from 1954*, *in* SOCIAL COMPARISON PROCESSES, *supra* note 159, at 1 (stating that "one's self-concept is based in part on how one compares to other individuals with regard to traits, opinions, and abilities"); *see also supra* note 153 and accompanying text (describing the effect of the absence of positive feedback from faculty on the self-esteem of female law students).

167. *Cf.* Richard H. Smith et al., *The Roles of Outcome Satisfaction and Comparison Alternatives in Envy*, 29 BRIT. J. SOC. PSYCHOL. 247, 254 (1990) ("[A] person's self-esteem is greatly affected by how he or she differs from others on valued attributes").

168. *See* Harrop A. Freeman, *Law Students and Law Examinations*, 4 STUDENT LAW., Apr. 1959, at 11, 12 (arguing that exam questions should span a range of difficulty to "separate the men from the boys").

169. GRANFIELD, *supra* note 1, at 100.

170. *Id.*

171. Institutional identification functions as a form of institutional legitimation, a process by which the institution infuses institutional values into the value systems of its members. *See* Laurie Davidson and Laura K. Gordon, The Sociology of Gender 11 (1979) ("Internalization of the values of a system through the socialization process is a powerful way to perpetuate that system"). One of the most pervasive values of the law school is the belief in individuation through hierarchy or stratification. More specifically, the law school perceives inherent value in rigidly rating students by ranking them against each other and in the hierarchy of station (teacher above student, dean above teacher, upper-level student above lower-level student, etc.) within the law school. *See* Duncan Kennedy, *Legal Education as Training for Hierarchy, in* The Politics of Law: A Progressive Critique 38, 50–58 (David Kairys ed., rev. ed. 1990) (discussing hierarchical relationships developed in law school and student response).

172. *See* Stephen C. Halpern, *On the Politics and Pathology of Legal Education,* 32 J. Legal Educ. 383, 383 (1982) ("The first-year experience serves to socialize the student to law school culture and to the norms of the profession"); *see also* David Dominguez, *Beyond Zero-Sum Games: Multiculturalism as Enriched Law Training for All Students,* 44 J. Legal Educ. 175, 175 and n. 1 (1994) (arguing that in law school the interaction among students is often experienced as a zero-sum game with professors acting as neutral third-party arbiters, in which status or success for one comes at another's expense, and suggesting that students are socialized by "intense competition for scarce commodities" into viewing everything in terms of one winner and multiple losers); *supra* note 165 and accompanying text (discussing the Socratic classroom and its effects on the connections that first-year students make with the institution of law school).

173. To a certain extent, we argue that success within the institution is predicated on the student's degree of self-identification with the institution. That is, the student must accept at least some of the norms of the institution in order to be acknowledged as successful. The student must sufficiently identify with the institutional definition of smartness to want to prove her own smartness. In this way, even students otherwise alienated by the law school have been able to do well precisely due to their spirit of gamesmanship. That is, they view success in law school as a game while keeping their core values untouched by the institution. This phenomenon seems to bear out Matsuda's outsider perspective. *See* Matsuda, *supra* note 46 at 8–9 (noting that people who are "outsiders," including women and people of color, embrace bifurcated thinking by adopting standard legal discourse for the classroom and reserving their race- or gender-consciousness for themselves and their support groups); *see also* Patricia J. Williams, The Alchemy of Race and Rights 89 (1991) (describing her sister's attempts as a black schoolgirl to deal with her "outsider" status); Van Praagh, *supra* note 118, at 141 (advocating cultural "bilingualism" as a means of mediating between traditional legal reasoning and the more emotionally meaningful technique of storytelling). It is the fact that their source of values and beliefs is outside of the institution that enables them to engage with and take risks within the law school.

Yet very few students enter the law school with such highly developed political beliefs, coping strategies, or a consciousness about the process of socialization into which they have entered. The majority of those who find little with which to identify must either mimic, in both form and content, what they believe are expected to say or be satisfied with poor grades (or both). Evidence from the Bartow Survey suggests that both situations occur with some frequency.

174. *First-year black student:* I just started to realize how important it is to hold on to what you believe in and how people can actually do that.

First-year black male: I think I have changed too because I have become much more pessimistic about what people's values are and what people in law school are trying to do. I think that many of them are just trying to get degrees to make more money and care nothing about changing the world [pause] have a good job and hopefully make a decent living. I hope—I know, in fact—I am not adopting the values that I see here.

175. Given the high student-faculty ratio and the large classroom format, at least some of the learning that goes on in legal education must take place within informal faculty mentoring relationships or in peer-to-peer contacts. Large lectures alone cannot provide for the needs of students. In addition, these informal settings allow for more interaction and thus cater to a different kind of learning. Small study groups or one-on-one discussions with faculty members force students to engage material more fully. To put it another way, small group learning encourages active rather than passive learning. *Cf. infra* notes 186–197 and accompanying text (discussing the development of mentoring relationships between faculty and students, as well as the effects of the presence or absence of such relationships); *see also* Dominguez, *supra* note 172, at 175 n.1 (positing that informal negotiation among students mimics the zero-sum model of the formal classroom, and that students "engage in direct zero-sum negotiation among themselves ... each trying to get as much help as possible without giving away too much in return").

176. Thus, in addition to our hypothesis that there exists either a formal or psychological link between class participation and academic performance, we theorize that women's alienation from informal academic networks also affects their academic performance. This latter hypothesis derives from the plaintiffs' claims that the Supreme Court endorsed in Sweatt v. Painter, 339 U.S. 629, 634 (1950) (stating that effective legal education requires "the interplay of ideas and the exchange of views"), and McLaurin v. Oklahoma State Regents, 339 U.S. 637, 641 (1950) (holding that the separation of the black law student from the white law student, even where formal education opportunity is provided to both, "impair[s] and inhibit[s the] ability [of the black student] to study, to engage in discussions and to exchange views with other students, and, in general, to learn his profession").

177. This is consistent with a study of graduate students, including law students, at the University of Illinois. *See* Berg and Ferber, *supra* note 129, at 638. The study found significant differences between men and women graduate students in their interaction with men and women faculty. For example, 78% of male respondents and 54% of female respondents reported they knew one or more male faculty members "quite well" in the course of their graduate studies. *Id.*

178. *See supra* notes 91–94 and accompanying text. Women emphasize the importance of faculty openness to questions outside of class and faculty who are friendly with and respectful of students. *See supra* text accompanying note 90; *cf. supra* note 88 and accompanying text (making a similar point regarding the higher value female students place on "treating students with respect").

179. *See supra* note 87.

180. *See supra* note 110 and accompanying text.

181. *See supra* note 176.

182. *See supra* note 122 and accompanying text.

183. *See infra* notes 198–205 and accompanying text (discussing the concept of

virtual tokenism); *see also supra* note 165 (positing social comparison as a source of status).

184. *See supra* table 6.

185. *See infra* notes 186–191 and accompanying text.

186. *See* AGNES K. MISSIRIAN, THE CORPORATE CONNECTION: WHY EXECUTIVE WOMEN NEED MENTORS TO REACH THE TOP 50–58 (1982) (suggesting that a mentor relationship can increase adjustment to and satisfaction with the mentee's environment); Berg and Ferber, *supra* note 129, at 638–39, 641, 643 (defining success as earning a graduate degree and finding a positive correlation among male students between success and being mentored); Cheryl Richey et al., *Mentor Relationships Among Women in Academe*, 3 AFFILIA 34, 37 (1988) (finding that a mentor provides a protégé with encouragement, advocacy, advice, and resources).

By "mentor" we refer to the one-on-one personal contact between an experienced or more powerful person within an institution and a novice learning the ropes. A mentor is a teacher in an interpersonal relationship. A mentor is a person of relatively high status, or simply a more accomplished person in terms of knowledge of the institutional mores who is willing to share that knowledge in guiding others. Unlike a role model, who simply demonstrates the possibilities of opportunities, the mentor actively engages in guiding, supporting, training, and educating others. *See* Chapter 3 (contrasting mentors with role models).

187. We draw this conclusion from the Bartow Survey data, the group interview data, and the graduation awards given by faculty. Data from other studies suggest that male faculty are more likely to mentor male students. *See, e.g.*, Berg and Ferber, *supra* note 129, at 631 (noting that men and women faculty tend to be more supportive of students of their own gender); M. Elizabeth Tidball, *Of Men and Research: The Dominant Themes in American Higher Education Include Neither Teaching Nor Women*, 47 J. HIGHER EDUC. 373, 383 (1976) (same); *cf.* EXECUTIVE SUMMARY, *supra* note 12, at 9 (reporting that 41% of women professors do not believe mentors are as available to them as to male faculty).

188. *See supra* notes 88, 90–94 and accompanying text (discussing data that show men to be more comfortable than women in speaking with male faculty, and noting that women perceive faculty to be aloof.)

189. *See* TANYA POTEET AND MICHELLE FONDELL, JOINT TASK FORCE ON GENDER FAIRNESS OF THE OHIO SUPREME COURT & THE OHIO STATE BAR ASS'N, SURVEY OF OHIO LAW SCHOOL FACULTY 11 (noting that mentors choose protégés who are of similar background, gender, race, and social class); Kathryn M. Moore, *The Role of Mentors in Developing Leaders for Academe*, 63 EDUC. REC. 23, 25 (1982) (explaining that, in the academic setting, mentors select protégés on the basis of "similarity of attitudes and behaviors as well as similarity of sex, ethnic origin, and religion"); *see also* Berg and Ferber, *supra* note 129, at 631 (noting that men and women faculty tend to be more supportive of students of their own gender); Tidball, *supra* note 186, at 383 (same); *infra* notes 195–197 and accompanying text (describing the difficulty people have penetrating informal networks).

190. *See* Costonis, *supra* note 144, at 160–61 (describing efficiency as one reason law schools employ large classroom instruction). Even more, they may disparage colleagues who approach teaching as a cooperative learning project on the grounds that teaching rigorous analytic thinking requires toughness on the parts of both the instructor and the student. Indeed, "the better a student's answer, the more [a good teacher] is personally challenged to find something wrong with it." D'Amato, *supra* note 149, at 473. D'Amato contrasts a hypothetical Professor Smith (the good teacher) who is confrontational, "combative," relentless, and makes his students feel insecure, with a hypothetical Professor Jones (the poor

teacher) who is attractive, "nice," and well-liked because he "accommodates" his students' entrenched and "sloppy" thinking patterns. *Id.* at 467–79. Although D'Amato's examples are of two male professors, his use of gender-laden language is quite impressive. "Aggressor" and "relentless" are terms that often describe men, whereas "patient," "attractive," and "accommodating" often describe women. *Id.* at 472–74. This may not be his intention, but it does highlight the ways in which certain kinds of teaching are perceived to be gendered, and thus perhaps the ways in which some men and women respond to different kinds of teaching. *Cf. id.* at 481 n.38.

As an example of instructional intimidation observed by the authors, one senior male professor has counseled more junior colleagues to follow up student comments in class aggressively. According to the male professor, where there are very good students and terrible students in a class, the role of the teacher is to identify for the students who falls into which category. In addition, this male professor's teaching philosophy holds that a stressful atmosphere is necessary for learning. In his view, students will not listen to each other unless the professor turns up the discomfort level so that students worry about and identify with the way their peers are being grilled.

Our point is not to argue that one teaching style works better in all cases for all students. It is to identify the costs of an intimidating pedagogy within and without the classroom for educating certain students, a disproportionate number of whom are women. *Cf.* Dominguez, *supra* note 172, at 175 (describing a harsh reality for losers at law schools where reigning dynamics work against their self-esteem and confidence).

191. *See supra* notes 91–94 and accompanying text (describing women's relative reluctance to approach faculty outside of class); *cf.* Banks, *supra* note 31, at 146 (questioning whether women and men "receive truly equal education" in law school, in light of findings that the law school environment tends to exclude women and discourage them from class participation); Betz, *supra* note 148, at 137 (stating that in an academic situation women are more negatively affected by a lack of encouragement than men).

192. Roberta M. Hall and Bernice R. Sandler, *A Chilly Climate in the Classroom,* *in* BEYOND SEX ROLES 503, 503 (Alice G. Sargent ed., 2d ed. 1985). As an example of the invisibility of these informal barriers, one male colleague at Penn invited all the students in his upper-level class to his home in the spring of 1992. Approximately thirty students were enrolled in the class; only fifteen accepted the invitation and attended the party. Of those who attended, none were women. The colleague reported this fact to Professor Guinier with some concern because he did not believe that he was conducting himself in a manner that overtly discouraged or disparaged his female students.

193. *See* Carrie Menkel-Meadow, *Portia in a Different Voice: Speculations on a Women's Lawyering Process,* 1 BERKELEY WOMEN'S L.J. 39, 40 (1985) ("Since our knowledge of how lawyers behave and of how the legal system functions is based almost exclusively on male subjects of study, our understanding of what it means to be and act like a lawyer may be misleadingly based on a male norm"); *see also* POTEET AND FONDELL, *supra* note 189, at 8 (finding legal education to be a "male-dominated profession").

194. *See infra* notes 206–207 and accompanying text (discussing the possibility that treating all students equally may affect women differently).

195. Kanter, *supra* note 15, at 8 (noting male lawyers' "preference for keeping power within a closed circle of socially homogeneous peers").

196. *See* Berg and Ferber, *supra* note 129, at 638–39 (studying graduate stu-

dents' comfort in approaching faculty); *cf.* Kanter, *supra* note 15, at 7–8 (noting a similar phenomenon of homogeneity in law firms, particularly the more prestigious firms).

197. *See, e.g.*, Richard Delgado, *The Ethereal Scholar: Does Critical Legal Studies Have What Minorities Want?*, 22 Harv. C.R.-C.L. L. Rev. 301, 314–16 (1987) (asserting that highly structured, rule-bound environments are more likely to give minorities relief from racism); Richard Delgado et al., *Fairness and Formality: Minimizing the Risk of Prejudice in Alternative Dispute Resolution*, 1985 Wis. L. Rev. 1359, 1387–89 (explaining why formal dispute resolution settings are more conducive to overcoming prejudice); Allan Lind et al., *A Cross-Cultural Comparison of the Effect of Adversary and Inquisitorial Processes on Bias in Legal Decisionmaking*, 62 Va. L. Rev. 271, 282–83 (1976) (finding adversarial proceedings a more successful means of overcoming preexisting bias than inquisitorial proceedings); *see also* Charles R. Lawrence, *The Id, the Ego, and Equal Protection: Reckoning with Unconscious Racism*, 39 Stan. L. Rev. 317, 341 n.100 (1987) (providing examples of informal situations in which racial decisions were made unintentionally).

198. Our ethnographic survey and archival study of women's experiences at this law school prompt us to review certain assumptions about assimilation based on theories of "critical mass." Women now represent more than 40% of the law student population—a critical mass of law students. *See* Rosabeth M. Kanter, Men and Women of the Corporation 208–09 (1977) (hypothesizing that a numerically strong "outgroup" of 15% will constitute a "critical mass" that will succeed in countering demeaning stereotypes and in changing an institutional environment to make it more conducive to the outgroup's success); Kanter, *supra* note 15, at 10–11 (defining threshold for dynamics of tokenism as 20%); Rosabeth M. Kanter, *Some Effects of Proportions on Group Life: Skewed Sex Ratios and Responses to Token Women*, 82 Am. J. Soc. 965, 966 (1977) (identifying the threshold for tokenism at around 15%). Despite the predictions of Kanter's critical mass theory, women at Penn are still relatively scarce in high-status positions, the positions which set and maintain the law school agenda. *See supra* table 3 and accompanying text (documenting women's proportionate underrepresentation with respect to honorary awards and activities at Penn Law, such as Order of the Coif, *Law Review* Member, *Law Review* board, moot court competitor, moot court board, and faculty-chosen graduation awards). As a result, women students—despite their numbers—remain a somewhat marginalized "outgroup" who are expected to succeed, to the extent they can, within the male-dominated hierarchy.

199. During the period of our study (1990–92), at least four white men joined the full-time faculty as either lateral or entry-level professors. Not a single tenure-track female professor joined the faculty during the same period. At the time, women faculty comprised seven of the approximately thirty-five full-time faculty. This number includes senior fellows and emeritus professors who teach first-year courses as full-time faculty members. It does not include visiting professors, adjuncts, or clinical instructors.

Five of the seven women were tenured; three of the seven regularly taught in the first-year curriculum; one of the seven was the law school's librarian, who does not teach a substantive law course. During the period of 1990–92, a minimum of one and as many as three of the women were on leave or visiting at other schools in a given semester.

200. *See supra* table 3; *supra* note 80 and accompanying text.

201. *See* Executive Summary, *supra* note 12, at 2–10 (reporting on findings from study of nine Ohio law schools); Berg and Ferber, *supra* note 129, at 631

(finding that women are more successful at earning graduate degrees in departments with more women faculty and suggesting that the "positive effect of women faculty on women students might be stronger if women faculty were . . . of higher rank and perceived as more successful"); *see also* M. Elizabeth Tidball, *Perspective on Academic Women and Affirmative Action*, 54 EDUC. REC. 130, 133 (1973) (finding that women students who study in departments with a relatively higher proportion of women faculty are more likely to go on to enjoy successful careers).

202. *See* Kanter, *supra* note 15, at 11 (defining tokenism in terms of proportional scarcity). Although Kanter hypothesized in this 1978 article that constructive or virtual tokenism could not exist if women constituted over 20% of an institution's population, our findings suggest that virtual tokenism was alive and well at Penn in the early 1990s and may continue to affect women in law school in the future.

203. Under this formulation, sexism is a societal and not merely a personal matter. Consequently, gender equality requires the transformation of a hostile learning environment, not simply the repopulation of the same environment with women struggling to become "honorary men." *See, e.g.*, Rhoda K. Unger, *The Personal Is Paradoxical: Feminists Construct Psychology*, 3 FEMINISM & PSYCHOL. 211, 211 (1993) (noting that tokens are the recipients of conflicting social demands to act both feminine and masculine; tokens may become "honorary men" by "identify[ing] with the aggressor," or they may choose to challenge the system to live up to its stated claims of genuine meritocracy); *see also* Judith L. Laws, *The Psychology of Tokenism: An Analysis*, 1 SEX ROLES 51, *passim* (1975) (examining tokenism in the academic profession, within the context of a gender/class system).

204. *See* Eve Spangler et al., *Token Women: An Empirical Test of Kanter's Hypothesis*, 84 AM. J. SOC. 160, 163–67 (1978) (finding that women who are tokens differ more significantly in performance than women who are proportionately represented, and that this performance differential affects academic achievement, voluntary class participation, and interaction with faculty); *cf.* Homer and Schwartz, *supra* note 31, at 39–40 (speculating that a lack of female faculty in part results in poorer grades for women).

205. This finding is consistent with a study done by Professor Catherine Krupnick of Harvard undergraduates in which she studied videotapes of student/faculty classroom interactions involving twenty-four different instructors (twelve female and twelve male). Female students participated in a manner proportionate to their numbers only in classes in which women were in the majority and the teacher was female. In other words, women's rate of participation increased commensurate to their numbers only in classes that did not represent "the predominant classroom circumstance . . . in which the instructor is male and the majority of students are male." Krupnick, *supra* note 152, at 18–19 (finding that female students at Harvard College "spoke almost three times longer" in classes with female instructors than in classes with male instructors). Perhaps not surprisingly, given how unusual it was to hear so many women's voices, in these cases the perception among the male students was that the female teacher favored the female students. *See* interview with Catherine G. Krupnick, *supra* note 86.

A study of law students at Boalt Hall revealed that women law students voluntarily participated in class less frequently than men and had lower grades. *See* Homer and Schwartz, *supra* note 31, at 37–41. The authors of the study recommended increased female faculty hiring as one way to address these discrepancies. *See id.*

206. *See supra* notes 148, 152, 163 (identifying male traits prized by legal education); *see also* Betz, *supra* note 148, at 137 (noting that even if neither males nor females are given encouragement to do well, the absence of encouragement is likely

to affect females disproportionately); *cf.* EXECUTIVE SUMMARY, *supra* note 12, at 9 (finding that although a majority of both male and female faculty recognize the importance of mentoring, nearly one-fourth of women faculty believed that a mentor is more important for new female faculty than new male faculty).

207. *See supra* notes 190–191 and accompanying text. Because women students disproportionately reported their disengagement with an adversarial learning style of the large classroom, even a gender-neutral teaching style may have a profoundly gendered impact. In this sense, women who are focused on relational thinking or contextual analysis may thrive in more intimate tutorial settings. *Cf.* TANNEN, *supra* note 148, at 42–44 (noting that young boys use aggressiveness as a way to invite participation and friendship); Jane Gross, *To Help Girls Keep Up: Math Class Without Boys*, N.Y. TIMES, Nov. 24, 1993, at A1, B8 (identifying different "learning styles" of boys and girls).

208. Berg and Ferber's study found a positive correlation between having at least one male faculty mentor and success in graduate school. *See* Berg and Ferber, *supra* note 129, at 643–45. Since the graduate schools studied had 44% female populations but few female professors, many of the female students were mentored by male professors. *See id.* at 644.

209. *Cf. supra* note 186 (contrasting role models from mentors). Elsewhere Professor Guinier and others have expressed reservations about the role model hypothesis, in part because of its relationship to the dynamics of tokenism. *See, e.g.,* Regina Austin, *Sapphire Bound!*, 1989 WIS. L. REV. 539, 574–76 (arguing that minority role models are not a substitute for a change in "material conditions"); Guinier, *supra* note 15, at 99–103 (describing why a more active minority mentor is preferable to a role model). *See* Chapter 3 in this volume.

210. We do not take a position as to whether women's gender identity is nature- or nurture-based. *See infra* note 214 and accompanying text.

211. "Unintentionally" suggests that the reasons for implementing the present system may not have been the conscious exclusion of women; although in using a male-oriented baseline, men enshrined their own values in both the law and legal education. We do not argue that the gendered nature of legal education results from an original self-conscious bias or intent. We do note, however, that our research provides valid evidence, albeit anecdotal, that some male students intentionally devalue women who step beyond traditional gender roles. *See supra* text accompanying note 108; *supra* note 120 and accompanying text (describing ways in which women who speak in class are ridiculed by their peers for transgressing perceptions about sexual boundaries).

212. Indeed, a few members of the Penn Law School faculty proffered this theory in response to a presentation of our data in May of 1992. *See supra* note 24 (describing context of that meeting). In the alternative, this response is an argument for the selection of only those women who are social males. *See* Littleton, *supra* note 13, at 1280–81 (noting that social males are those in whom cultural maleness has been layered on to biological gender identity).

213. Other versions of this response are that "lawyers are assholes and maybe women just don't want to be assholes," *see* interview with Dr. Joseph Torg, Director of the University of Pennsylvania Sports Medicine Clinic, in Philadelphia, Pa. (Feb. 16, 1993), or that women opt out of the ranking for other professional and nonprofessional reasons (their social life is more important; they are multidimensioned people unlike their male counterparts; they sought a legal career to help people and then got turned off when public interest jobs were not available); *see also* Eccles, *supra* note 102, at 151 (finding that women place more importance on fam-

ily than men do); Robert Fiorentine, *Increasing Similarity in the Values and Life Plans of Male and Female College Students? Evidence and Implications,* 18 SEX ROLES 143, 148 (1988) (finding that college women value domestic and nurturing activities even as they pursue career goals similar to men). *But cf.* Joan Z. Spade and Carole A. Reese, *We've Come a Long Way, Maybe: College Students' Plans for Work and Family,* 24 SEX ROLES 309, 318 (1991) (finding that college males and females have equally strong commitments to family and work).

214. We follow the lead of Professor Christine Littleton in attempting to address the consequences of gendered differences, and not its sources. *See* Littleton, *supra* note 13 at 1297 ("It is the *consequences* of gendered differences, and not its sources, that equal acceptance addresses").

215. *See* our discussion of "asshole bingo," and a description of the role that attitudes about sexual orientation play in policing women's behavior, *supra* note 120; *cf.* Granfield, *supra* note 31, at 11, 23 n.11 (describing a similar game at Harvard Law School called "turkey bingo").

216. *See supra* note 15 (describing role of "gentlemen of the bar"). This transformation might explain the difference in survey responses between first- and third-year women regarding criticism of bias within the institution itself and regarding career aspirations. *See supra* notes 87, 101–102 and accompanying text (illustrating that third-year women perceive less gender bias than do first-year women, and that, whereas over one-fourth of first-year female students aspire to public interest jobs, only around one-tenth of third-year female law students share that goal, preferring work in private law firms by a wide margin). Of course, some view this same information differently. *See supra* note 139 and accompanying text (suggesting, as alternative interpretations of these data, that bias might diminish over the course of three years among male students; that bias might be less prevalent among upper-level, as opposed to first-year, instructors; or that women who can choose their upper-level courses simply might avoid those instructors who are more openly biased).

217. According to the criteria on which the law school presently relies, including the LSAT, GPA, and the other so-called objective indicia of law school performance, women should perform in law school as well as men. *See supra* notes 67–73 and accompanying text. Maybe, the argument goes, these criteria simply overpredict women's future success. *Cf.* Leslie G. Espinoza, *The LSAT: Narratives and Bias,* 1 AM. U. J. GENDER & L. 121, 127 n.34 (1993) (citing a Law School Admission Council claim that LSAT scores predict academic success in the first year of law school). Alternatively, our data support the conclusion that the entry criteria, especially the LSAT, are weak predictors more generally. *See supra* note 74 and accompanying text. *See also* Susan Sturm and Lani Guinier, *The Future of Affirmative Action: Reclaiming the Innovative Ideal,* CAL. L. REV. 1 (July 1996) (describing limits of test-based prediction).

218. We are not condemning all alternative explanations of our data. Indeed, we have investigated several different hypotheses before drawing these conclusions. The point is simply that women's difference, despite equivalent entry credentials, should not alone be used to justify the status quo in which the existing relationships inevitably leave women at the bottom of the hierarchy.

219. *See* Cort and Sammons, *supra* note 149, at 400 ("[T]he objective of legal education is the preparation of lawyers for lawyering. The problem which underlies the debate [often defined as whether law schools should teach law or lawyering] ... is defining good lawyering and testing means of producing it"); *see also* Barbara B. Woodhouse, *Mad Midwifery: Bringing Theory, Doctrine, and Practice to*

Life, 91 Mich. L. Rev. 1977, 1978 (1993) (expressing "concern about the health of legal education" and proposing potential solutions). *See generally* MacCrate Report, *supra* note 1, at 327 (making "recommendations for improving and integrating the process by which lawyers acquire their skills and values").

220. One study analyzed the academic credentials of candidates for the North Dakota bar in the years 1902 to 1913, inclusive, to determine whether or not law school grades were an adequate means of predicting success in the practice of law. *See* Lauriz Vold, *Legal Preparation Tested by Success in Practice*, 33 Harv. L. Rev. 168, 169 (1919). Generally, those with high marks in law school did well in actual practice (focusing on litigation practice), but those with the top law school grades (those in the top decile) did not do as well in practice as those whose grades were in the next highest group:

> Grinds [scores over 90th percentile] have been more successful than the next scholarship group in handling Supreme Court litigation, where the issues depend largely on intellectual power; but they have been surpassed by the next scholarship group in the matter of securing cases, and in the matter of winning in the trial courts, instances where the so-called human qualities as opposed to mere intellectual power come more largely into play.

Id. at 175.

221. This problem is not just with the case-study method, but rather with the law school's overall approach to teaching students about what lawyers do. *See, e.g.,* MacCrate Report, *supra* note 1, at 330–34 (suggesting steps to enhance professional development during law school); Gerald Korngold, *Legal Education for Non-Litigators: The Role of the Law Schools and the Practicing Bar*, 30 N.Y.L. Sch. L. Rev. 621, 622–23 (1985) (arguing that the greatest failing of current legal education is its focus, through the case-study method and clinics, on appellate cases and adversarial law, ignoring nonlitigation activities that often consist of attempts to find common ground). Of course, the focus on the case method does not necessarily mean the law school is preoccupied with developing adversarial skills. Law schools could use this method to sharpen analytical skills rather than to reinforce the sense of "ritualized combat." Nevertheless, the choice of method in the context of large classes with high student-to-faculty ratios implicitly endorses a highly competitive approach, which is often internalized by students.

222. First, "students are given the impression that trial and appellate work is the bulk of what attorneys *actually* do and what they *should* be doing." Korngold, *supra* note 221, at 622. Second, the case method of instruction teaches students to analyze and respond in the adversarial context. *See id.* Third, the appellate focus of the curriculum leads students to the conclusion that a third party will ultimately resolve all disputes. *See id.* at 622–23. Korngold further notes that even law school clinical work focuses on litigation experience. *See id.* at 623; *see also* Dominguez, *supra* note 172 at 196–97 (suggesting that a nontraditional "negotiable" learning experience for law students would force them to learn how to "work through . . . racism, sexism, and other forms of bigotry").

223. *See, e.g.,* Steve H. Nickles, *Examining and Grading in American Law Schools*, 30 Ark. L. Rev. 411, 412 (1977) ("[L]egal education has paid insufficient attention to the problems and issues of student evaluation [and has relied upon] procedures and techniques which have been discredited by research in education and psychology"). In its "Statement of Fundamental Lawyering Skills and Professional Values," the MacCrate Report identified two analytical skills that form the conceptual foundations for almost all legal practice: problem solving and legal analysis. *See* MacCrate Report, *supra* note 1, at 135. The report also identified five

skills that are essential for a wide range of legal specialties: legal research, factual investigation, communication, counseling, and negotiation. *See id.*

In addition, many critics of legal education such as Judge Harry T. Edwards of the Federal Appeals Court of the District of Columbia Circuit assert that law schools do not provide enough practical training for their students and do not perform cost/benefit analyses to determine useful educational tools. Instead, law schools rely on the desires of the faculty to determine the shape and function of the curriculum. *See* Harry T. Edwards, *The Growing Disjunction Between Legal Education and the Legal Profession*, 91 MICH. L. REV. 34, 35–36 (1992).

224. *See, e.g.,* Lisa Bernstein, *Understanding the Limits of Court-Connected ADR: A Critique of Federal Court-Annexed Arbitration Programs*, 141 U. PA. L. REV. 2169, 2172–74 (1993) (describing the increased use of alternative dispute resolution as either a precondition to, or substitute for, judicial resolution of federal and state litigation).

225. *See* Michael J. Saks, *Do We Really Know Anything About the Behavior of the Tort Litigation System—and Why Not?*, 140 U. PA. L. REV. 1147, 1212–13 (1992) (stating that more than 90% of lawsuits filed result in negotiated settlements prior to trial).

226. *See* Robert Keeton, *Teaching and Testing for Competence in Law Schools*, 40 MD. L. REV. 203, 215–17 (1981) (recognizing that traditional law school education emphasizes legal analytic skills rather than communication and learning skills); *cf.* TANNEN, *supra* note 148, at 132 n.6 (stating that women initially perform better as psychotherapists because women possess the interactive skills essential to the practice of the profession; once men acquire these skills, the difference in their performance levels off); Stacey Burling, *Study Finds Gender Gap Among Doctors*, PHILA. INQUIRER, Oct. 17, 1994, at A2 (reporting the findings that female doctors spend more time with their patients; that patients of both sexes talked more to female doctors and asked them more questions; and that women's communication techniques are associated with better patient compliance and understanding).

227. For example, only 47 members of the graduating class of 1992, 18 of whom were women and 29 of whom were men, obtained judicial clerkships, and only 29 of these clerkships were at the federal level (10 by women, 19 by men). *See* University of Pennsylvania NALP Report for Graduating Class of 1992. Similarly, only 42 members of the class of 1993 took judicial clerkships—19 women and 23 men—and only 26 of these were with federal judges (11 women and 15 men). *See* University of Pennsylvania NALP Report for Graduating Class of 1993.

228. From the institutional perspective of the law school, the purposes of evaluating students through examinations are to monitor the effectiveness of the institution in meeting its educational objectives, provide a feedback mechanism for professors on their own teaching, and enable the institution to keep track of students as they progress towards a degree. *See* Nickles, *supra* note 223, at 419–20.

Other catalogues of the functions of law examinations include the measurement of "learning and/or competence of the examinees," motivation and feedback, assessment, feedback to professors, bar preparation, and teaching lawyering skills. Motley, *supra* note 150, at 725. Philip Kissam notes that law school exams also have the more pragmatic function of preparing students to take (and pass) the bar. *See* Philip C. Kissam, *Law School Examinations*, 42 VAND. L. REV. 433, 463 (1989) (discussing "the practical consequences of exams and grades").

Although we do not have data documenting the structure of law school examinations or their relationship to the dominant pedagogy, the issue deserves more serious attention.

229. Instead, the law schools may simply be operating as "gatekeepers to the profession." Cramton, *supra* note 160, at 323 (noting that law schools should pay more attention to the different ways in which legal skills can be developed); *see also* Costonis, *supra* note 144, at 174 (noting that law school programs employ a pedagogy that inadequately addresses the full range of skills and values needed for legal competence).

230. *See* Costonis, *supra* note 144, at 174–77 (describing role of experiential skills training in lawyer competence); *see also infra* notes 237, 242 and accompanying text (describing the traditional assumption that law schools train legal minds, but law firms train lawyers).

231. In other words, women are ranked by an evaluative methodology that ignores their ability to learn, practice, and apply the law in areas other than traditional academia or appellate advocacy. Moreover, the ranking system may disable women from participating in the formal educational pedagogy, or from learning the skills that are not being taught in law school but may be necessary to the practice of law. *See, e.g.,* Keeton, *supra* note 226, at 215–17 (acknowledging that law schools traditionally emphasize analytic skills over communication and learning skills).

By "educated," we therefore mean two things. First, if the Socratic dialogue is the primary educative tool, it does not engage a substantial and identifiable group of students when it is practiced in an intimidating environment. By their in-class silence and relatively weak exam performance, these students are disengaged from the "training" or educational methodology. They presumably are not being "trained" as effectively as their more vocal colleagues. Second, the law school, even to the extent it attempts to train legal minds, is not necessarily preparing students for the different kinds of skills they may need in the workplace. As Professor Nickles has observed,

> The law school examination is given with the intent of deriving a grade, and thus any distinct purposes of the examining process in law school are subsumed within the larger functions served by the grading system. Especially within the context of legal education, the objectives of examining logically cannot be separated and analyzed apart from those of grading.

Nickles, *supra* note 223, at 415.

232. Although the differences in academic performance data are statistically significant, these differences may appear minimal to some observers. Even small differences, however, become important when women are denied the opportunity to receive the on-the-job training they need to become lawyers. Many employers use this information to determine who among Penn graduates gets the opportunity to learn the practice of law. *See* Johnson, *supra* note 151, at 1246 (noting that law firms "depend on the sorting process of elite law schools' admissions decisions," a sorting process that values a uniform first-year curriculum and grading policy and analytical thinking); *see also supra* note 151 and accompanying text (suggesting that elite law schools fail to prepare their students in the aggregate for actual legal practice.)

233. *See* Lepow, *supra* note 119, at 70 (noting that society views lawyers as being less influential than in the past and that many people perceive the work of lawyers as a "destructive force").

234. *Cf.* Michael Winerip, *Merit Scholarship Program Faces Sex Bias Complaint,* N.Y. TIMES, Feb. 16, 1994, at A18 (describing a complaint against the Educational Testing Service and the College Board, who developed and administer the Preliminary Scholastic Aptitude Test (PSAT), charging gender discrimination in

awarding National Merit scholarships because *it provides test scores* to the scholarship organization, making "a significant assist in discrimination against females," in violation of Title IX).

235. For some law students, the hierarchy of the Socratic classroom and the grading system creates a dysfunctional level of stress. *See supra* note 150 and accompanying text; *see also supra* notes 109, 117 and accompanying text (noting a gendered psychological distress among law students that is absent in studies of medical students); *supra* note 223 (discussing the possibility that the dominant methodology in legal education has outlived its usefulness); *supra* note 232 (noting that even small differences in grades can have a great impact on future career prospects). Professor Nickles explains:

> Examinations typically mean grades, and grades mean everything. In American law schools grades have become negotiable. They will purchase more than the expected individual pride in accomplishment which reinforces confidence and initiative. Grades will buy a spot on the dean's list, membership in honor fraternities, enrollment in specialized classes and programs, and a place on the law journal staff. Upon graduation these prizes can be exchanged for associations with the better law firms, clerkships with prestigious courts, or acceptance by the elite graduate schools. The snowball continues to roll, and these initial professional ties become cherished springboards to others that are still bigger and better.

Nickles, *supra* note 223, at 411–12; *see also* Ann C. Scales, *Surviving Legal De-Education: An Outsider's Guide*, 15 VT. L. REV. 139, 141 (1990) ("The grading policy... is dictated by big law firms.... [A] partner in a big east coast firm... characterized the first year as The Race. To do well in the first year is to win The Race, and to secure your success in law firm practice forever").

236. By suggesting an analogy to employment discrimination, we neither urge litigation to resolve the problems we identify nor contend that doctrinal approaches easily comprehend the complex relationship of the relevant variables. Our reference is triggered by the apparent relevance of principles of validation. *Compare* Civil Rights Act of 1991 § 703(k), 42 U.S.C. § 2000e-2(k), as amended by Pub. L. 102-166, 105 Stat. 1074(k) (Supp. IV 1992) (detailing business necessity and job relatedness defenses) *with* Education Amendments of 1972 § 901, 20 U.S.C. § 1681(a) (1988) (providing that "[n]o person in the United States shall, on the basis of sex, be excluded from participation in, be denied the benefits of, or be subjected to discrimination under any education program or activity receiving Federal financial assistance" (exceptions omitted)). For analogous case law, compare Dothard v. Rawlinson, 433 U.S. 321, 331–37 (1977) (describing the business necessity defense) and Griggs v. Duke Power Co., 401 U.S. 424, 432 (1971) (same) with Sharif v. New York State Educ. Dep't, 709 F. Supp. 345, 361–62 (S.D.N.Y. 1989) (describing the educational necessity defense).

237. Law school exams have several functions. *See* Nickles, *supra* note 223, at 422 (discussing a survey of evaluation methods of every law school in the United States as of 1973, such surveys having been sent to the deans and student bar association presidents as well as the editors-in-chief of all law journals listed in the foreword to the Index to Legal Periodicals [1975]). The cultural and societal functions of exams are certification (the law degree functions as a standard of qualification), selection (the law graduate is worthy of representing the profession), and prediction (of competency in field). *See id.* at 416–17. "Students who received better grades readily are assumed to know better how to think like lawyers and therefore to be better lawyers in practice." *Id.* at 417–18. This same assump-

tion is held by law professors. In fact, 68% of faculty surveyed by Nickles agreed that there was a significant correlation between academic success and success as a practitioner, whereas only 36% of law review editors and 14% of student bar association presidents believed this to be the case. *See id.* at 429 n.52. As Janet Motley points out, "[w]hether or not student perception is accurate, it does give us some information about the credibility of our evaluation method in [the eyes of students]. It certainly should tell us that the motivation which is engendered by the examination process is not related to desire to become a successful practitioner." Motley, *supra* note 149, at 730 n.11 (commenting on the statistics cited by Nickles). The student-related purposes of examinations are to gauge learning and to establish a mechanism for competition for top grades. *See* Nickles, *supra* note 220, at 418–19. It is an open question whether traditional examinations test or predict performance as a lawyer. For example, some within legal education might argue that it is not part of the law school's mission to train law students to be lawyers. They defend the law school curriculum and examination methodology on the grounds that anonymously graded, issue-spotting examinations test—to the extent the examinations are solid evaluative mechanisms—abstract analytic ability. To put it somewhat crudely, law school trains legal minds, law firms train lawyers. It is after graduation that law school students arguably learn to be lawyers through on-the-job training.

Training law students to "be lawyers" does not occur until the students are on the job. After all, Penn Law School is not a trade school or even a mere professional school. This, some might say, is the last opportunity for most law students to get a "liberal education." Yet, even those who defend law school—as the last opportunity to "train legal minds"—acknowledge that at least some part of the law school's responsibility is to place its students on the job market.

Moreover, even if law school simply trains a student to "think like a lawyer," this skill is presumably correlated with success in the profession, yet academic performance on timed examinations graded on a mandatory curve may not, in fact, measure accurately what it takes to be a lawyer. Given the multidimensioned kinds of law practice and the vast range of skills employed even by Penn graduates who are hired by large corporate law firms, it no longer seems possible that one type of examination methodology accurately predicts success in a multifaceted profession. As a result, some posit that law school "socializes" rather than educates lawyers. In this hypothesis, differential examination performance is used to distribute the real opportunities to learn to become lawyers; students who do well are then hired by law firms whose mission is actually to train lawyers "on the job." As Professor Coutts remarked,

> There are those who have tried to show statistically that "success in practice has been, on the average, roughly in proportion to the scholarship shown in preparation"; but such statistics can be explained by the fact that the best law firms take, and give the best opportunities to, those with the highest honours degrees.

J. A. Coutts, *Examinations for Law Degrees*, 9 J. SOC'Y PUB. TCHERS. L. 399, 401 (1967). Finally, issue-spotting skills are not the same as analytic or reasoning ability. "[Issue spotting] often does not involve the demonstration of the ability to prioritize issues, nor the discussion of problems of proof, practicality of remedies, nor the numerous other skills which practicing attorneys must use in resolving real-life problems." Motley, *supra* note 150, at 737.

238. *See* 1 MICHAEL JOSEPHSON, LEARNING AND EVALUATION IN LAW SCHOOL 5–6 (1984) (discussing the characteristics of a "good test").

239. In other words, an evaluative methodology should ensure that all important aspects of a job are encompassed in its assessment mechanism. In addition, even if the school can show that its methodology is valid, there may be room to show that there exists a less prejudicial educational and evaluative methodology alternative. *See* Albemarle Paper Co. v. Moody, 422 U.S. 405, 425–26 (1975) (demanding significant correlation between challenged practice and important elements of job).

240. *See Dothard*, 433 U.S. at 329 (concluding that plaintiffs may only show the existence of less discriminatory alternatives if the employer proves that challenged requirements are job related).

241. A new American Bar Association report has, however, articulated such a list. *See* MacCrate Report, *supra* note 1, at 135–221 (enumerating ten fundamental lawyering skills and four professional values). In articulating this list of fundamental skills, the task force suggests that law schools may put this list to use "as a focus for examining proposals to modify their curricula to teach skills and values more extensively or differently than they now do." *Id.* at 128. Concurrently, the list could be used to develop criterion-referenced exams.

242. *See* M. Ray Doubles, *Law School Examinations*, 8 AM. L. SCH. REV. 254, 254 (1935) ("[The] law school examination should be both prepared and graded with the object of testing and ascertaining whether the student can 'think straight' on legal problems"). J. A. Coutts, a British law teacher, remarked that "[a] typical American claim is that examinations should show whether the candidates have acquired legal information and have learnt to 'think like lawyers,' to analyse facts and to apply legal principles." Coutts, *supra* note 234, at 401 (1968); *see also* Keeton, *supra* note 226, at 219–22 (stating that law school exams are "aimed at testing the skill of legal analysis as well as a body of doctrine").

243. Law schools, it seems, simply inherited this methodology. *See* Nickles, *supra* note 223, at 446 (noting that essay examinations were seen as a complementary form of evaluation to the case-study method).

244. For example, practicing law in an increasingly adversarial and competitive way may contribute to minimization of ethical obligations, client dissatisfaction, and general public distrust. *See* Clark D. Cunningham, *The Lawyer as Translator, Representation as Text: Towards an Ethnography of Legal Discourse*, 77 CORNELL L. REV. 1298, 1301 (1992) ("Litigant discontent is pervasive and notably independent of outcome; 'winners' are as critical as 'losers' "); *see also* TOM R. TYLER, WHY PEOPLE OBEY THE LAW 178 (1990) ("[I]n evaluating the justice of their experiences [people] consider factors unrelated to outcome, such as whether they have had a chance to state their case and [have] been treated with dignity and respect"); Tom R. Tyler, *Client Perceptions of Litigation; What Counts: Process or Result?*, TRIAL, July 1988, at 40, 41–42 (discussing concerns about the "fairness of the process").

245. We recognize, of course, that this proposal may require some faculty members to reevaluate their attitudes toward mentoring. In addition, the material costs of altering or eliminating the Socratic method of teaching may prove prohibitive. Large lectures which depend on using examples of dialogue between the faculty member and one student to teach a particular principle to the entire class are considerably cheaper than smaller classes that give all of the students some individual attention. *See* Costonis, *supra* note 144, at 160 (suggesting that the Langdell law school of high student/faculty ratios, large classes, low per-student expenditures, and tuition-driven financing may rely on the case method as an "economic" rather than "pedagogical" phenomenon).

246. *See, e.g.*, Cort and Sammons, *supra* note 149 at 397 (discussing Antioch School of Law program designed to produce better "lawyering" by teaching, testing, and evaluating competencies identified as crucial to being a good lawyer); Dueker, *supra* note 146, at 120 (advocating "connected teaching," which begins with what the students already know and employs a "building," rather than a "banking," process); Steven Hartwell and Sherry L. Hartwell, *Teaching Law: Some Things Socrates Did Not Try*, 40 J. Legal Educ. 509, 511–14, 519 (1990) (describing experimental study formats taught in conjunction with a typical, large-section class, but finding that exam grades did not differ according to the learning format); Kissam, *supra* note 228, at 493–502 (suggesting reform of the law school examination process); John B. Mitchell, *Current Theories on Expert and Novice Thinking: A Full Faculty Considers the Implications for Legal Education*, 39 J. Legal Educ. 275, 277–97 (1989) (proposing application of various learning theories to the method of legal instruction to improve student comprehension); Motley, *supra* note 150, at 749–60 (suggesting reform of the law school examination process); Stephen Nathanson, *The Role of Problem Solving in Legal Education*, 39 J. Legal Educ. 167, 181 (1989) (arguing that the primary method of study in law school should be problem-solving exercises, since the ability to solve problems is the most important skill a lawyer possesses); Nickles, *supra* note 223, at 460–79 (arguing that the traditional methods of evaluating law school performance rely upon theories which have been discredited by education and psychology research); Thomas L. Shaffer and Robert S. Redmount, *Legal Education: The Classroom Experience*, 52 Notre Dame Law. 190, 190–201 (1976) (examining the influence of classroom environment on learning); Van Praagh, *supra* note 118, at 113 (discussing method of legal instruction that takes into account emotion and personal perspective); *see also* MacCrate Report, *supra* note 1, at 128 (proposing modifications of traditional legal curricula to emphasize the development of professional skills and values); Dominguez, *supra* note 172, at 177 (proposing a format of "dynamic multicultural negotiation between small groups of students modeled after integrative bargaining in the commercial context").

247. Interview with Ralph R. Smith, Associate Professor of Law, University of Pennsylvania, in Philadelphia, Pa. (Apr. 7, 1993).

248. *Id.*

249. *See* interview with Catherine Krupnick, *supra* note 86 (describing this and other approaches that seek to minimize the ability of boys to dominate classes by being quicker than girls to raise their hands).

250. *See* Charles L. Finke, *Affirmative Action in Law School Academic Support Programs*, 39 J. Legal Educ. 55, 63–70 (1989). In Finke's study, groups of twelve first-year students participated in weekly meetings conducted by trained third-year students. *See id.* at 63–64. These first-year students also participated in monthly meetings in groups of three. *See id.* The groups discussed all first-year substantive courses. *See id.* at 63. Students in these groups outperformed many of their nonparticipating peers, even though those participating students had weaker entry-level credentials. *See id.* at 66–70.

Finke's success may reflect evidence that retention of learned material drops precipitously after two weeks, from approximately 60% to 17%. Interview with Lawrence D. Salmony, legal education consultant, in Philadelphia, Pa. (Mar. 30, 1993).

251. *See supra* note 1 (describing findings of the MacCrate Report).

252. The notion that all disputes are best resolved by disinterested advocacy in a hierarchical, competitive, win/lose approach is under challenge from activists

and scholars who value a more collaborative environment. *See* Dominguez, *supra* note 172, at 177 (advocating an approach in which each party looks to build relationships and to improve "its ability to anticipate and make adjustments for long-term challenges"). Many now question traditional notions of a competitive meritocracy in which "the cream rises to the top." For example, branches of Eastman Kodak, General Motors, and AT&T are seeking more egalitarian approaches based on teamwork. *See* Claudia H. Deutsch, *Less Is Becoming More at A.T.&T.*, N.Y. TIMES, June 3, 1990, at F25 (stating that teamwork is becoming the norm for the 1990s employee); Andrea Gabor, *Take This Job and Love It*, N.Y. TIMES, Jan. 26, 1992, at F1 (noting that some managers believe a merit system "nourishes short-term performance," rivalry, and politics instead of long-term planning, teamwork, and the search for quality and solutions). Some companies now claim that rewarding a handful of winners may be consistent with the ingrained culture of American individualism, but it discourages cooperation and may damage morale. *See id.* Even those preaching entrepreneurial government emphasize the importance of encouraging responsive results rather than "hierarchical" process. *See, e.g.,* DAVID OSBORNE AND TED GAEBLER, REINVENTING GOVERNMENT: HOW THE ENTREPRENEURIAL SPIRIT IS TRANSFORMING THE PUBLIC SECTOR 138 (1992) (advocating a "result-oriented" government).

253. *See supra* notes 73–83, 216–28 and accompanying text.

254. *See supra* notes 108, 112–18, 120–21 and accompanying text.

255. Interview with Judge Edmund B. Spaeth, Jr., Lecturer, University of Pennsylvania Law School, in Philadelphia, Pa. (Spring 1993).

256. *See, e.g.,* Cunningham, *supra* note 244, at 1301 (suggesting that client satisfaction would improve if attorneys developed better listening and communication skills); Menkel-Meadow, *supra* note 193, at 57 (suggesting that a greater sense of empathy is vital to serving client needs and objectives satisfactorily); *cf.* Burling, *supra* note 226, at A2 (describing women doctors' superior communication skills).

257. Professor Krupnick found that the men in one college class occupied classroom space much differently from the women. *See* Catherine G. Krupnick, *Meadows College Prepares for Men*, in GENDER AND PUBLIC POLICY: CASES AND COMMENTS 137, 147 (Kenneth Winston and Mary J. Bane eds., 1993) (quoting one instructor who noted that when students gave oral presentations "all of the women stayed at their seats," but "each of the men got up, walked to the front of the room, used the [black]board, used the map, and moved me out of the way"); *see also supra* note 249 (discussing an attempt to compensate for the classroom tendencies of male and female students). Deborah Tannen suggests that men and boys feel more comfortable talking at angles to each other, whereas women and girls face each other directly and sit much closer together. *See* TANNEN, *supra* note 148, at 89–99. This supports the assertions of Krupnick and others that the physical layout of a classroom—the way people and space are organized—can affect the way the class proceeds, who participates, and how they participate.

258. *See* Krupnick, *supra* note 257 at 143–47 (discussing the semester-long evaluation of four college classes, consisting of 2 men and 15 women, 4 men and 11 women, 2 men and 16 women, and 4 men and 14 women, respectively, in which the men participated at disproportionately high rates).

259. *See* interview with Catherine G. Krupnick, *supra* note 86; *see also* Krupnick, *supra* note 254 (describing male domination of seminar classes in which the professor follows a hierarchical structure).

260. Uri Treisman's work on why African-American and Latino students do not perform well in university-level calculus classes makes poignantly clear the

need for further study of the ways students learn. *See* Treisman, *supra* note 126, 372. Treisman conducted a survey of his colleagues' beliefs about why students failed to perform well in their mathematics classes; he found that most of the profession held similar beliefs (low income, low motivation, poor academic preparation, and lack of family support), but that all of those beliefs proved to be false. *See id.* at 364–67.

Had Treisman designed a tutoring program based on the incorrect assumptions about learning held by concerned and well-informed professors in the field, he would have created a program that attempted to correct for problems that did not exist. Instead, Treisman looked at why Asian students did well and African-American and Latino students did not. This process uncovered the different ways in which these groups of students studied, disproved early assumptions about failure, and led to the designing of a program encouraging peer group study sessions that dramatically improved the performance of African-American and Latino students in calculus. *See id.* at 366–69. The law school must understand how its students learn, formally and informally, before it attempts to design programs to help their learning.

261. Indeed, all law students might benefit from a greater emphasis on studying law as problem solving. *See, e.g.,* D'Amato, *supra* note 149, at 465 n.8 (advocating the study of mathematics as the ideal problem-solving model for studying law). Students might also benefit from experiments with cooperative learning. *See, e.g.,* Vernellia R. Randall, *Comparative Learning: Practical Advice,* LAW TCHR., Fall 1994, at 6–7 (describing cooperative learning as legal training "in which small groups of students work together on an academic task" using structures that "ensure student-student independence").

262. *See* Robert E. Fullilove and Philip U. Treisman, *Mathematics Achievement Among African American Undergraduates at the University of California, Berkeley,* 59 J. NEGRO EDUC. 463, 463–78 (1990). In examining why Asian students did better in math than African-American students, the authors found significant differences in the way they studied. *See id.* at 466–67. When the university introduced a tutoring program that integrated the studying styles of the successful Asian students, the African-American students did much better. *See id.* at 472–75. Kristine Knaplund and Richard Sander, in their evaluation of different kinds of tutoring and academic support programs at the UCLA Law School, found that some kinds of intensive small group instruction worked better than other support methods. *See* Kristine Knaplund and Richard Sander, *The Art and Science of Academic Support,* at 57 (Jan. 1994) (unpublished paper, on file with authors) They found that relying on traditional methods of academic support, such as tutoring and exam workshops, only worked in certain ways and under certain circumstances. *See id.* at 32–37. Their study could help the law school design programs that work by showing what has not worked in the past at other institutions. Both studies indicate that the law school can and perhaps should intervene in how the students are studying, with an eye towards teaching them new and more successful studying strategies and styles. *See also* Shanfield and Benjamin, *supra* note 117, at 73 (advocating "sanctioned peer support groups" and other support groups directed by outside leaders to help students "anticipate and master" law school problems).

263. What our data highlight is that simply adding women's bathrooms is not enough. Christine Littleton has called this the "add women and stir" phenomenon. *See* Littleton, *supra* note 13, at 1280. The problems with the institution are structural, not facial.

264. The Bartow Survey questions reproduced in this appendix were presented

as multiple choice questions, with a variety of answers provided. Generally, these answers represented ranges of frequency, such as "never," "only occasionally," "at least once a month," "at least once a week," "at least once a day," and "no opinion." Answers to other questions represented ranges of attitude, such as "always affected" (or "very satisfied"), "sometimes," "never," and "no opinion." Another subset of responses represented perceptions of the equality of treatment of male and female students, with answers such as "men more often," "equally," "women more often," and "no opinion." Yet another subset offered respondents an unrestricted number of choices from a list of answers; the various answer choices to these questions are reproduced in their entirety alongside the accompanying question in order to show more clearly the range of available responses.

CHAPTER III. MODELS AND MENTORS

1. *See* Daley, *Little Girls Lose Their Self-Esteem on Way to Adolescence, Study Finds*, N.Y. TIMES, Jan. 9, 1991, B6 (survey of 3,000 adolescents concluded that black girls in high school draw apparent self-confidence from their families and communities rather than the school system; in order to maintain high self-esteem, black girls must disassociate themselves from school experience).

2. Mari Matsuda, *When the First Quail Calls*, 11 WOMEN'S L. REPTR. 7 (1989).

3. *See* W. E. B. DU BOIS, THE SOULS OF BLACK FOLK, vi, 16–17 (1903): [T]he Negro is a sort of seventh son, born with a veil, and gifted with second-sight in this American world,—a world which yields him no true self-consciousness, but only lets him see himself through the revelation of the other world. It is a peculiar sensation, this double-consciousness, this sense of always looking at one's self through the eyes of others, of measuring one's soul by the tape of a world that looks on in amused contempt and pity. One ever feels his twoness,—an American, a Negro; two souls, two thoughts, two unreconciled strivings; two warring ideals in one dark body, whose dogged strength alone keeps it from being torn asunder.

4. In movements for social change, those at the bottom often have the real interest and the most information. Mari Matsuda, *Looking to the Bottom: Critical Legal Studies and Reparations*, 22 HARV. C.R.-C.L.L.REV. 323, 346, 348 (1987) ("Those who are oppressed in the present world can speak most eloquently of a better one").

5. Adeno Addis explores these and other explanations for the cultural and political valence of contemporary role models. *See Role Models and the Politics of Recognition*, U. PA. L. REV. 1377 (1996).

6. Adeno Addis also explores the distinction between role model and mentor: "One cannot be a mentor to the world, nor can one be a protege of an individual who shows no personal interest in oneself or one's work." *Id.* at 1389. Addis also distinguishes between the terms "hero" and "role model": "One of the distinguishing features of a role model is that he or she inspires the possibility of emulation. On the other hand, a hero instills admiration and respect for the qualities he or she displays and the achievements he or she has attained." *Id.*

7. Renewed calls have been made for more black women law professors to be role models for black women students. Indeed, my original decision to write this self-reflective essay was precipitated by debate that abounded during Professor Derrick Bell's spring 1990 protest at Harvard Law School. Claiming he could not function as a role model for women students, Bell refused to accept his Harvard

Law School salary until a woman of color was hired as a professor. *See* Butterfield, *Harvard Law School Torn by Race Issue,* N. Y. TIMES, April 26, 1990, A20 (as a male, Bell said, he could not serve as a role model for female black students; quoting first-year student: "I'm coming from the perspective of a black woman, and we need black women role models"; and second-year student: "We need black women mentors to tell us what it is like out there when we join a firm and start trying to get clients"); *see also* Suzanne Homer and Lois Schwartz, *Admitted But Not Accepted: Outsiders Take an Inside Look at Law School,* 5 BERKELEY WOMEN'S L. J. 1, 62 (appendix B, question 21A of *Boalt Hall Student Questionnaire,* April 1988: "Do you think the lower number of professors at Boalt who are people of color has deprived you of significant role models in the field of law?"; *id* at 54: "Has the lower number of *female professors* at Boalt deprived you of role models in the field of law?"; at least 75% of the women of color answered in the affirmative to both questions).

See generally Berenice Fisher, *Wandering in the Wilderness: The Search for Women Role Models,* 13 SIGNS 211 (1988). When Fisher first heard in the 1970s "the claim . . . women . . . needed female role models to make [their] way through the world," she was very angry because the emphasis on role models "sets women up for co-optation when the powers-that-be offer us role models instead of justice" and "perpetuates the logic of domination by encouraging us to look *up* to 'special women' rather than to look around us for the women with whom we might act." *Id.* at 212. *See also* Anita Allen, *On Being a Role Model,* 6 BERKELEY WOMEN'S L. J. 22, 25 (1990–91) ("One problem with the role model argument is that while it trumpets our necessity, it whispers our inferiority"); Angela Harris, *Women of Color in Legal Education: Representing La Mestiza,* 6 BERKELEY WOMEN'S L. J. 107–109 (observing that "[t]he price of specialness is the gilded cage of the token").

8. Iris Marion Young, *Justice, Democracy and Group Difference* 9–15 (unpublished paper prepared for presentation to American Political Science Association) (Sept. 1, 1990) (describing communicative discourse).

9. *Id.* at 12.

10. *See, e.g.,* Kimberlé Crenshaw, *Foreword: Toward a Race-Conscious Pedagogy in Legal Education,* 11 NAT'L. BLACK L. J. 1 (1989); Mari Matsuda, *Affirmative Action and Legal Knowledge: Planting Seeds in Plowed-Up Ground,* 11 HARV. WOMEN'S L. J. 1, 14–16 (1988) (use of black girl's memories of civil rights movement in American legal history class; use of an Alice Walker essay in torts class).

11. Letter from a former student, Dec. 26, 1990 (on file with author). *See* Young, *supra* note 8 at 13–14: "By having to speak and justify his or her preferences to others who may be skeptical, a person becomes more reflective about them, accommodates them to the preferences of others, or perhaps becomes even more convinced of the legitimacy of his or her claims."

12. According to Ann Bartow's 1990 survey of students at Penn Law School, 93.1% of women respondents chose "treats students with respect" as one of three most admired qualities in a professor, while 82.3% of the men preferred professors who express their ideas clearly; with this exception, the choices were the same for men and women respondents for the other two most admired qualities, knowledge of subject matter (94.8% of women, 88% of men) and enthusiasm for teaching (92.5% for women, 80.7% for men).

13. Kendall Thomas, AALS Annual Meeting, Law and Interpretation Section, Washington, D. C. (Jan. 4, 1991).

14. *See* Harlon Dalton, *The Clouded Prism,* 22 HARV. C.R.C.L.L.REV. 435, 444 (1987). *See also* Richard Delgado, *When a Story Is Just a Story: Does Voice Really Matter?,* 76 VA. L. REV. 95, 99 (1990) (describing outsiders' accessibility to and stake

in disseminating information that persons without their experiences may not have).

15. *See* Derrick Bell, statement reprinted in *Section on Minority Groups Newsletter 4* (May 1990) (advocating on behalf of black women role models and mentors).

16. *See* Alan Freeman, *Antidiscrimination Law: A Critical Review*, THE POLITICS OF LAW, 96, 110 (David Kairys, ed. 1982) (role models "bourgeoisify" sufficient number of blacks to legitimate basic social structure); Richard Delgado, *The Ethereal Scholar: Do Critical Legal Studies Have What Minorities Want?* 22 HARV. C. R.-C. L. L. REV. 301, 310 (1987) (role models demonstrate that the system is formally fair; the person who occupies a position of power, therefore, deserves it; "In a meritocratic society, the cream rises to the top"). *Compare* Roy Brooks, *Life After Tenure: Can Minority Law Professors Avoid the Clyde Ferguson Syndrome?*, 20 U. S. F. L. REV. 419, 423 (1986) (arguing that black middle class is in position to speak on behalf of black problems in general).

17. Addis (*supra* note 5, at 1418) writes,
Viewed this way, the concept of role model diverts attention away from the problems of power and social structure. On the one hand, the message for the intended emulator seems to be that, because there are no institutional or structural impediments to success, if individuals adjust their erroneous perceptions to the contrary, work hard, and possess the necessary natural endowment, success will surely follow. On the other hand, the message to the individual selected as a role model is quite often that he or she achieved that position not because of merit, but because of his or her representational and symbolic value. Praising the supposed role model to his or her intended role model followers as an example of success is, therefore, insincere.

18. Allen, *supra* note 7.

19. Richard Delgado, *Storytelling for Oppositionists and Others: A Plea for Narrative*, 87 MICH. L. REV. 2411, 2423–2427 (1989) (describing conventional concern that a black professor who causes trouble by stirring up students "wouldn't be a good role model even for the minorities").

20. *See* Regina Austin, *Sapphire Bound!* 1989 WISC. L. REV. 539 (describing firing of young black woman "role model" for being an unwed mother). As Austin argues, role models are "black people who have achieved stature and power in the white world because they supposedly represent the interests of the entire black community. Such role models gain capital (literally and figuratively) to the extent that they project an assimilated persona that is as unthreatening to white people as it is (supposed to be) intriguing to our young." *Id.* at 575.

21. *See* Patricia Hill Collins, *We Don't Need Another Dr. King*, N.Y. TIMES, Jan. 19, 1991, 31 (exposure to role models does not guarantee emulation of their ideas and actions; it may instead simply encourage dependence and a sense of paralysis; in sum, role models are no substitute for transformation through institutional strategies).

22. "Lifting as I rise" is the motto of the black clubwomen affiliated with the National Association of Colored Women's Clubs who serve as mentors and advisors to hundreds of youth clubs. *See* Karen De Witt, *For Black Clubwomen, a New Era Dawns*, N.Y. TIMES, Aug. 4, 1996 at 44. *See also* Richard Delgado, *Affirmative Action as a Majoritarian Device: Or, Do You Really Want To Be a Role Model?*, 89 MICH. L. REV. 1222, 1230–31 (1991):
You can do other more honorable, authentic things. You can be a mentor. You can be an "organic intellectual," offering analysis and action programs

for our people. You can be a matriarch, a patriarch, a legend, or a provoca-
teur. You can be a socially committed professional who marches to your
own drummer. You can even be yourself. But to the ad, ROLE MODEL
WANTED, the correct answer, in my view, is: NOT ME!

23. Claudia Deutsch, *Less Is Becoming More at A.T.&T.*, N.Y. TIMES, June 3, 1990,
at F25 (the "perfect" 1990s employee would practice interdependency, neither
placing blame nor accepting full responsibility and developing own strategy for
recovery; teamwork would become the norm: "an interdependent store manager
[of a store suffering sluggish sales] would sit down with people from marketing,
production and other departments to discuss how the product could be better designed, priced—and sold").

24. Coproduction is political science professor Jack Nagel's term for a leadership relationship that is communicative and interactive. JACK NAGEL, PARTICI-
PATION (1987).

25. Quoted by Patricia Hill Collins, N.Y. TIMES, Jan. 19, 1991, at 31.

26. Although the law school admits a class of almost one-half women and, for
the first time in 1990, one-third non-white, my upper level courses have always
consisted primarily of white men. This is not surprising considering the small absolute number of African-American, Asian-American and Latin American students, and the relatively small percentage of these students in other than the class
of 1993.

27. Addis, *supra* note 7, at 1386. Addis concludes,

Thus, when we talk about educational role models in a race and gender specific sense, we do not mean that role aspirants will master a particular body
of knowledge faster and better when they learn it from a supposed role
model of the same race or gender. Nor do we mean that the supposed role
models will or should define the good and virtuous life for emulation by the
potential role model follower by serving as comprehensive role models.
Rather, we mean that the presence of members of traditionally excluded
groups will provide visible reassurance to the aspiring role occupant that
the dominant group does not devalue them and their horizons of significance and that they "share[] with all other members of [their] community the qualities of . . . morally accountable subject[s]."

Id. at 1430.

28. This process was aptly described by Berenice Fisher when she observed that
"the meaning of being a role model grows out of discovering shared struggles and
shared vulnerabilities in relation to the world." Berenice Fisher, *Wandering in the
Wilderness: The Search for Women Role Models*, 13 SIGNS 211, 232 (1988).

Above all, a mentor conveys her confidence in the ability of the student to succeed. The moment an adult intellectual takes a student seriously is often the moment the student takes her own intellectual ability seriously. *See supra*, Chapter 1,
notes 17 and 38 and accompanying text.

29. *See* Harlon Dalton *supra* note 14, at 439 n.12; Delgado, *Storytelling, supra*
note 19, at 2414 (1989) (most who write about storytelling focus on its
community-building functions: building consensus, common culture, and ethical
discourse).

30. *See* Kimberlé Crenshaw, *Race, Reform, and Retrenchment: Transformation and
Legitimation in Antidiscrimination Law*, 101 HARV. L. REV. 1331, 1336 (1988) (describing blacks' greatest resource as the ability to speak and share experience of
racism, to "name our reality"). As a black woman who has experienced minority
status and stigma associated with my race and/or gender, I am self-conscious

about both race and gender. However, multiple consciousness is not a claim for essentialism. *See, e.g.*, Angela Harris, *Race and Essentialism in Feminist Legal Theory*, 42 STAN. L. REV. 581, 608 (1990) (the opposite of essentialism is multiple consciousness, in which self is multiplicitous, differences are relational rather than inherent, and wholeness is an act of will not passive discovery). *See also* Delgado, *Storytelling, supra* note 19, at 2425.

INDEX

Adaptive work, process of, 5, 6, 18, 23
Addis, Adeno, 93, 97, 165nn. 5, 6, 167n.17, 168n.27
African Americans. *See* Minorities
Age, gender difference for, 55, 139n.127
Alexander, Sadie T. M., 98
Alice's Adventures in Wonderland (Carroll), 99, 101
Alienation: and academic performance within the formal structure of the institution, 58–62, 143nn.147, 148, 144n.150; and exclusion of women from informal learning networks, 62–66, 149nn.175, 176; women's alienation from law school, 48, 49, 58–62, 135n.111
Allen, Anita, 93, 165n.7
American Bar Association, 73; MacCrate Report task force, 15, 107nn.26, 27
Asian-American students. *See* Minorities
Asshole Bingo, 68, 137n.120, 155n.215
Austin, Regina, 154n.209, 167n.20
Awards. *See* Honors and awards

Balin, Jane, 1, 5, 8, 89, 92, 96, 101
Banks, Taunya, 34, 115n.31, 117n.41, 139n.127, 151n.191
Bartow, Ann, 1, 8; Bartow Survey, 30–32, 42–46, 47, 62, 78–84, 112nn.19, 20, 21, 114nn.28, 29, 115n.30, 164n.264; video documentary, 6–7, 42
Bell, Derrick, 165n.7, 167n.15
Berkeley Law School study, 33, 34, 121nn.57, 58, 60, 61, 62, 145n.154, 153n.205
Biculturalism, 53, 67, 68, 136n.118
Black students. *See* Minorities
Bowie, Niko, 24
Brown v. Board of Education, 85

Career aspirations, public interest law, 7–8, 12, 45, 46, 98, 133n.101, 134nn.102, 103
Civil rights lawyer, 98–101
Class size/classroom space, 74, 163n.257
Clinton, William Jefferson "Bill," 1, 4, 26, 99
Collins, Patricia Hill, 167n.21, 168n.25
Color, students of. *See* Minorities
Communicative discourse, 91, 166n.8
Comparative Labor Law Journal, 42
Counseling, 48
Crenshaw, Kimberlé, 135n.114, 166n.10, 168n.30
Critical mass theory, 64–65, 75, 152n.198, 153n.202
Critical perspectives seminar, 31, 114n.25
Criticism of survey methods, male, 56, 140nn.131, 132, 133

Dalton, Harlon, 103n.4, 166n.14, 168n.29
Discrimination: against women, 56, 142n.139; employment, 70–71, 159n.236
Dissonance, 50, 51
Diver, Colin (Dean, University of Pennsylvania Law School), 8, 31, 57, 142n.144
Diversity, 5, 21

Diversity Advantage: How American Business Can Out-Perform Japanese and European Companies in the Global Marketplace, The (Fernandez), 6
Double-consciousness, 87
Douglas, William, 8, 103n.6
Drucker, Peter, 16
Du Bois, W. E. B., 87–88, 100–101, 165n.3

Ebersol, Dick, 14
Elite schools: elite law school education, 58–59, 144n.151; gender disparities in, 12–13
Employment discrimination, 70–71, 159n.236
Entry-level criteria, 8–9, 36
Examinations: law, 70, 71, 157n.228, 159nn.235, 237, 161nn.242, 243; LSAT, 6, 8–9, 15, 31, 35, 36, 38–41, 104nn.7, 8, 9, 105n.12, 124n.74; one-size-fits-all tests, 11, 17

Faculty: female, 64–66, 152nn.198, 199, 201, 153nn.202, 203, 204; interaction with, 63, 149nn.177, 178; and mentoring relationships, 63–64, 66, 74, 150nn.186, 187, 189, 190, 154n.208; qualities in law professors, 12, 44, 92, 131nn.89, 90, 91, 94, 166n.12; women of color law professors, 85–97
Fairness, 5; sameness and, 6, 11, 12
Feminism, being called a feminist, 59, 145n.157
Fernandez, John P., 6
Fine, Michelle, 1, 5, 8, 23, 76, 89, 92, 96, 101
Focus groups, 31, 34
From Gladiators to Problem-Solvers (Sturm), 18

Gender: bias in the classroom, 45, 132nn.95, 96, 97, 98, 99; gender differences, 54–55, 138n.123, 139nn.125, 126, 127, 140nn.128, 129, 130; gender hierarchies, 61–62; gender-neutral language, 45,

131n.94; gender-related issues and male law students, 56, 60, 142n.140; narrative data, 46–56; quantitative data from the Bartow Survey, 42–46; quantitative data on academic performance, 35–42; studies of gender in law school, 33–34, 120n.56
Gentlemen: "gentlemen" model, 146n.163; use of term, 29, 85, 111n.15; women who do not become gentlemen are less valued members of the law school community, 66–71, 154nn.211, 212, 213, 214
Gilligan, Carol, 33, 117n.43, 118n.46
Giovanni, Nikki, 95
Grade point average (GPA): college GPA mean statistics for incoming students, 35; law school GPAs, 36, 37, 122n.69; LSAT and law school GPA, 39–40; undergraduate, 31, 36
Grading, "Q quotient," 42, 59, 129n.84
Group-based learning teams, 2, 103n.2, 154n.207, 162n.250, 164n.262

Harassment: from male students, 56, 59, 73, 141n.137, 145n.158; sexual, 7
Harris, Angela, 165n.7, 168n.30
Harvard College, 10, 11, 87, 106n.19, 144n.152, 153n.205
Harvard Law School, 109n.1, 110n.10, 120n.56, 142n.141, 142n.144, 165n.7
Hazing, by male peers, 59, 63
Heifitz, Ronald, 4–5
Hierarchies, gender, 61–62
High school: extracurricular activities, 10, 106n.17; "planning backward" movement, 20
Honors and awards: 41–42, 63, 126nn.75, 76, 77, 78, 127n.80, 128nn.81, 82, 83
hooks, bell, 5

Invisibility of informal barriers: 64, 151n.192

Journal of International Business Law, 42

Krupnick, Catherine, 13, 106n.19, 130n.86, 141n.135, 144n.152, 153n.205, 162n.249, 163nn.257–259

Law Review, 41, 42, 47, 126n.78, 128nn.81, 82
Law school: studies of gender in, 33–34, 120n.56; and undergraduate performance, 9, 104nn.11, 13; women in, 33, 116n.39; women who do not become gentlemen are less valued members of the law school community, 66–71, 154nn.211, 212, 213, 214
Law School Admission Test (LSAT): 6, 8–9, 15, 31, 36, 104nn.7, 8, 9, 105n.12, 115n.34, 155n.217; LSAT scores and law school performance, 38–41, 124nn.73–74; mean statistics for incoming students, 35
"Lay Lawyering" (Lopez), 15
Leadership: as "adaptive work," 4–5; in the corporate world, 16, 107nn.29, 30; female leadership in student organizations, 63; female students in leadership positions, 54, 138n.122; students in leadership roles, 4
Learning networks, alienation and exclusion of women from informal, 62–66, 149nn.175, 176
Learning styles: cooperative styles of learning, 3; group-based learning teams, 2, 3; learning theory, 154n.207, 156nn.221, 223, 158n.231, 162n.246; student learning, 74, 163n.260
Legal education: changing, 69–70, 156nn.221, 222, 223; diverse approaches to, 5; grading system, 159n.235; new approaches to, 72–75, 161nn.245, 246, 162n.252, 163nn.257, 260, 164n.262; restructuring, 72
Legitimation, 61, 148n.171
Lehrer, Jim, 23

Lesbian-baiting, 54, 59, 137n.120
Lewis, Marilyn McGrath, 10
Listening, 14, 17
Lonsdorf Index, 35, 36, 122n.67
Lopez, Jerry, 15
Lorde, Audre, 27
Los Angeles Police Department, Christopher Commission Report, 18–19, 108n.33
Lottery selection, 106n.18

MacCrate Report of the American Bar Association, 15, 107nn.26, 27, 109n.1, 142n.144, 156n.223, 161n.241
MacKinnon, Catharine, 33, 118n.45
MacNeil, Robert, 23
MacNeil/Lehrer News Hour, The, 23
Madison, James, 100
Matsuda, Mari, 33, 87
Menkel-Meadow, Carrie, 16
Mental health, 52, 136n.117; inquiries, 48–49
Mentors and role models, 22, 109nn.37, 38, 39; black, 85–97, 165nn.6, 7, 167nn.20, 21, 22, 168nn.28, 30; faculty mentoring, 66, 74, 154n.208; female police officers of color, 18; mentoring relationships, 63–64, 106n.17, 150nn.186, 187, 188, 161n.245; need for women role models, 66, 154n.206
Merit, 11, 21
Mertz, Elizabeth, 106n.19, 107n.23
Minorities: academic needs of black students, 3, 14, 103n.2; Asian-American students, 3, 95; black mentors and role models, 85–97; dissonance and alienation, 51–52; informal barriers, 64; LSAT and, 15; race and academic performance, 124n.73, 146n.161; students of color and the Socratic method, 50, 135n.114
Moot court board, 41, 42, 128n.83
Multiple consciousness, 87–88

Narrative data, 46–56
National Public Radio (NPR), 23
NBC Sports, 14, 106n.22

New York City police officers, 18, 19,
108n.32
New York University School of Law,
142n.143

Ohio Law Schools study, 111n.12,
152n.201; survey of Ohio Law
School faculty, 150n.189
Olympics: Olympic gymnasts, 3,
103n.1; women viewers and the
1996 Summer Olympics, 14,
106n.22
One-size-fits-all approach, 1, 4, 11,
17, 18, 20
On-the-job training, mentoring and,
23
Open-ended narrative space, women
students' use of, 56, 141n.134
Open-ended questions, 47
Order of the Coif, 41, 126n.75,
142n.143

Pacts, women's formation of, 49, 63,
134n.110
Paper-and-pencil tests, 6, 11, 106n.18
Participation, class, 14–15, 107n.23;
asking questions/volunteering
answers in class, 12, 13–14, 43,
106n.19, 129n.85, 130n.86; class
size and, 74, 163n.257; differing
rates of participation, 44–45,
131nn.88, 89, 90, 91, 94; speaking
in the classroom, 59, 144n.152;
women's lower rates of, 28, 32, 58–
62, 115n.31; women's sexuality
and, 53–54, 68, 137n.120; women's
silence in the classroom, 33, 59,
61, 117nn.41, 42, 145n.154
Peer groups, 14
Peer policing, 68, 74
Peer relations, 59
Performance: academic performance
data, 32, 35–42; alienation and academic performance within the formal structure of the institution,
58–62, 143nn.147, 148, 144n.150;
gendered academic performance
differential, 70, 158n.232; of law
students, 11; on-the-job, 11, 23
"Planning backward" movement, 20
Police officers: female, 18–19,

108n.33; height requirement, 19–
20
Positive feedback, absence of, 59,
144n.153
Price, Hugh, 105n.15
Problem solving, 4, 5, 6, 15, 161n.234,
162n.246, 164n.261; litigation-as-
combat model of, 73, 107n.27,
162n.252
Professors, law. See Faculty
Public Broadcasting System (PBS),
23
Public interest law, practice in, 7–8,
12, 45, 46, 98, 133n.101, 134n.102

"Q quotient," 42, 59, 129n.84
Qualifications, assessing, 5
Qualitative data, 31, 32, 113nn.22, 24
Quantitative data: on academic perfor-
mance, 35–42; from the Bartow
Survey, 42–46
"Quota Queen," 99

Ranking, 4, 61, 70, 148n.172,
158n.231; rank in college and
mean statistics for incoming students, 35; students in top fiftieth
percentile of the class, 37, 38,
123nn.70, 71; students in top ten
percentile of the class, 37–38, 39,
123n.70
Rape, discussing rape in criminal law
classes, 56, 141n.136
Role models. See Mentors and role
models

Sameness, fairness and, 6, 11, 12
Scholastic Assessment Test (SAT)
(formerly Scholastic Aptitude
Test): 10, 103n.2, 104n.10,
105n.12
Self-esteem, women's, 59, 60–61, 91,
107n.23, 136n.116, 144n.153,
145n.160
Sexism, 45, 60, 133n.100
Sex-related issues in class, 56
Sexual harassment, 7
Sexuality, women's, class participa-
tion and, 53–54, 68, 137n.120
Silence, women's, 33, 59, 61,
117nn.41, 42, 145n.154

"Social males," 68
Socratic method: faculty mentoring
    and Socratic-style instruction, 64;
    in classroom instruction, 28, 50,
    66, 110n.10, 111n.12, 135n.112,
    154n.207; new approach to, 72, 74,
    161n.245; Socratic classroom and
    women's academic performance,
    58, 60, 147nn.164, 165, 159n.235;
    Socratic exchanges, 15, 91; tech-
    nique of Socratic teaching, 13
Stachel, Deborah, 1, 114n.24
Stanford Law School study, 33–34,
    119nn.48, 51, 52, 53, 120n.54,
    142n.144
Student organizations, 63
Sturm, Susan, 18, 103n.5, 105n.12,
    108n.32, 155n.217
Success, correlating, 10, 11

Tokenism, 64–65, 152n.195,
    153nn.199, 154n. 209, 200, 201
Treisman, Uri, 3–4, 14, 95, 103n.2,
    139n.126, 163n.260, 164n.262
Turning Around (video), 7

University of Michigan Law School,
    134n.110
University of Oregon Law School, 73
University of Pennsylvania Law
    School, 1–2; admissions criteria,
    68, 155n.217; alienation and aca-
    demic performance within the for-
    mal structure of the institution,
    58–62; alienation and exclusion of
    women from informal learning
networks, 62–66; analysis and rec-
    ommendations, 57–75, 142nn.141,
    142, 143, 144; entry-level creden-
    tials, 8, 9; on gender, 35–56; law-
    yer model, 50, 135n.113; male and
    female undergraduates, 54,
    139n.124; narrative data, 46–56;
    preliminary research about, 27–
    29, 109nn.1, 3; quantitative data
    from the Bartow Survey, 42–46;
    quantitative data on academic per-
    formance, 35–42; recommenda-
    tions, 71–75; related research, 32–
    35; research methodologies, 30–
    32; three windows into the law
    school, 30–35; treatment of law
    students, 11–12; women who do
    not become gentlemen are less val-
    ued members of the law school
    community, 66–71
University of Texas School of Law,
    104n.9

Varsity sports, participation in, 54,
    138n.123, 139n.125
Voices, women's stolen, 48

Williams, Patricia, 148n.173
Women's Law Group, University of
    Pennsylvania Law School, 31, 47,
    114n.26
Workforce 2000 Report, 25
Working group format, 72

Yale Law School, 33, 85, 87, 98,
    120n.56, 134n.110, 142n.144
Young, Iris Marion, 91, 166n.8